ALBERT SLOSMAN

THE ORIGINS TRILOGY
I
THE GREAT CATACLYSM

In those days lived Isis and Osiris

Albert Slosman (1925-1981)

THE ORIGINS TRILOGY I
The Great Cataclysm
In those days lived Isis and Osiris

LA TRILOGIE DES ORIGINES I

Le grand cataclysme

First edition Robert Laffont, Paris, 1976

Translated and published by
OMNIA VERITAS LTD

www.omnia-veritas.com

© Omnia Veritas Limited – 2025

All rights reserved. No part of this publication may be reproduced by any means without the prior permission of the publisher. The intellectual property code prohibits copies or reproductions for collective use. Any representation or reproduction in whole or in part by any means whatsoever, without the consent of the publisher, the author or their successors, is unlawful and constitutes an infringement punishable by articles of the Code of Intellectual Property.

... BY WAY OF PROLEGOMENA	11
ALBERT SLOSMAN	12
FOREWORD	13
CHAPTER ONE	32
IN THE BEGINNING GOD!	32
CHAPTER TWO	53
MATHEMATICAL-DIVINE COMBINATIONS	53
CHAPTER THREE	73
CREATION	73
CHAPTER FOUR	87
THE ORIGINAL SYMBOLISM OF CREATION	87
CHAPTER FIVE	103
SYMBOLIC DIGITAL TERRESTRIAL	103
CHAPTER SIX	115
AHA-MEN-PTA ("THE ELDER-HEART-OF-GOD")	115
CHAPTER SEVEN	132
A MEETING OF THE GRAND COUNCIL	132
CHAPTER EIGHT	149
GEB THE LAST MASTER!	149
CHAPTER NINE	168
LA REINE NOUT	168
CHAPTER TEN	185
OUSIR AND ISET	185
CHAPTER ELEVEN	207
SIT: SONS OF THE ("MESIT BETESOU")	207
CHAPTER TWELVE	229
THE GREAT CATACLYSM	229
CHAPTER THIRTEEN	248
MANDJIT	248
CHAPTER FOURTEEN	263
CHRONOLOGY OF AHA-MEN-PTAH	263

BIBLIOGRAPHY **283**
   THE MAIN DOCUMENTS STUDIED FOR AN ANAGLYPHIC UNDERSTANDING OF THE
   TEXTS 283
   OTHER TITLES 287

... BY WAY OF PROLEGOMENA

> Perhaps you have heard the name Atlas spoken, and that of the race that descended from him in many generations? It is also said that the many families that make up our race descended from him. Alas! They were once a happy nation, cherished by the gods for as long as they honoured the heavens.
>
> Jérôme FRASCATOR
> (Syphilidis, song III)

> The theogony of the Atlanteans, reported by Diodorus of Sicily, probably found its way into Egypt in the great irruption mentioned in Plato's Timaeus.
>
> BUFFON
> (Epochs of Nature)

> The sinking of Atlantis can be viewed with equal reason as a historical point. The shallowness of the Atlantic Sea as far as the Canaries could well be proof of this event, whose islands could be the remains of Atlantis.
>
> VOLTAIRE
> (Dict. phil. des changements arrivés sur le globe)

> Why shouldn't the Canaries and the Azores, islands in the Atlantic Ocean, be the remains of the land called Atlantis? They show the most solid mountains of the parts that were the highest. The humbler hills and intermediate valleys were submerged when, as a result of the earthquakes and the flood, this continent disappeared into the waters of the sea.
>
> Father Athanase KIRCHER
> (The Underworld, Volume I, 3)

> Rational thought, without the help of the Divine particle constituting the impalpable Soul can only lead to a philosophy of Nothingness.
>
> A. S.

Albert Slosman

Passionate about ancient Egypt and Atlantis. Professor of mathematics and expert in computer analysis was involved in NASA's programmes to launch Pioneer to Jupiter and Saturn.

His intention was to rediscover the source of monotheism and write its history.

His search for the origins of everyone and everything led him, by curious and unexpected paths, to fix his attention on the ancient Egyptian civilisation, whose formation and development were approached with an open and independent mind throughout his short life.

Albert was a member of the Resistance during the 2nd World War, was tortured by the Gestapo and later suffered an accident that left him in a coma for 3 years.

Slosman was a person of extremely fragile appearance and health, but animated by an intense inner strength that kept him alive, motivated by the desire to complete a work in 10 volumes that was intended as an immense framework of the permanence of monotheism through time, and which his premature death did not allow him to conclude.

A minor accident, a fractured neck of the femur, following a fall on the premises of the Maison de la Radio in Paris, took his life, perhaps because his body (his human carcass, as he liked to say), already well shaken, could not withstand another assault, however insignificant it may have been.

Foreword

> *Those of the ancient Egyptians who wished to attain Knowledge first learned the type of lettering known as epistolographic; secondly, hieratic, which was used by the hierogrammatists; and finally,* hieroglyphic. *There are two types of hieroglyphic: one is cyriological and uses alphabetical letters; the other is* symbolic. *The symbolic method is subdivided into three types: one represents objects in their own right, by imitation; another expresses figuration in a tropical manner; the third, expressed by allegory, defines certain enigmas.*
>
> CLEMENT OF ALEXANDRIA
> *(Stromates, V, 657)*

For the past two thousand years, one text has been the subject of much ink, and it continues to be so, if only because of this book, which begins by quoting it: the famous Timaeus by Plato, whose other philosophical accounts are also internationally renowned. But in 'Timaeus', the author was inspired by the poem in verse by the sage Solon, which he readily admits.

Hundreds of more or less debatable and discussed books have appeared, not to mention Pierre Benoit's very fine novel, which alone inspired so many researchers... and dreamers! Atlantis, to keep its Platonic name for the time being, has been found in practically every part of the world! We won't go into the humorous side of things here, so as to devote as many chapters as possible to the history of the lost continent itself, and under its true name, as taught to us by ancient hieroglyphic texts, in their anaglyphic subtitles, i.e. in their second sacred meaning, i.e. Aha-MenPtah, which means: Elder-Heart-of-God.

This is why the survivors of the Great Cataclysm that engulfed the country called it Amenta, Kingdom of the Dead, when they landed on African soil.

This was why the survivors, on arriving at Ta Merit, the Beloved Place, could only baptise it, through their first king: Menes, as Ath-Ka-Ptah, which means: Second-Soul-of-God, and which became phonetically by a grace that only the Greeks understand: Ae-Guy-Ptos, or in French: Égypte...

Numerous texts formally attest to this ancient origin. But before discussing them in detail, let's look at the Platonic account of the events that took place on this sunken continent. Critias speaks:

"I'll tell you an old story I heard from an old man. For my grandfather was then, as he said, close to his ninetieth birthday, and I was no more than ten. It was the day of the Coureotis, during the Apatouries.[1] On this occasion, the ceremony took place in the usual way for us children: our fathers invited us to recitation competitions. We recited poems by force, and as Solon's poems were still new at the time, many of us sang them. Now, one of my brothers, either because that was his taste at the time or because he also wanted to court our grandfather, declared that Solon seemed to him not only to have been the wisest of men in all other respects, but also, in terms of his poetic talent, the noblest of all poets. The old man, as I recall, was delighted and, smiling, replied: "Yes, Amynander, if Solon had not written verse simply as a hobby, if he had applied himself like others, and if he had finished the story he had brought back from Egypt, if he had not been forced by seditions and other calamities he found here on his return to neglect poetry completely, in my opinion, neither Hesiod nor Homer, nor any other poet, would ever have become more famous than he was.

- And what was this story, O Critias?

- It dealt with the greatest exploit of all, and one that would rightly have deserved to be the most illustrious of all those that

---

[1] An Ionian festival in October, lasting four days, during which young men were inducted into the various phratries.

this city has ever accomplished. But due to the passage of time and the death of the actors, the story has not reached us.

- Repeat it from the beginning," asked Amynandre. What was it? How was it carried out? And from whom did Solon learn it and report it as true?

This is a prologue to the Platonic account of the Timaeus, thus attesting to the authenticity of the account given by Solon more than a century earlier. We know from many echoes of authors who were contemporaries of the Hellenic sage that his unfinished verse poem dealt with the history of Egypt in great detail and with great precision, and was revealed for the first time; During his long stay on the banks of the Nile, he learned to read the hieroglyphs in the text itself, which recounted the tragic and real adventure of a continent engulfed by a Great Cataclysm, whose survivors founded, through their descendants, the Egyptian families, then those of the Semites, Phoenicians and Greeks, among others.

Before getting to the heart of life in Aha-MenPtah, let's continue reading Plato's interpretation of the prose story, so that we have it in some sort of concordance in our memory for the rest of this book:

> There is in Egypt," says Solon, "in the Delta, towards the tip of which the course of the Nile divides, a certain Nome which is called Saïtique, and whose largest city is Saïs. King Amasis reigned there.[2] For the people of this city, it was a certain goddess who founded it; in Egyptian, her name is Neith. But in Greek, they say, it's Athena. These people are great friends of the Athenians and claim to be in some way related to them. Solon recounted how, when he arrived among them, he came to be held in high

---

[2] During the 6th century BC, the Libyans in the west were fighting against the Egyptian army of General Apries and against the Dorian Greeks from Cyrene, who were themselves up against the rebels of Amasis, famous for his drunkenness and vulgarity. After various battles, Amasis was crowned Pharaoh!

esteem, and how, when he asked the priests who knew the most about antiquities one day, he discovered that neither he nor any other Greek knew anything about them. And once, wishing to induce them to talk about old things, he set about telling them about the most ancient things we have here. He told them about Phoroneus, who is called the first man; about Niobe, the flood of Deucalion and Pyrrha, and the myths about their birth and the genealogies of their descendants. And he tried, by guessing the years in which the events took place, to calculate their date. But one of the priests, who was very old, said: "Solon! Solon! You Greeks are always children: a Greek is never old! At these words, Solon hastened to ask: "How do you hear it? And the priest replied: "You are young, all of you, through the Soul! For, in the Soul, you have no old opinion, no old tradition, no science whitened by time. And here is the reason: men have been destroyed, and they will still be destroyed in many ways. By fire and by water, the most serious destructions took place. But there were lesser ones, in a thousand other ways. For it is said that once upon a time, Phaeton, the son of Helios, having harnessed his father's chariot but unable to steer it along his father's path, set fire to everything on Earth and himself perished struck by lightning. The truth is this: a deviation sometimes occurs in the bodies that circulate in the sky, around the Earth. And, at widely spaced intervals, everything on earth is then destroyed by the overabundance of fire. Then all those who dwell on mountains, in high places and in dry places, perish, rather than those who dwell near rivers and the sea. But for us, the Nile, our saviour on other occasions, also protects us from this calamity by overflowing its banks. On the other hand, on other occasions, when the gods purify the earth with the waters and submerge it, only the herdsmen and shepherds of the mountains are saved; but the inhabitants of the cities where you live are swept into the sea by the rivers. On the other hand, in this country, neither then nor in other cases, do the waters descend from the heights into the plains, but it is always from beneath the earth that they rise quite naturally. It is said that this is why the oldest traditions have been preserved here. But the truth is that in all places where there is neither excessive cold nor scorching heat to entrench it, there is always a race of men, sometimes more, sometimes less numerous. And so, whether among you, or here, or in any other place of which we have heard, if something beautiful, great or remarkable in any other respect has been accomplished, it has all been written down here since Antiquity, in the temples, and the memory of it has thus been preserved. But with you and other peoples, every time things get a little organised as regards writing and everything else that is necessary for States, here again, at intervals regulated like a disease, the floods of heaven fall on you and leave only illiterate and ignorant people surviving among you. So, periodically, you become young again, without knowing anything about what happened here, or at home, in ancient times. For these genealogies - which you quoted just now, O Solon - or at least what you have just read about events in your own country, differ very little from children's tales...".

There is no doubt that all these words are taken from the poem written by Solon. It really speaks of what the Wise Man saw and heard in Egypt. The truth comes out of his mouth, having verified the hieroglyphic texts himself. The facts stated by the Priest are therefore accurate.

But if Plato had faithfully copied the words of his very wise ancestor up to that point, he was clearly going to introduce a bravura piece of his own invention into the rest of the 'Timaeus', which would be the prelude to the philosophical path he would chart in 'The Republic' and 'The Laws', to the glory of the perfect state - and the Greek state, of course!

The politico-social organisational scheme becomes increasingly clear in the next paragraph, where Plato idealises the City and Army of his country! Thus, in the following passage, the Atlantean country ceases to be a continent and merges in the Past with all-powerful Greece! For the Present, in which the author is struggling, needs a serious helping hand if it is not to sink!

Let us listen to the fable invented for this purpose, and told - is unthinkable in reality - by the Egyptian Priest of the Initiatic Temple of Sais:

"And you don't know that the best and most beautiful race among men was born in your country, or that you and your whole city are descended from them, because a little of their seed has survived. You don't know because for many generations the survivors died without being able to express themselves in writing. Yes, Solon! There was a time, before the greatest destruction by the waters, when the city that is now that of the Athenians was the best of all in warfare and the best policed in every respect. It is said that the finest feats were accomplished here. It had the best political organisation of any city we have ever heard of.

Obviously, this passage was bound to put the Greeks in the right frame of mind, and encourage them to become once again what they were supposed to be!

To achieve this tour de force, Plato spares no effort, no expense! He opened wide the fictitious mythological archives of the Athenian gods, bringing in the benevolent Athena to found Saïs, where she took up residence under the name of Neith! Forgetting that this protector of the Saïtic Nome already existed there long before the first stone of the Parthenon in Athens was laid! But it doesn't matter to him, the Greek renaissance has demands that take precedence over reality! But let's listen a little more to this unorthodox Egyptian priest *(sic)*:

"I will not be reticent, but for your sake, O Solon, for the sake of your city, and even more so for the sake of the goddess who protected, nurtured and taught your city and this one, I will tell you this wonderful story. Of our two cities, yours is the older, by a thousand years, for it received your seed from Gaia and Hephaestus. This one is more recent. According to our sacred writings, eight thousand years have passed since our country became civilised. It is therefore of your fellow citizens of nine millennia ago that I am going to tell you briefly about their laws, and among their great deeds, I will tell you the most beautiful thing they accomplished."

Let's stop there with this most emphatic of Platonic descriptions, because the famous writer gives free rein to his own visions and philosophical precepts about the various classes of this ancient society, where the Hellenic combatants had a predominant and privileged place! This is the most absurd nonsense from the mouth of one of the most erudite Egyptian priests, whose hieroglyphics never included the word war because the people of his country had no soldiers!

The rest of Plato's account is more reminiscent of the Second Medieval War, which Aeschylus dramatised in The Persians. Our author, to make up for his homily and really return to Solon's Atlantis, describes how the venerable grandfather Critias recalled his memories. But this has no further place in our preface. If any reader curious about the continuation of this glorious piece so desires, the innumerable translations of the Timaeus that exist on the book market will amply satisfy him.

So let's return to the continent of Aha-Men-Ptah, from its human origins. To do so, we will also have to go back to the Origin itself, as conceived by its inhabitants and handed down to us on the banks of the Nile by their great-grandchildren.

The Origin with a capital O; the Origin of each of us, of everyone, of everything: of heaven and earth, of their containers and their contents! Whether we are believers or atheists, our thoughts have at least once been directed towards this common, unique Origin and its Creator, whether He is called God or simply 'chance'! And who could be more qualified to speak of this Origin than the very people who lived it and recounted it to their descendants, who engraved it in stone for all eternity?...

The aim of this book is therefore to enable readers of all spiritual persuasions to form their own opinions by reading the story - and not a story! - of Aha-Men-Ptah, who was wiped off the face of the earth in a matter of hours by the Great Cataclysm!

To get back to this Origin, we need to go backwards through the analytical chronology of the sunken continent. And while it may seem complex to go back so far into the past, the task is by no means insurmountable! There are many extant writings that recount the Annals of Aha-Men-Ptah, even if they are in anaglyphic hieroglyphics, and they go back a long way into antiquity! Whether these texts are engraved on raw or baked brick, then on stone; whether they are printed in clay or painted on leather skins that have barely been tanned before being written on papyrus, it is easy to see that *they all* agree in defining a single, highly spiritual and essentially monotheistic Origin.

The surprisingly clear metaphysics, both liturgical and theological, that emerges from this predynastic Egyptian knowledge makes it perfectly logical to say that their authors represented a superior civilisation, arriving there as the result of an Exodus and descending from an infinitely more ancient people who had lived elsewhere.

How can this preface convey the vital need of this dying race to communicate its Origin, both its achievements and the Unic God who made them possible, so as to give future generations the means to do the same by harmonising with His commandments?

How can we bring home to the people of the twentieth century this innate need for ancient communion that Souls had as Divine parcels coiled up in mortal carnal envelopes, with their Fathers, during their non-eternal earthly lives?

How can we make contemporary minds, too complexed by their environment, which they themselves are destroying, accept this vital need to harmonise every act of daily life with the natural commandments of a single God: Ptah?

Nowadays, how can we fail to shake our heads in amazement at this rigorous ethic that compels man to commit nothing that could be held against him at the "weighing of the soul", on pain of not being able to reach the Amenta, that "beyond death", to enter the "Kingdom of the Blessed"?...

All these questions are not without answers, however, because the oldest history of mankind has handed them down to us, transcribed by successive generations of scribes! They are there, in a multitude of inscriptions, engraved on the walls of the oldest tombs: at Saquarah, at Denderah, at Thebes, or on the foundations of the oldest Temples, "copied from ancient texts". In his own way, Mena, or Menes in Greek phonetics, who was the first king of the first dynasty, recounted the history of his ancestors. The year was 4303 before the beginning of the Christian era! The unifier realised the dream cherished by his great-grandparents: to build a Temple to the glory of God, *around which would be built the capital of the second Homeland thus founded*. The religious edifice was called Ath-Ka-Ptah, or Second-Soul-of-God.

This second soul, or 'second heart', soon became the name of the country, which was phonetised as: Ae-guyptos in Greek and Égypte in French. During the first two dynasties, it was also the name of the capital, which later became Aneb-Hedj or Les-Murs-Blancs, which the Hellenes turned into... Memphis...

The simple logic of this primordial denomination of Ath-Ka-Ptah is to admit that there was a first heart, a first soul, *elsewhere;* an ancient heart, an 'Elder Heart' of God: Aha-Men-Ptah.

The origins of this people can thus be traced back unquestionably to a Son of God who placed creatures made in the image of the Creator in an earthly place as a civilisation, around thirty-six thousand years before the birth of Jesus. In that place, an Adam learned to speak and to use his hands to work. The Word was incarnate! For more than four millennia, the Pharaohs were considered to be the distant descendants of Adam, the name coming from the hieroglyph Per-Aha, which means precisely: Descendant of the Elder!

By the end of this gruelling Exodus, which ended with the crossing of the torrid Libyan desert, the early pioneer had a growing and almost unconditional Faith in the God who had so severely punished his ancestors. By building the Second Heart under the enlightened guidance of Menes, he knew in his heart that he could now live in peace with other men and in harmony with his Creator, whose image he was. He knew the tasks to be accomplished during his earthly life, and the sins not to be committed on pain of dreadful penalties beyond Human Life. He had learned by experience what it cost to transgress the Divine commandments! Once the loss of their Eden, in the sun of this privileged land that had been Aha-Men-Ptah, was more than enough! He would only get it back a second time by totally abdicating his own personality for the benefit of the community. In this way, hope would be reborn, as would everyone's right to Eternal Life.

This notion of Divinity, as it existed at that time, undeniably required a cycle of abstract thought that was both dominant and decisive, formed precisely by a long accumulation of observations, reflections and meditations over many millennia.

This explains, in a way, why on the day when this maximum of intense spirituality was reached, a certain very human force of inertia was established, hovering over everything and every act of life repeated daily. The lofty, ancient thoughts that linked the Soul to its God were submerged at that precise moment, and gave way to a purely reasoning, materialistic mind! Something the Priests of the Second Homeland never wanted to see again under any circumstances! Hence the abundance of prohibitions and 'gods', or rather protectors of the provinces, who kept an incessant watch on every moment of the lives of everyone and everything.

But from Menes onwards, the imperative religious dogmas faded again over the centuries, only to fade completely as the millennia passed! After the invasions that preceded the beginning of the Christian era, and the Greek penetration, all that remained was mythology based on fantasy...

Thus were confirmed the words of Imouthes the Wise, whom the Hellenes named Asklepios: "*O Egypt! Egypt! All that will remain of your religion are fables! Even your children will no longer believe in it. Nothing will survive but words engraved on stones that alone will remember your pious exploits.*"

This is proving to be rigorously accurate! For who today cares to explain, or even more simply to study rationally, what specialists call "mythology"? Since no one can, or wishes to, go back in time within a more or less biblical chronology that necessarily predates Noah's flood, this even more ancient narrative remained a simple fable!

At a meeting in 1958, they advised all specialists to look into this thorny historical problem.

For we must not forget that until Ezra, around the middle of the fifth century BC, the Jews had no sacred writings or canonical rules from a religious authority, especially as the Great Synagogue did not yet exist.

There were certainly the laws transcribed by Moses, and reiterated by his successors who wished to create a stricter observance of the Commandments. There were also the speeches of the prophets who excited the Hebrew people and called for greater piety and virtue. Finally, there were many poets, who entrusted an illusory glory to epic songs... But this was no substitute for *an ecclesiastical authority* to choose and designate as such the writings of the Divine Will, inspired by It!... When for more than four thousand years these had already been in force in Egypt!

Moreover, Ezra was not content simply to gather together in the five books of the "Pentateuch" the laws that he was trying to bequeath to the Jews as the work of Moses, but he added to them legends common among the Chaldeans of his time, which themselves were based on Egyptian texts demonstrating the Power of God on Earth, particularly concerning the Great Cataclysm, the appalling transcription of which became the Universal Flood. The same was true of all creative things, as we shall see in detail later.

Despite many vicissitudes, the Jews, like the Greeks after them, had a History that was carefully preserved in a language that was precise because it was totally familiar, and above all highly embellished and perfectly commented on! How would it have been possible to penetrate the intimacy of a much more learned nation, the mother of the other two, but extinct, completely gone? First swallowed up with its knowledge in Aba-Man-Ptah, it was razed and destroyed a second time in Ath-Ka-Ptah, with its monuments and libraries...

So, as the reader plunges deeper and deeper into the past, he or she will have to make the effort to imagine, deep down, the many details of ancient life that are unfamiliar to him or her, and that have been blurred, melted away, erased, even hammered out of the texts on the monuments; in a few words, the reader will have to substitute his or her spiritual eloquence for the ruined deficiency of the barely visible traces!

That's why the colossal constructions of the most ancient dynasties that have come to light bear witness to a civilisation that came from elsewhere, from a distant, sunken land, where the East suddenly became the West, changing the face of things! They are the link between this prestigious past and our present, which is resolutely concrete and materialistic, while they are a reminder of the end of a people who believed themselves to be the creator of all things!

So the Almighty Divine Power plunged the survivors into an extreme Exodus, made up of adaptations and settlements, amalgamations and mixtures, which ended in a new land with the reintroduction of "clans" and "castes"! As for the indigenous tribes living on the spot, still in the age of carved stone, they welcomed these foreigners, the Nubians, without restraint, and they included everyone in their family circle, just like those they met during their long march towards the Light: Ath-Ka-Ptah.

No one was enslaved, but the newcomers understood that they needed a kind of supremacy to maintain order and unity. They encouraged the mystery that surrounded their Divine Origin, creating a superstitious fear that led to the foundation of the monarchical form that would last for over four millennia.

And so their second people were "reborn", made up at the top by the "Descendant of the Elder" and his "Cadets", with pinkish skin and either brown or blond hair. Then there were the "Ethiopians", black-skinned, with frizzy hair and little intelligence, but with the ability to adapt quickly! Finally there were the 'Kussites', who had taken the newcomers for gods and served them with devotion and faith. Later, it was these same Kussites who, wanting to keep the same God in their hearts, kept two of the three hieroglyphs of the name of the country in total perdition, in order to define their simple eternal belief: Ka-Ptah, the Copts, or the Hearts of God.

Within two or three centuries, a new people had been born under the leadership of Menes, the first "Per-Aha", or Pharaoh. They left behind their flint tools and precarious shelters, and embarked on the path of obedience to God for a better life. He even quickly formed new civilisations, both in the Near East and further east, while retaining intellectual supremacy against all odds for over four thousand years, with Ptah as Supreme Power.

The harmony was ideally achieved by the location chosen when a retirement plan was drawn up. Various locations had been explored, but only the one that had been given the beautiful name of: Ta Méri, "the beloved place", proved to be a perfect match. Even the locations reserved for the "Mathematics Combinations", perfectly suited to the same climatic conditions, were situated on the same parallels! Long before reaching this promised land, all the advantages had been rationally determined. This territory was without doubt the new link that would enable a Second Alliance with the Eternal.

The Nile was the vital axis, all the more so as, taking a new course, it had become even more aligned with a parallel Heaven-Earth axis. It was for reasons other than those often put forward for climatological reasons that the "River" was called "a gift from God". In fact, this long liquid mass that flowed across the entire country was the perfect earthly replica of the Milky Way, hence its anaglyph: Hapy. He called the Nile the Milky Way, as well as a special type of scarab beetle, the emblem of Isis, still known in Latin as 'the Flying Bull'. We will, of course, come back to all these elements, which are as subtle as they are logical, but it is easy to verify, for anyone who has been on the banks of the "Great River" under a starry sky, that the Milky Way is the Great Celestial River, a faithful reproduction of the Nile, because a long, milky white streak crosses the sky in all its width, stretching eastwards in two stringy sections - like the White Nile and the Blue Nile - and disappearing on the western horizon in a triangular lactoid cluster - like the famous terrestrial delta.

The harmonic link between Heaven and Earth is therefore no mere figment of the imagination, and any of the pioneers of the predynastic era could easily see for themselves the identity of the two Hapy, from the very first evening, simply by looking up. The bridgehead for God's recognition of the Second Homeland had finally been established...

To perfect it, they had to settle on this land in the same way as the stars were settled on the banks of the Great Celestial River: in geometrically-configured clusters, which sailed slowly after the driving Sun, like the Mandjit boats - the unsinkable ones - that had saved all the survivors. And their descendants followed the course of the "Great Earth River" to colonise the banks in "clans".

Up above, the zodiacal constellations, those 'celestial clans', vital elements of the fabric that makes up the Soul of every being, that Divine particle: the Ray Life that grants the Active Force, could begin their Action. They emitted - and still do through their central Sun - a radiation so colossal, and so powerful though invisible, that a Siberian Soviet laboratory calculated that it pierced the Earth at its greatest diameter, in $1/200^e$ of a second... Each of these twelve Suns, broadcasting at particular wavelengths, forms characteristic patterns and wefts, , which the "Masters" of the "Divine-Mathematical Combinations" obviously knew in their entirety. As more will be said about this later, we won't go into the details here.

"The first thing to emerge from this preface is the religious meaning of the engraved or painted texts."

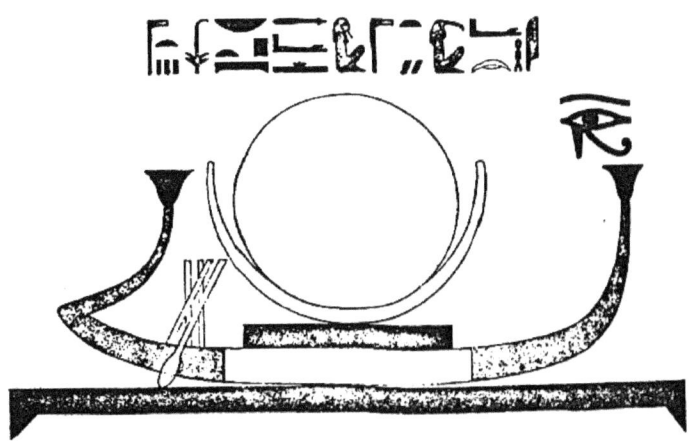

Here the Sun sails in a new direction across the upturned sky after the Great Cataclysm, led by the Sacred Eye.

In front of these "stellar canvases", the Sun sails backwards, introducing the precessional cycle of the "Great Year", the perfect number of which is 25,920 years. This figure has been astronomically and scientifically demonstrated. It is the second link in the chain linking the Earthly Soul to Heaven, and it too, along with many others, will be amply explained.

The third link fell to the builders who established themselves on the predestined land so that, through the buildings they erected to the glory of God and to ward off the evil spell cast by Him on His first creatures, they could achieve the Covenant. To do this, they built the Mansions of God, making them shine with all the riches available. But they also modelled in the rock an enormous Aboul'Hol, or "Father of Fear", a nickname that the Arabs still give him, whispering it with respect and terror! He is the father of all the reproductions that proliferated over the following millennia, all symbolising the Great Cataclysm. Their purpose was to remind everyone of Divine Law and the instructions for obedience, the only guarantees of Good Understanding and of no return from such an upheaval. That's why it was carved in the mass: to resist Eternity itself...

For the people as much as for Pharaoh, "the Ancestor", there was absolutely nothing enigmatic about this statue, especially as his temple, dug into the foundations, was there, all alabaster and pink granite, ready to favour all the intercessions that would allow an earthly life free from a second cataclysm. That's why all the generations that succeeded each other during the first twelve dynasties would laugh themselves to death if they could have been present when the Greek elites, then the super-intelligences of our Christian era, tried to find out what the Sphinx was!

The first thing that must emerge from this preface is the religious meaning of the phrases engraved or painted by the workers commissioned by the scribes, who were themselves faithful servants of the Priests who carried out the work of the Pontiff. And these hieroglyphic and anaglyphic texts, which are therefore quite hermetic for neophytes, were obviously intended only for the ancient Egyptians, not for modern Egyptologists. It should also be added, to better convey the ardour of the builders, that in forming the silhouette of Aboul'Hol, they thought they were also raising towards the sky, in the same axis as the "pyramids", a beneficial double, symbolising the same figuration of the reclining lion of the constellation of the same name! For the Great Cataclysm had taken place, as mentioned above, on July 21 9792 BC, at the very moment when the Sun was apparently passing through this stellar configuration, and also when, through the phenomenon of equinoctial precession and the pivoting of the Earth's axis, being in its cycle of the "Great Year", it began to move backwards instead of forwards. This is what it is still doing after twelve thousand years!

The symbolism of the two lions leaning against each other with the Sun rising between them, as well as this Aboul'Hol, or lion lying down and "father of fear", provides indisputable confirmation of facts that at the time were not at all a matter of proving, since everyone knew them, but simply of conjuring them up. The date of that month of July provides the argument and justification for all the iconography of the Egyptian Leonine. The catastrophic flood that irrevocably disrupted the lives of the survivors, leaving them with memories of earthquakes, tidal waves and titanic volcanic eruptions, in this month when the Sun was twice in Leo, remained synonymous with complete change.

So it seems that the protection requested of Leo has nothing to do with royalty itself, but more simply with the majesty of the sun, which is asked to sail in peace as long as it is in the constellation of Leo! For the mathematically proven precessional phenomenon was always likely to recur! Hence the incessant imploring of an entire people desiring real harmony in order to avoid the return of a new and equally appalling upheaval.

The problem posed by the precession of the equinoxes is a simple one. The Earth turns on itself in almost twenty-four hours. In other words, almost three hundred and sixty-five days a year: about six hours more, which should be added and which is in fact added every four years to give an extra day.

Time thus appears to be in harmony with Space. In practice, however, the situation is quite different. The second movement that drives our globe is the one that causes it to retrograde precessionnally. In other words, it also causes our planet to move backwards in space, by fifty seconds of arc per year. Now, since there is no Atlas giant to prevent the Earth from going backwards, and since in this precise case terrestrial mathematics is strictly useless, it takes 25,920 years for the Earth to complete one full rotation of its precessional movement, at the rate of ONE degree every seventy-two years. Which *is very* slow.

After completing a cycle backwards on itself, it will find itself back at a zero point, fixed on the day of the beginning of spring and known as the vernal point. This scientifically established truth is, however, unverifiable in human terms, given the length of this "Great Year" in space, except by an accumulation of astronomical observations made generation after generation. This is what has brought to light, through the chronological annals, a disruptive element in the system that can halt the harmonic unfolding of the movement: a cataclysm, for example.

The ancients knew all about the highly complex "Mathematical Combinations" that made up the well-oiled cogs! This is absolutely certain thanks to the documents that have come down to us through the Temple of Denderah, the Temple of the Lady of Heaven: Isis. In fact, the name is Greek! Its hieroglyphic name means Iset. A whole chapter will be devoted to her, as will the primordial meaning of the Denderah texts. A planisphere, in particular, transformed into a 'zodiac', has been the subject of controversy among scholars, who, divided into three groups, have been bent on proving that this astral configuration dates back only three hundred years before Christ, or two millennia, or even fifteen thousand years before that!

Today, it's easy to see that all three groups of scholars were equally right! It's also easier to explain the causes of the cyclical cataclysm. When the precessional recession reaches 180 degrees, 12,960 years have passed, and it was inescapable, for the Masters of the "Divine-Mathematical Combinations", that the imbalance of the human Soul would lead to a break in equilibrium during the geological imbalance!

What does this mean? It's that a permanent imbalance reigns within the earth as 'matter'. The precessional retreat of the Earth's crust is slower or slower than that of the burning mass compressed within it. This means that the magma, this colossal mass of some fifteen billion billion tonnes, most of it metallic, undergoing the attraction more or less slowly than the crust that encloses it, will undergo a different mode of pressure.

And when, as a result of this precessional phenomenon, the progress of which is felt differently by the crust and the magma, any point protruding from the one meets any point protruding from the other - perhaps by several thousand metres - the scraping that first occurs is transformed into the bursting of the crust, whose thinness and softness of matter cannot withstand the formidable pressure of the magma.

The entire History of Aha-Men-Ptah and Ath-Ka-Ptah will develop into a trilogy that the length of Time Past makes necessary.

Diodorus of Sicily, in his "Historical Library", tells us, in chapter XXIII, among other things: "I have learned here, commonly, that one must reckon between the time when Osiris and Isis lived, and the reign of Alexander, founder in Egypt of the city that bears his name, a period of ten thousand years."

This first volume, which will take us all the way to the "Great Cataclysm", will still speak of Osiris and Isis, for they were born under the last King of Aha-Men-Ptah: Geb. So we will stop this preface here, in order to penetrate into the Original reality, and go on from page to page, until the "Great Cataclysm".

CHAPTER ONE

IN THE BEGINNING GOD!

No one claims that a statue or a painting cannot exist without a sculptor or a painter, and that this creation has no Creator? Take care, my son, not to deprive the work of its creator. Instead, give God the name that best suits him; call him the Father of all things!

HERMES TRISMEGISTUS
(Book I, chap. 5)

*The Universe, to tell the truth, embarrasses me!
It moves like a clock with its hands!
I cannot imagine that this clock exists,
and that it has no clockmaker!*

VOLTAIRE
(Reviews)

The moment of the "Weighing of the Soul", which was crucial to obtaining the green light for *the Amenta*, was the main preoccupation of the Egyptians during their earthly lives. It was dreaded because the judgement was final! Only those who had lived without sin could join the 'Kingdom of the Blessed', where all the ancestors who had lived in this sunken Aha-Men-Ptah had found themselves, their faults having been forgiven by God. This Eden, lost forever to the living, became accessible to the 'pure', on the other side of Life, in the form of Amenta: the Beyond of earthly life.

In His infinite goodness, the Eternal One, who had given each human image a piece of Himself, thus allowed every just and good Soul, i.e. of the same weight as when it arrived on Earth, to pass unhindered through the limits of the carnal envelope.

This fear of disappearing 'afterwards', under floods of water and in appalling torments, just as much as the fear of never being able to rejoin the Blessed Ancestors who had undoubtedly had access to it, made the people malleable to the type of life recommended by the Priests without unleashing Divine wrath a second time: the communion of spirit and action ordered by God's commandments!

At every level of this Wise Society, none of the components gifted with a Soul, knowing that this Divine parcel linked them to their Creator, would have wanted at any price to attract His Wrath another time! And so it was that harmony reigned once again for millennia in Ancient Egypt.

The sceptical reader, and there are always some, will question this state of mind, especially in our contemporary materialistic world, for it seems absurd that an entire people, *without exception,* should chain themselves morally and physically as much as spiritually, thus subjecting themselves to the most rigorous ethics. I can well see the shrug of the shoulders and the pout of the modern man who feels clearly superior and much more intelligent for having freed himself from these retrograde prejudices that... that... etc.

But in fact, without even thinking about philosophising about the conception of a way of life, this species of intelligence no longer has a conscience or a Soul! For at present, 'freedom' is no more than the right to carry out one's own desires, even if it means inconveniencing others by forcing them to be prisoners of their personal actions! This 'liberal' form of life obviously no longer obeys any commandment whatsoever, and all licences - not freedoms - are encouraged... and they become a dictatorship *for everyone else*! This kind of freedom is nonsense and shows that something is already cracked. The end of the true way of life is near, if not the end of the world, and reasonable people are turning a blind eye, while the priests try to make God's commandments coincide with the unbridled desires of a youth that the elders themselves have driven to revolt!...

We are now at the point where the last royalty was in Aha-Men-Ptah. Everyone openly mocked the institutions, questioning everything out of place before the final tragedy. That's why this story deserves to be told... and pondered!

My aim is not to frighten people, or to preach about the future; that would be impossible, because the future will be created as and when people shape it by their own actions. This is why the protests of rising youth, covered up by adults, are in no way liberating for future generations!

My aim is to recount the past, as a historian, as it has unfolded since the origin of Aha-MenPtah, without making up facts that are often reminiscent of passages in the Old Testament.

My aim will therefore be to introduce you to this way of life, which is common to an entire people, in order to encourage you to reflect and perhaps preserve the future, which seems to be quite compromised in human terms, due to the psychic imbalance that is causing a rupture between heaven and earth, brought about by the rupture between God and His image. For all the current rantings preaching all sorts of freedoms are in fact abolishing the only freedom possible in this world in perpetual motion: freedom in accordance with God's commandments, and therefore in accordance with the rules that govern cosmic harmony.

It is clear that the injustices and vices that are becoming more and more widespread, despite the efforts made to eliminate them, have led to a crisis of faith, both among young people and among the priests themselves. The balance has been upset, but it could be restored if there were a real awakening to reality before the scales weighed all the souls, as happened at the end of Aha-Men-Ptah!

We will therefore go back to the Beginning, in order to better understand the creative work and its environmental process, so that humanity, the ultimate goal of the work, remains in constant harmony with its Creator.

Atheists and sceptics are already fidgeting in their seats, getting ready to let these inane pages fall by the wayside! Let them do nothing with them, at least for a few more chapters!

So let's imagine, along with non-believers of all kinds, that God is not the Creator, that He does not exist; that Creation is a mere "chance", a "coincidence", or anything else!

Having had no theological training myself, I can still conceive of this abstraction; but having had, on the other hand, a solid mathematical and logical foundation as a computer analyst, this hazardous conception cannot last more than half a second!

The denial of the Divinity of Creation is absolutely illogical! Thousands of "coincidences", adding up to millions of concrete results over hundreds of millions of years, cannot be the result of "chance"!

For the whole Universe, and not just our little earth, is governed by a system, highly complex of course, but dependent on a single Law. There can be no doubt about it, except for those who are afraid of the Truth. Indeed, when we say Law, or system, we mean: "Someone enacting the Law and being responsible for the system! But there you have it... and that's where the fear comes from!... No man has ever been able to formulate this Law, because it is billions of years older than he is!

This Law causes the Earth to revolve around the Sun, as well as the other planets, in a series of complex but interacting movements. The entire solar system rotates within a stellar group, which itself rotates around a central galactic nucleus, in a spiral movement lasting some two hundred and fifty million years.

Each galaxy in turn has an enormous sense of direction, propelling it at dizzying speeds towards the Quasars, for which new measurements had to be invented: 'units' of Time and Space, such as the megaparsec! The megaparsec is equivalent to 10^6 parsecs, each worth *3,260,000 light-years*. Which, to understand in our tiny Earth mathematics, gives a total of: 101,399,040,000,000,000,000 kilometres!... And this figure is tiny compared with the distance between *one* quasar and another!

Millions of galaxies, made up of billions of constellations encircling myriads of solar systems, move, attract each other, rotate in the same way, around the same Beginning, from which Creation made the Universe, this Space where masses far more enormous than our little Sun interact with each other to define Time.

What does Man represent in this incommensurability?... Strictly nothing! Whether he lives or not will in no way change the Harmony that reigns under the Law of His Creator, unless the biped with a soul takes himself for his equal and tries to create a danger himself by playing the sorcerer's apprentice! He has been the life-giving force behind the Great Work, and he must not become its devastator, even if, on Earth, the human being is everything... or almost everything!

After all, just a moment's reflection: all these movements of the globes, which no one disputes, all these phenomenal distances covered at dizzying speeds by the Earth alone: all these incessant movements apparently do nothing to change the behaviour of your body, because when you are at rest, you have the impression of being completely motionless! When you're moving forward, walking at a leisurely pace, putting one foot in front of the other, you're convinced that you're only going five kilometres an hour! Not to mention the fact that you may well be upside down, looking up at the sky above your scalp!...

Man is so convinced of the accomplishment of ordinary gestures that he no longer even thinks about the miraculous achievement represented by the simple natural act of walking! The ancients studied the philosophy behind it in detail, but the modern soul, materialistic to the extreme, is no longer in tune with God or any philosophy other than that which concerns its own well-being!

The body is on its way to becoming a mere mortal mechanism, with interchangeable parts: the heart has already been grafted!... The body is nothing but dust, and to dust it returns! This maxim is certainly becoming increasingly true, but what about the soul? Human evolution is accelerating at such a pace that it is deliberately rejecting all sentimentality and all spirituality.

The "thinking reed" of the Pascalian era already foresaw the progress it could make in the future; faced with the dizzying prodigies that have been achieved, it sees itself today, its hopes having been far exceeded, as the size of a "thinking oak"! That's why he tends to think he's indestructible, that anything is possible: and he thinks he's a demigod... But alas! Three times alas! May God preserve us from demigods! For intelligence is only intelligent if it cultivates and develops its vital force, impalpable but real, which links it to God: the Soul.

Intelligence in no way means "working for the Good"; it can also represent the personification of Evil, or even a mixture of the two, which is hardly the best solution! Knowledge combined with learning has never produced Wisdom. By refusing to look his conscience in the face, Man loses his soul, and loses himself too! That's why the worst calamities could inevitably result if mankind continues to accelerate the already delirious pace of Life! Because the natural geological movements of the Earth can be disrupted by this, due to the very fact that the Divine Work, and the Law that flows from it, evolves according to its own immutable rhythm, which is not the same as the one that human intelligence alone is trying to impose!

"I am all that ever was, is and will be". This unchanging maxim, engraved above the entrance portal to the initiation hall of the Temple of Sais, already impressed the Sage Solon, inspiring him to the same desperate reflections two and a half thousand years before us. Since then, the world has moved on even faster...

To demonstrate logically and mathematically the Divine Law used to conceive and create the multitude in immensity required as much patience as meditation, both of which I was forced to do because of my physical immobility ! Two serious accidents forced me to take long rests, but they enabled me to compile, compare, explore, extract and extrapolate the synthesis of numerous documents. I was also able to calculate, with and without the help of computers, on hundreds of assumptions and basic data, based on the same analogical principle as Pascal: "The multitude that does not reduce to unity is only confusion".

The first concrete glimmers of this unification appeared during my convalescence. Ever since I became a computer scientist, I've been convinced of this reality, which Pythagoras himself, long before the advent of computers, recalled in the motto engraved on the pediment of his school in Crotone: "God drew ONE from ZERO, just as he drew the Earth from nothing.

The Beginning of Time fits into this original framework, by virtue of the Divine Law that develops it. And if the sceptics are too quick to snigger, rubbing their hands morally as they already perceive a contradiction as big "as a mountain", let them be disillusioned... the demonstration they have in mind is false! Just because there is a beginning doesn't necessarily mean there is a beginning. Let me explain: ZERO is the beginning of a series of numbers; ONE begins the additional calculations.

Since Eternity has no beginning and no end, the Eternal One is indeed God when He begins a new beginning, because He perpetually recreates the Universe with His cosmic breath, at His rhythm, which is essentially different from that of our conception. Its duration is infinitely "other" than a time calculated quantitatively according to our earthly schedules. But its rhythm, all things considered, depends on the same coordinates. A *Great Cycle*, reduced to a solar scale, gives the Great Year; on a human scale, it becomes: quite simply, the DAY.

This explains Creation in SIX DAYS, which depend on this Law that applies to the whole of the Cosmos: Heaven and Earth. Each of these daily pulsations is endowed, in addition, with a triple movement, which the hieroglyphic texts call "respiratory", a term that admirably suits the details of the six days of Creation. These are the inhalation, or contraction; the time of rest, the horizontal plane; and the exhalation, or expansion, which gives the "Great Breath", expressed by the hieroglyphic symbol: △MER, or the

Beloved. This sign also symbolises the triple movement of the sun: rising to the zenith, descending towards sunset, and sleeping horizontally at night. It is the link between Heaven and Earth; the vital radiant element that protects: the Magnet. Why was it called a "pyramid" by the Greeks, a name that means absolutely nothing? No one can explain!

At the Beginning, therefore, Divine Time, setting in motion a new cycle, began again in $T-10^{12}$ (or 0,000 000 000 001) bringing about a new Origin of the Creation of the entire Cosmos. Going back in time to 1975, this date gives 168,121,464,064 years for the duration of a cosmic cycle: a Great Cycle of 168,121,464,880 years.

These figures, presented so abruptly, may seem the most extravagant! As a whole chapter is devoted to Creation, it is only mentioned here for documentary purposes, in order to clarify the moment when "Light bursts forth from Darkness", once again.

In $T-10^{12}$, God came out of his rest in the Uncreated: Chaos, creating Light at the same time, instantaneously. Matter then came through energy, culminating in matter-Spirit, the culmination of the cycle engendered in the image of the Creator.

So there was only God resting before this time $T-10^{12}$, in the Chaos that had returned! So it was not a Beginning that occurred then, but a recommencement: a new act of perpetual eternity!

When the Divine Breath resumed its work and its cosmic rhythm, it brought forth the Light, creating and procreating, through cyclic reactions and controlled interactions, the order of all things and beings, in the balanced harmony of the Universe.

This justifies the words: "God created man in His own image". But it is Man who no longer justifies his appellation as a Divine parcel! He tends to become a biped without a soul, looking strangely like the Beast of the Apocalypse! Here too, other eras have handed down texts that leave us dreaming; here's one of the most edifying extracts: "The children of princes are thrown against the walls. The families of nobles are thrown into the streets. The rich grieve and the poor rejoice. Every town declares: "Let's do away with those who exercise any kind of authority over us ." The priest, distraught, says: "If I still knew where to find God, I would kneel down and pray." Justice now exists in name only, and men do evil while claiming to be good. The old order has disappeared, and the noise will not subside. But it's not the laughter you hear: it's the murmurs and cries that fill the land. Young and old say: "Oh, if I could only die! And the little children add: "My father should never have given birth to me!

Is this passage taken from a document dating from the revolution of 1789, or from a manifesto of the 1968 protest movement?... Of course not! Not from either, but from a papyrus dating back to the fall of the pharaoh Mentuhotep, in 2195 BC! Chaos was about to sweep away the reigning dynasty.

Horapollon, a native of the first centuries who taught Greek in Alexandria, provides explanations of the Beginning, Creation and Chaos, among other things, in his initiatory work "The Hieroglyphics" that Christian exegetes would certainly not disavow, despite the antiquity of the symbols, which date back at least seven thousand years in Egypt alone!

But this ancient author fell into complete oblivion until the 16th century, when he was revived by his uneducated detractors, who consigned him to anonymity for three hundred years! Mr A. Wolff called him "an ignorant writer, whose work contains only a detestable explanation of hieroglyphics, certainly contrary to the spirit in use in high antiquity".[3]

Mr Wyttenhach, for his part, delivered the coup de grâce: "This is an inane compilation by a Greek of the Late Empire, who has

---

[3] *Vorlegen ber die Geschichte der Grieschischen Literatur*, vol. II

tried to give his wicked writing a higher profile by decorating it with the divine name of Horapollon!⁴"

He had to wait for Champollion, who, seeking inspiration in the Antiquities, was seduced by the interpretation of the texts given by this scholar. He demonstrated the close connection between Horapollon's "Hieroglyphics" and the system he was developing.[5]

As Champollion's understanding of the hieroglyphs seems to me to be, to say the least, marred by a multitude of errors, as well as by enormous gaps that need to be filled, I have turned my attention to Horapollon's writing itself. It should be noted that the author was an Egyptian grammarian who taught Greek in Alexandria during the reign of Theodosius. This speaks to the culture and seriousness of the character. Indeed, Suidas wrote of him: "He was a man skilled in his art, who was second to none to the most famous grammarians of Antiquity. This also enabled him to write remarkable commentaries on the works of Homer and Sophocles.

Fabritius, another historian of the same period, goes , saying that the text, translated by the Greek Phi lippe, came from a work in the famous library of Alexandria, and reproduced as such, because the very name Horapollon includes the hieroglyph Hor, which means Horus, and whose Greek look-alike is none other than Apollo! It would therefore be Horus himself, in predynastic times, who composed it for the use of the High Priests.

Clement of Alexandria, for his part, drew on other copies of texts saved from the first library fire to provide the real elements for understanding the 'Hieroglyphics', in his 'Stromata'. It was from these that I was able to extrapolate the key to the 'anaglyphs'. They

---

[4] *Dict. Histor.et Phil,* vol. I, 3-8.

[5] As a result, the last edition of this work, *Horapollonis Niloi Hieroglyphica,* appeared in Amsterdam in 1835, in Latin only.

are an inalterable well of intelligent and intelligible solutions to all the acts that accompany everyday life, just as much as the Sacred Life of religious acts.

This is why, throughout the centuries leading up to the Christian era, there was an invasion of Egypt, which, peaceful though it was, encumbered the Priests of Thebes, Heliopolis, Sais and Memphis! The thirst for Knowledge of the newcomers from all sides repelled the learned Egyptian Pontiffs, who often realised that all Wisdom was excluded from the souls of the seekers!

As a result, most of them only returned home with a tiny parcel of the Knowledge that had taken them all the way to the banks of the "Great River". But whether in astronomy, mathematics, algebra or various medical and philosophical disciplines, the 'crumbs' that were brought back opened up an abyss of thought for the Greek 'scholars'!

Hipparchus and Eudoxus, not to mention Eratosthenes, brought back many elements that enabled them to found astronomy on solid conjectural foundations. But the most important axioms of the 'Divine-Mathematical Combinations' had not been revealed to them. In particular, those concerning the Earth's retreat in space: in other words, the retrogradation due to the precession of the equinoxes.

In this respect, no definition more remarkable than the one obtained by simply observing the facts on the terrace of the Temple of the Lady of Heaven at *Denderah*, many millennia before our era, has ever been written! It is reproduced in the "Encyclopédie Méthodique et Mathématique", published in 1820, in the article entitled "Precession": "Precession is the almost invisible movement by which the equinoxes continually change place, moving from east to west very imperceptibly, causing the Sun to appear ever retreating in the course of a Great Year of about twenty-six thousand years, in the constellations, known as zodiacal, which encircle the celestial equator."

We would say today that the precessional movement is demonstrated by the successive increase in the longitude of the stars, which increases by one degree every seventy-two years, the vernal point thus moving backwards continuously by fifty seconds of arc on the celestial equatorial circumference, returning to a ZERO point every 25,920 years.

From this perfect, cyclical Number, let's remember a few key points:

-The Man-Day; from the moment of his birth until his death, the Man who lives on Earth will normally breathe according to the same regular rhythm, which is an average of eighteen breaths of air per minute. In other words, for one day on Earth: 18 breaths/minute× 60 minutes× 24 hours = 25,920 breaths/day.

-Man-Year; from the moment of his birth until his death, Man lives on average on Earth for seventy-two years. That's for the duration of an Earth Life: 72× 360 days = 25,920 days/life. This corresponds to ONE degree of equinoctial precession, and already provides a fairly remarkable mathematical evaluation scale for the different days of Creation:

25,920 years of the Great $= \frac{1}{1}$

25,920 days $= \frac{1}{360}$

25,920 per day $= \frac{1}{9\,331\,200}$

This first numeration in the enumeration of the Numbers of the Beginning is thus provided by the number 25,920, determined by the Great Cyclic Year, which itself periodically modifies the terrestrial criteria by its extremely precise data, generating them one after the other, changing in turn the configurations, the seasons, the "combinations" which provoke them, thus obeying this immutable Divine Law which goes back to the Beginning!

The modifications made to the places reserved for Life were therefore very necessary and even vital for those who wished to live in harmony with God, and therefore in harmony with the Universe, and could not therefore leave the architecture of their monuments in a false orientation, making it evolve according to the combinations of the sky. The foundations of many Temples preserve the plans for the modifications to be made at each new sothian cycle in order to remain directly under the radiant influence of this primordial star, Sirius. And it is to the credit of Newton, who was so often criticised for his false interpretation of Egyptian chronology, that he was the first to think of applying the retrograde calculation of the precession of the equinoxes to historical events, even though, unfortunately for this intuitive genius, the facts were wrong!

M. Bailly, in his "*Astronomie*" (p. 509), dryly notes this failure: "The idea of regulating chronology by the ancient determination of the retrograde equinoctial and solstitial points was beautiful and great, and worthy of a man of genius such as Newton. But he was mistaken in the application he made of it, and the resulting system fell because it was contrary to the facts".

Here the overriding factor of Logic comes into play! Simple logic, without any calculation or guesswork, should have proved to Newton the falsity of the short Egyptian chronology he was trying to demonstrate, whereas Laërce showed the existence of the Pharaohs forty centuries before his time, and Herodotus spoke of an origin going back more than twelve thousand years!

But neither will Logic demonstrate the absurd! And the Numbers of Creation will not be used for operations of the kind already condemned by Irenaeus: "The teachers who make you see clearly the supracelestial origin of Jesus by a calculation of this kind: given that the letters of Christ (ΙΗΣΟΥΣ) read as numbers, and added together, make 888; and that on the other hand the Greek alphabet which is used to translate numbers, includes eight letters used to write the units, plus eight tens and eight hundreds, which gives the same sum of 888. Jesus ren therefore closes in his essence all numbers, and therefore all perfections.[6]

Throughout these pages, no "far-fetched" tricks will be used to prove the calculations. In addition, perhaps a few mathematical curiosities will add some pleasure to the proofs! Like the unfortunate example given above with the number 8!

In Egypt, it was the Sacred Number: that of the Ogdoade, the Divine College. Eight was the number of perfect order and balance: that of Justice, and therefore of the scales that weighed souls.

The mathematical proof of this perfect balance is provided by the following rule: the eight numbers (the nine minus the number 8) multiplied by themselves give these results:

$$1 \times 9 \times 1234567.9 = 111\ 111\ 111$$
$$2 \times 9 \times 1234567.9 = 222\ 222\ 222$$
$$3 \times 9 \times 1234567.9 = 333\ 333\ 333$$
$$\text{etc.}$$
$$9 \times 9 \times 1234567.9 = 999\ 999\ 999$$

As for the symbolism of the Ogdoad itself, depending on the Ennead (i.e. 8 + 1 = 9, or God + the multitude), it shows its real possibilities as much as its mathematical supremacy, by the following demonstration:

$$0\ 9+8=8 \times$$
$$9 \times 9+7=88$$
$$98\ 9+6=888 \times$$
$$987 \times 9 + 5 = 8888$$
$$9876 \times 9 + 4 = 88888$$
$$98765 \times 9 + 3 = 888888$$
$$987654 \times 9 + 2 = 8888888$$
$$9876543 \times 9 + 1 = 88888888$$

---

[6] Book 1, 15, 2.

$$\times\ 987654329 + 0 = 888888888$$
$$\times\ 9876543219\ \text{-}1 = 8888888888\ \text{etc.}$$

In addition to the mathematical jugglery and mental subtlety it represents, this ancient technique has a very valuable philosophical component, but it is too far beyond the scope of this book to go into. Let us simply note here the very solid foundations of arithmetic and logic in the association of numbers.

And if Man, with his fatuity and selfishness, quickly forgot the Divine foundations of Creation, new cataclysms would cyclically remind him to be less proud and more considerate of God's work, even if the result remained mediocre! The name of the Divinity would change or be modified; the Son redeeming sins would always be burdened with the chains of humans going blind again; and the celestial movement would return to its initial point, changing only the form of thoughts and actions, but not the substance itself! The conclusion of human folly was the tragedy brought about by the Last Supper, and the sad but admirable reality that followed!

A similar drama, many millennia earlier, in a different form, preceded the end of Aha-Men-Ptah. And before we delve any further into the hieroglyphic texts, we need to understand that the Scribes responsible for writing down Tradition, the "Chebet", had been brought up and educated solely for this purpose! And they spoke only the Truth.

During the Exodus, the descendants of these Scribes were brought up to be able to mentally retain the texts that were transmitted to them orally, since all books were destroyed! It was only gradually that Scripture took over again. The first writings, hastily painted, are nevertheless exact reflections of Reality.

Although the meaning of the writing characters evolved, returning to its anaglyphic origin, the interpretation of the "Book" never changed! Whether it was under Narmer, i.e. before the first dynasty, or under Sesostris, two and a half thousand years later, or even under the Ptolemies shortly before the beginning of the Christian era: the formulas for the man who had to remain pure in order to enter Ameuta "Beyond Life" were always the same for seven millennia!...

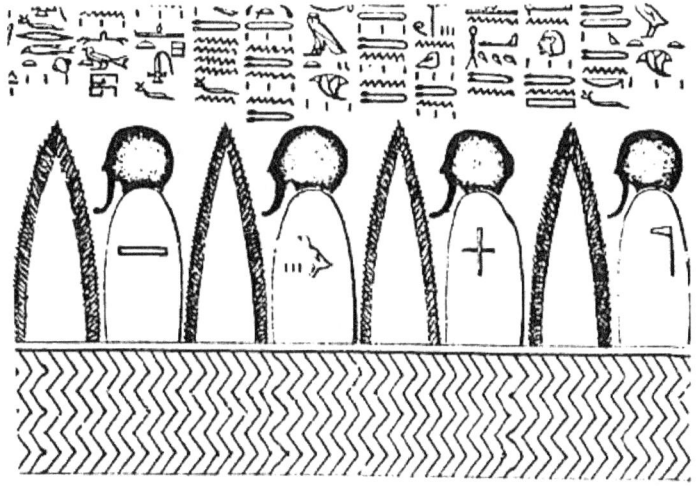

The first writings, hastily painted, are nevertheless accurate reflections of reality. Here, from right to left: Usir (Osiris) son of God, then father of believing men, then Father of Sons, finally the Justifier for the "weighing of Souls".
(Between each effigy, a stylised sycamore).

The date of arrival of the first survivors in the territory of Ta Méri, or "l'Aimé", is still hard to pin down to within a few hundred years. It's all become so remote, so implausible! Imagine asking a scribe used to translating Ovid to do the same with a story by San Antonio! This less conformist French slang is as far removed from the Latin version as the traditional writings of the first dynasties were from those in use under Ramses in the 19th dynasty!

So, taking bits and pieces from here and there, and adding end to end gleams that are as confused as they are diffuse, transformed here and there by the centuries and changed customs, a homogeneous text has emerged under my pen, coordinated by a most logical mathematical framework, which, I hope, is in line with early monotheistic theology, at least in its broad outlines.

Here too, a comparison is tempting in the face of the profusion of "religious" groupuscules claiming to be followers of Jesus and/or God, if not of the devil! A Pontiff of *Denderah*, faced with the display of impious worshippers of animal idols, or even true priests trained in his own school of religious novitiate, who worshipped Amun: a Ram!... Or Apis: a Bull!... That was five thousand years ago... And the celestial mechanics were distorted by a kind of devotion that drowned all real faith in God in a tasteless mysticism! The result was the upheavals that shook Ath-Ka-Ptah with each new royal era! Between the Old and Middle Kingdoms, in particular, which favoured the invasions of the Persians in the 6th century BC.

Since historical events, like other events, are repeated under the same conditions, the hundred or so coincidences that follow owe nothing to "chance"! Everything was created in a precise order, adding a partial result to a fragmentary sum awaiting evolution; and this: thousands and thousands of times to culminate in the creation of Humanity in its environment.

We are therefore going to go back in time, step by step, so that the chronology of Creation becomes clear, even if it is not accepted by the irreducible sceptics! Please don't let them be like the Judges of Hycetas and Copernicus, not to mention Galileo, in condemning what remains outside their understanding!

Anyone can doubt anything, of course; but we shouldn't sneer at things that are not understood! Herodotus has been there! And yet! And yet: Egyptian chronology takes the step backwards that he spoke of in his journey. Remember:

> "Up to this point in my story, the Egyptians and their Priests showed me that, from their first King to the present day, there had been 341 generations, as many High Priests and as many Kings. Now, 300 generations make ten thousand years, because three generations are worth 100 years. And the 41 generations that remain beyond 300 make 1,340 years. They added that during these 11,340 years, no god had manifested himself in human form, and

that nothing like this had ever been seen, either in times prior to this period, or among the other kings who reigned in Egypt in later times. They assured me that, in this long series of years, the Sun had risen four times outside its ordinary place, including twice where it is now setting, and that it had also set twice where we see it rising today.

It is obvious, and easy to criticise, that from a mathematical point of view, Herodotus was at odds with the simple calculation of data concerning generations! Three per century multiplied by 41 makes 1,366 years, not the 1,340 announced. In fact, it was the figure of 11,340 years that everyone was laughing at! With the exception of Manetho, all Egyptian chronologies were based a third of this figure! The most adventurous dated it back to 4300 BC. wasn't until the Predynastic tombs that specialists finally opened their eyes! No one would dare, in this case, even to simply smile when hypothesising a beginning ten millennia earlier.

Mathematically established by cross-checking the texts and by obtaining the exact date of the point at which the equilibrium of our globe broke down: 27 July 9792 BC, the Egyptian chronology can be more easily identified, in almost perfect agreement with that calculated by Herodotus! As for the solar upheavals mentioned by the author at the end of the extract quoted, it is quite clear that it was the Earth, by tipping over, that led the survivors to believe that it was the Sun that was falling!

Today, men have forgotten; they claim to be the only masters, using God's image as a mark to make Him fit them!

In the beginning: God breathed in a Divine particle, the Soul, so that His image would be differentiated from the animals and could rise in His Peace to live in peace! The "Luminous One", as the ancients called her, was indeed the receptacle of the benefits of her Creator; but today, she is a selfish complex, driven by a mental routine that avoids the slightest meditation!

It has to be said, however, that the contemporary "Masters" of thought, whether priests or philosophers, are challenging the dogmas of Christianity at the end of the millennium, even though they are totally necessary because every detail of the rite has been carefully thought through.

Monumental churches are now no more than a convenient name for hundreds of buildings in which the Divinity and Jesus, the Poor One, are totally absent in the Spirit! Perhaps crosses will soon be deemed unnecessary!

The Christian era 'coincided' with the retrograde entry of the Sun into the constellation of Pisces. The rallying sign of the first Christians was a fish, and a whole mystical and harmonic symbolism has gravitated around it since the birth of this Son, this Saviour, who came to redeem the sins of the world.

The vernal point of this constellation, Pisces, will occur in around forty years' time, and not in the year 2000, as the enlightened ones so fervently predict: what will be left of Christianity by then? And after that, our solar star will continue its retrograde course by entering the constellation of Aquarius, whose name is so predestined and well chosen, since for thousands of years it has indicated the moment of choice!

The celestial representation of Denderah indicates that Aquarius is ending a "Great Year", and shows a venerable old man holding a vase in each hand, visibly hesitating as to which one he will spill onto the Earth: he is Aquarius-Water!... The Flood in the making! But only in power, because he is at the moment of choice, depending on the conduct of Humanity. Will it be the Apocalypse, or the Golden Age?... The Golden Age: the good...

At the same time as the end of the Piscean cycle, the end of the Christian era is already foreseeable because of the nonsense that has reigned for some years among the 'Masters' Christian thought! Too much freedom in religion also leads to another, more pernicious form of slavery, and a far more serious one for the future!

As if under the wand of a perverse witch, the Soul is transformed in the believer himself, into an unconscious and carefree reason, since the Priests indicate that the Way taken is good! And Reason, supported by unreasonable reasoning, no longer reasons... with reason! The Soul is no more!

But perhaps this is done precisely so that the final choice between Good and Evil only becomes clearer?

During my enforced rest periods, I read and reread Jamblicus' Mysteries, as well as other Greek texts taken from Egyptian authors. But in 'The Mysteries', there is this passage that appeals to me enormously: "Just as the separate pilot of the ship stands at the helm, so the Sun stands at the rudder of the whole world. In the same way that the pilot directs everything from the stern, quickly giving the first impulse for the road that comes from him; in the same way, much more superior, God, from above, from the bosom of the first principles of nature, indivisibly gives the first active causes of movements. This, and many other things, are thus signified by navigation in a boat.

As in the time of Jamblicus, the perfect link between the Ancient and the Modern, God remains the Eternal Pilot. And the mystery of the boat, found more or less symbolically everywhere in Egypt, is not a mystery, any more than the "sphinx" or the planisphere at *Dendera*. The solar boat *at Abousir,* an enormous brick construction, always means the same thing, and is part of the overall context defining the Divinity's benefits to the Rescued of Aha-MenPtah. The full chapter on the "Mandjit", the unsinkable boats, will provide the full explanation.

Science is driving human civilisation forward too quickly for us to take the time to reflect on the past, and that's a mistake, because so many misfortunes could have been avoided!

The earth's environment is no longer sufficient to create new conditions for life, or even survival, for any species whatsoever, at the current rate of destruction of Nature. Because harmony in all things is equivalent to a balance established after a billion years and millions of additions! These additions, plant and animal, are all necessary to each other, one for the life of the other!

This is where the "Servants of God" are guilty: because they have learned about Divine Creation, and they let it happen with full knowledge of the facts. Perhaps because the Priests are beginning to doubt the validity of their Faith! Maybe because they don't want to fight against an active minority of their own for fear of upsetting their flock, when in fact they are driving them towards those who mock them!

Today, the free will of the soul is nothing more than a delusion, due to the growing influence of a very small minority, thanks to propaganda skilfully orchestrated by modern media such as newspapers, radio and, above all, television!

The brainwashing, the irony, the sarcasm and the ranting are increasingly getting the better of the simple common sense that inhabits the majority of the human race, which is pushed back, powerless to defend itself. And the chaos is becoming clearer by the day, the extremely slippery slope of which, once reached, can never be climbed again! In the beginning, there was God; and in the end, there will also be God!

Let's listen to Mentuhotep again, in another extract from his papyrus; it will be a good introductory thought for the rest of this book:

> "The country is filthy, and no one wears white linen any more. In the courts of justice, law books are thrown outside the walls and trampled underfoot in the public square. Offices are robbed, civil servants are murdered and their documents are burnt. What will my children do if another Divine Saviour does not come to bring a little freshness on earth to all that is feverish? But will the flock still exist?..."

CHAPTER TWO

MATHEMATICAL-DIVINE COMBINATIONS

> *The Universe is so resplendent with Divine poetry,*
> *because a Divine mathematics,*
> *a Divine Combination of Numbers,*
> *animates its movements.*
>
> His Holiness Pius XI
(Extract from his last Easter homily)

> *Perhaps later, if human thought*
> *Reaches the bottom of the mystery by pulling its chain,*
> *The dull number that we have read in heaven, Long buried as a*
> *null value,*
> *Must emerge glorious in the unique formula*
> *From which the whole problem will be solved.*
>
> Sully Prudhomme
(From Free Will)

The "Divine-Mathematical-Combinations" represent the geometrical figures and mathematical calculations of the celestial movements "of the wandering lights in relation to the fixed luminous ones". Cosmic harmony is achieved through these combinations, which are not supputative but depend on a single Law that forms the Universe.

It was this Sacred and Secret teaching that the Pontiffs who succeeded one another for millennia in the "House of Life" adjoining the Temple of the Lady of Heaven, at *Denderah*, dispensed sparingly to the High Priests alone!

This ancient "School", whose origins date back to the very arrival of the first survivors, is authenticated not only by texts, but also by the tombs unearthed under the Pontiffs' Hill, less than three kilometres from the Temple. There "rest" the "Sages among the Sages", the Blessed with the Knowledge of God. Among them, one taught under a "Master" of the 2nd dynasty, another under Khufu, the famous Cheops! The Royal Scribe of this pharaoh reports that the Temple was rebuilt by his Master "according to the data that were found in the original foundations, written on gazelle-leather scrolls by the "Followers of Horus", i.e. by the Elders themselves, long before the first King of the first dynasty ascended the throne!

It was therefore through these direct descendants that Divine Law was transmitted, whose "MathematicalCombinations" were to enable humans to direct themselves in Justice and Goodness. To understand these facts, we need to go back well before this second Homeland! Some twenty thousand years earlier!

The ancient Pontiffs were already teaching that the Earth, before being an earth, was something else: matter already awaiting creativity. It was combined in a different way, only becoming a receptacle for Souls, cycle after cycle, by virtue of this Divine Law acting evolvingly, ceaselessly, on all things and all beings. When a cycle came to an end after a certain number of periods, or eras, after a time of rest, the eternal movement was reborn, bringing Life once again, but in a different 'projection' in Space.

Which means that it - the Earth - is never identical to itself, any more than it was the day before, or the second before! Nor are all the things and all the living beings on it. For the Earth evolves with everything that lives from it, in it and on it, in Time and Space, following the solar rhythm and the precessional rhythm that coincides with the apparent movement of the twelve celestial constellations. These geometrical and mathematical 'combinations' lead day by day, second by second, to new c combinations:. which prepare not only for the next moment, but also for the tomorrows that will sing... or be disillusioned!

This study was undoubtedly deviated from its original meaning, first by Plato, who, returning from Egypt and speaking of these "combinations", introduced the word astronomy". Aristotle then opted to call these suppositions "astrology"! Fortunately, Hipparchus, and later Ptolemy, re-established the truth somewhat by teaching their fellow Hellenes that the learned Egyptians taught the sciences of the heavens to their students in sections of "special mathematics". In fact, Ptolemy used part of this term in the title of his main treatise, "Mathematical Compositions". But there is no doubt that Pythagoras was the great reporter after his seventeen-year initiatory stay in Egypt!

The sole aim of these disciplines was always to reduce to the smallest possible number, the simplest expression, from which the coordinates of the Law began. So, instead of speaking, of using the Word to solve movements, they used Numbers to describe and write these "Combinations".

Thus the numerical explanation of the Beginning, of Creation, of the process of the development of the worlds, and of Humanity on Earth itself, appeared, demonstrating the real power of the Creator over all things and all beings. It also proved the propitious moments for ruptures of equilibrium, which "coincided" with the periods of possible decadence in blinded humanity.

Many millennia later, in *the Book of Revelation*, Saint John prayed: "He who has an ear, let him hear", adding a little later: "I will give him a stone with a new name engraved on it". This seems to have no common meaning, but here again, by listening with the soul, the word pebble returns to its original etymology, which was: "calculi", meaning: to count with pebbles, or to calculate with Numbers.

It may seem tiresome to keep coming back to this numerical notion, but it was it that enabled this ancient civilisation to remain on the path of Wisdom for ten thousand years and to live in Peace! The archives of the Temple of the Lady of Heaven at *Denderah* contained treatises, of which only a few snippets have survived, the hundreds of originals still buried in an underground chamber whose entrance has never been found! In very long mathematical lists, all the 'combinations' are described, with the mental means of remembering them, and in which the Numbers display all their calculative properties.

A small glimpse does exist, however, in some museums, from copies of ancient papyri that were 'books' of elementary mathematics, with the answers to the problems posed, for use by primary school pupils. The four specimens: a leather manuscript, two wooden tablets and two ancient copies of ancient papyri!

These last two documents are the famous Rhind and Moscow mathematical papyri. They are vital for a perfect understanding of the very mentality of the teachers, as well as the marvellous subtlety of those who devised the exercises!

The Moscow papyrus, which measures 544 centimetres by just 8 centimetres, contains twenty-five problems. The interesting thing about this document of nine fragments brought back to the U.S.S.R. by the Russian Egyptologist Gulenitschef is that, although it dates from the 19th dynasty, as the scribe's signature attests, it is only a copy of an original papyrus dating back another sixteen centuries, which had been written by a Pontiff for the use of a Pharaoh's son!

In other words, this ten-year-old boy was literally juggling with mathematics and numbers 3,500 years before Pythagoras, Thales and even Euclid began to glimpse the axioms and theorems that they would become the European promoters of, and which were already in popular use at that time!

And there is only one mathematical discipline in this papyrus... Here's an example: "Type of calculation of a pyramidal trunk".

If you are given a trunk of a pyramid 6 high, with 4 for the lower side and 2 for the upper side: you calculate by taking the square of this 4, which gives you 16. Double the 4, which gives you 8. Then calculate the square of the 2, which gives you 4. Add the 16 together with the 8, then with the 4, which gives you 28. You then calculate $\frac{1}{3}$ from this 6, which gives you 2. So you double 28, which gives you 56. There you have it: you've found the exact answer, which is 56.

When you put it like that, the calculation is astonishingly simple! And the numbers involved prove that this was the true intention of the authors of the text. But remember your own experience of mathematics! For the same problem, we used, and are still using, the 'modern' cabalistic formula for the volume of a square-based pyramidal trunk, which is: $V = (a^2 + b^2 + ab) \cdot \frac{h}{3}$

For this problem, what is the most intelligent way to teach a young person this type of calculation?... Five thousand years ago, or today? It goes without saying that the operations performed are strictly the same in both cases! I leave it to you to answer...

Another more complicated example? Here it is. Taken from the same papyrus:

If you are given a basket with an opening $4\frac{1}{2}$ let me know its surface area. You calculate $\frac{1}{9}$ from 9, since the basket is $\frac{1}{2}$ egg, and that obviously gives you ONE. You calculate the rest, which gives you 8. You calculate $\frac{1}{9}$ from 8. This gives you $\frac{2}{3}\frac{1}{6}\frac{1}{18}$,[7] You calculate the rest subtracting these $\frac{2}{3}\frac{1}{6}\frac{1}{18}$, which gives you $7\frac{1}{9}$ Finally, you calculate $7\frac{1}{9}$ times $4\frac{1}{2}$ you 32. There you have it: you've found exactly the answer, which is 32.

The imaginary representation of the shape of the basket, which is ovoid and therefore similar to half an egg, is also symbolised hieroglyphically *by a half-sphere* (⌂). This will inevitably remind the young mathematician of our time of this more abstract formulationfor an identical calculation of the area of a half-sphere:

---

[7] This "Treatise on arithmetic" adopted fractions with a *unit* numerator, in order to better develop mental arithmetic. Instead of writing $\frac{3}{4}$, the student would write: $\frac{1}{2}\frac{1}{4}$

$$S = \left[\left(2d - \frac{2d}{9}\right) - \left(\frac{1}{9}\right)\left(2d - \frac{2d}{9}\right)\right] d.$$

The best method of calculation may not be the current one...

The second papyrus, purchased in *Thebes* in 1858 by Egyptologist Rhind, was also copied from an ancient manuscript. The scribe Ahmose explains at the beginning of his transcription: "I copied this treatise on calculation in the year 33, the fourth month of the flood, from the twelfth day, from a manuscript of the time of the Most Great King, to the Righteous Voice: the Elder Nêmarê".

It dates back to an even more remote antiquity, to the origins of Knowledge, when Knowledge was compiled on leather scrolls! It brought together all the elementary problems relating to Numbers and Measurement, the Science that was to become the study of "Divine Mathematical Combinations". Their teachers at *Denderah* were, in order of study: the 'Masters of Heaven', the 'Masters of Calculation', the 'Masters of Mysticism', and when the novitiate was completed and the Pontiff judged the student worthy of taking the final step, he was left in the company of the 'Master of Mathematical Symbolism', thus reaching the final stage of Sacred Initiation, entering the secret, hidden room reserved for this elevation.

It was with this Pontiff: the An-Nu, the "Great-in-Divine-Knowledge", that the final step was taken. It was in this sanctuary that the young priest learned the reason for the immense triangular volumes, erected with the sweat of the brows of the entire population united in the Faith, and which had a perfectly clear and precise meaning, which their names popularly explained: they were: the Seqt-BENMer-Shoum, i.e. "*the Beloved towards whom the Light descends*", in other words: the Pyramids!... That's right! This primordial symbolic monument took the name of "pyramid" (sic) by the grace of the Greeks, nobody knows why, or how, even becoming, as a sign of explanation (?) grain silos in Joseph's time!...

In these calculations of the trunks, which we will continue to call "pyramidal" for want of a better term, and which are described, as we have seen, in the Moscow papyrus, *the hieroglyphs are explicit about the names!*

- The half-diagonal is: SEQT ;
- the perpendicular to the height is: BEN ;
- the angle and its edge which gives the cosine: SHOU;
- the line ratio is: MER.

The whole becoming: "L'Aimé-vers qui-descendla-Lumière", or SEQT-BEN-MER-SHOUM, which in popular parlance simply became: MER, or... pyramide (?)!... MER = the Beloved, which is quite a programme! The chapter devoted to... pyramids will explain exactly what they mean.

As everything became mere appearances as soon as a new civilisation displaced the previous one, the Greeks paid absolutely no attention to the real issue raised by the Pharaonic enigma, contenting themselves with trying to solve it from their own perspective, thousands of years younger than they were, and not with the rigorous logic that should have guided their steps! So they invented a mass of gods similar to their own, babbling on and on about meanings they didn't understand at all! So let's not even talk about modern Egyptologists! Occasionally, however, scholars from other disciplines show glimmers of light that are of little interest to their colleagues, who are obsessed with the animal representations in ancient engravings. Laplace, the famous astronomer, wrote: "Seduced by the illusions of the senses and of his own self-esteem, man has long regarded himself as the centre of the movement of the stars; several centuries of work have caused the veil that covered the system of the world to fall from his eyes. He then saw himself on a planet that was almost imperceptible in the universal system, itself a small invisible point in the immensity of space. The results of this discovery are apt to console him for the rank that it assigned to the Earth, by showing him his greatness in the smallness of the base used to measure the heavens".

It was this first human perception that undoubtedly led the ancients to translate the movement of the stars into mathematical form, into a series of numbers, after they had suffered several catastrophes that had given them ample food for thought! The result was a law which, despite its apparent complexity, demonstrated a complete organisation such that it could only have been the work of the Creator Himself, His image: Man did not appear on Earth until billions of years later!

Even if a super-Einstein had existed somewhere "elsewhere", a formulation as brief as $E = MC^2$ would have been simpler than the Law!

Since Einstein's name has just been mentioned, let's take up his axiom, which clearly expresses, although it cannot yet be demonstrated, that the Cosmos cannot be defined solely by three dimensions (width, height, length) and that a fourth must necessarily be included.

Following this same principle, the ancient mathematicians expressed the fact that the Universe could not be defined solely by three components (space, time, matter) and that it was logically appropriate to add a fourth that animated the other three: the Eternal Creative Radiant Force of God. other words, God's Time.

Here's a very simple example!

As we all know, light emerges from space at a speed of 300,000 kilometres per second. The sun's rays therefore reach the Earth in approximately eight minutes. This means that we can perceive the luminosity eight minutes after its original emission.

So let's imagine - and this makes perfect sense - that as you're reading this, someone suddenly walks into the room and exclaims: "The Sun has exploded! We haven't got a minute to live! Don't laugh at the sudden madness of the person speaking, given that at the same moment you see the star of the day shining brightly!... For it is possible that this is the Truth...

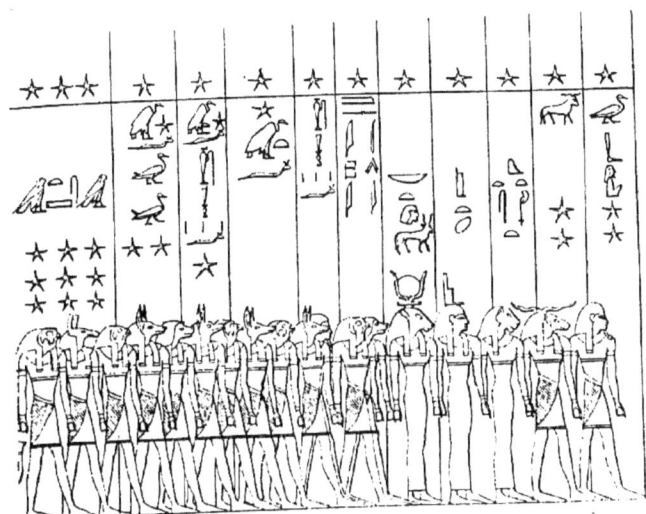

The fourth Time, that of God, is the vehicle of Souls, the divine parcels that regulate earthly time.
Here: *Isis leading the survivors of the Great Cataclysm to her second homeland: Ath-Ka-Ptah, Egypt.*

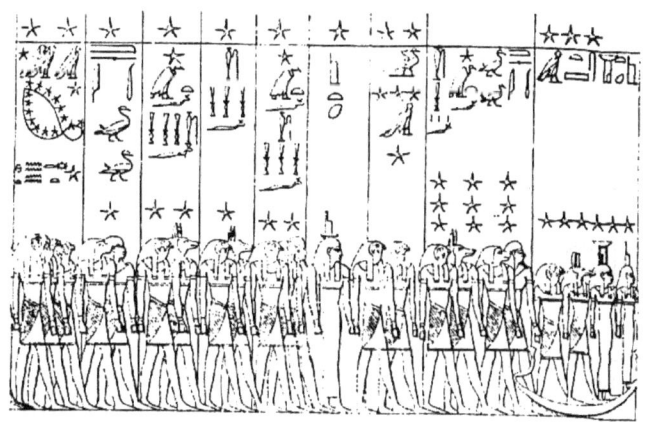

In fact, the Sun we see is just a photo, a pure and simple projection of the solar image that existed eight minutes earlier!

So, even though it's in sight, in full view of you, it may have exploded seven minutes ago, in which case you'd only have a few seconds of respite to get right with God before the Earth itself vanishes into thin air!

This is by no means science fiction, because it happens at least once a century in another system of the Universe. There are even supernovas that explode... two thousand light years away: in other words, they vanished two thousand years ago, and we can only now see the impact on our retinas or on the ultra-sensitive film of electronic cameras.

So there is without question a fourth element, that of the ancients: the Time of God. It is the vehicle of the Divine parcel: the Soul, and can guide it during its earthly sojourn.

In his Timaeus, Plato comments on the phrase engraved at the entrance to the Temple of Sais: "to be and to have been", which neatly sums up the notion of the Fourth Era. "The days, nights, months and years did not exist before the sky came into being; and it was by organising the sky that God himself brought them into being. These are all parts of time, and these expressions: to have been, to have to be, designate species of time that has begun, although without thinking about it, we apply them to eternal existence, to which they are no longer appropriate.

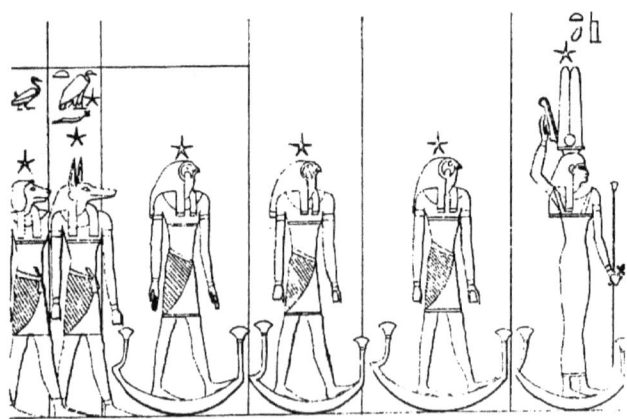

Isis bringing Osiris (triple because he will be the Father of the survivors. All triple hieroglyphs signify the plural).

Two certainties follow from the introduction of this fourth Time:

- Everything visible in space is necessarily visible in time, but not in the same Time;

- Everything perceptible in space is not visible in the same Time, but in a "parallel" time-continuum.

The purpose of this article is not to demonstrate the continuum advocated by so many scientists, but to show that the formidable Radiant Force spoken of by the ancients, and which comes from the celestial equatorial constellations hundreds of years away, can propel its energy towards the Earth through the said continuum.

To simplify things, let's say that this force, R, is a vector quantity. As it will always come from space according to the same directional harmonic law, the rules for calculating it will be extremely precise.

Starting from the premise that every action produces a reaction, whatever the energy deployed, R is the product of the interaction of similar but inverted elements: like man and his image reflected in a mirror. It was this incessant duality between Good and Evil, of Man and his double, depicted by the Wise Scribes in red and black on their hieroglyphs, that the Pontiffs calculated the 'Divine-Mathematical-Combinations' regulating the various combinations of the influxes coming from the enormous Suns of the twelve constellations, in order to quote in absolute numerical values the means of countering Evil and strengthening Good.

In more practical language, here's a typical example: when, during the fifteen minutes of physical training in the morning, springs fixed to a wall are stretched, it's easy to calculate the force with which the muscles of the hand pulled on the rubbers; but it's also easy to calculate the force with which the springs pulled on the hand! This brings us to the fundamental Principle of Creation: everything is complementary to everything else.

Just as it is now accepted that any particle of matter has a similar particle of antimatter 'elsewhere', so everything has its complementary double or 'anti'.

As far as Force R is concerned, it has been established that the propulsion speed of its movement can be defined as the translation performed by any other energy for one unit of time. Its displacement is therefore a vector oriented in the same direction. It should not be forgotten, in fact, that since the force of friction is zero in the sidereal void despite the great apparent speed, the speed of R will be constant for each of its straight lines until they are disturbed, or stopped, by some body.

This is the case when the carnal envelope of the human newborn arrives, as described by the Ancients at the beginning of the courses on the study of "combinations". As soon as the umbilical cord is cut, and therefore the maternal impulse is no longer involved in the creation of the carnal envelope, a primary pattern strikes the cervical cortex at that precise moment. The R-Force takes the place of the mother; the receiving brain will be indelibly impressed by this particular pattern, with colossal power, but not visible to the human being who has been impregnated by these very influences since birth. But the baby will give its first cry in the face of this intrusion, which will be the first reflex of a new Soul coming to Earth Life, now in its place.

For the Ancient Sages, these influences form the Divine thread that personalises each soul. It can be precisely calculated, since the basic canvas was exactly reproduced according to the same coordinates as those that impressed the cortex. The human soul can thus be in perpetual liaison with the creative celestial soul, if it does not itself break the agreement pre-established at birth.

The Priests of Aha-Men-Ptah had defined the problem very well, while at the same time pinpointing the direct powers they attributed to the various combinatorial solutions, having gone back a long way in time to provide solid support for their observations.

Let's take a step back into this created space, until the day when the Cosmos once again began to expand. It is said that Light springs from Darkness, separating Day from Night, Matter from Nothingness, generating millions of planets with their own movements, always rotating and oscillating in opposite directions, while revolving around millions of Suns at the centres of systems, themselves endowed with circular movements around millions of galactic nuclei, forming galaxies with billions of stars each! They themselves are...

But let's stop there, as this list could go on for another two hundred pages! Instead, let's look at an astonishing "coincidence"! That of all the galaxies that populate the known Universe that is our own: they are listed by astronomers in four categories, all four in spiral formation:

1) Normal spiral galaxies: these are galaxies whose arms start from a central nucleus;

2) "Barred" spiral galaxies: these are galaxies whose arms start from a diametrical "bar";

3) The ellipsoidal spiral galaxies: range from the almost complete sphere to the so-called "lens" type, such as our own, whose centre, the nucleus, is bulging, and whose Milky Way, so well observed by the ancients, occupies an outer edge;

4) Irregular spiral galaxies: these are galaxies that have probably been caused by supernova explosions, creating new worlds, and are currently the focus of a great deal of research using radio sources.

Now, the hieroglyph of Creation is a spiral emerging from the wave:

Today, this spiral means exactly what it did many millennia ago: the Creative Principle, the Law. For all things. including rocks and minerals: stones being considered beneficial or evil by the Ancients. In the Bible, we already see Moses fleeing Egypt carrying the breastplate with the twelve stones of beneficial influence.

They were considered to have accumulated in themselves, over thousands of millennia, the beneficial R-Force that was special to them. And why shouldn't that be possible?

"We have never been able to discover any juices circulating in rocks, but could we conclude from this that they are not organised? I don't think so; it is more natural to assume that their organisation, which is as simple as their composition, is perhaps just as difficult to observe. Apart from that, as we know that there are stones that are greasy to the touch, that there are others that let a lot of moisture escape when heated, that there are still others that become concave when cooled, that there are also some that become charged with electricity when heated; could we not admit that there is some subtle fluid that can circulate in them?... Perhaps an invisible, radiant force even creeps through them, like the magnetic fluid that rolls through iron.

This beautiful page is due to the curator of the Geneva library, Mr Jean Sènebier, who wrote the extract above, taken from the introduction he wrote as an addition to his translation of the opuscules of "La Physique animale et végétale", by Abbé Spollanzani. And this curator needed a good dose of audacity to write such sentences at the time he did! Did I mention that this work dates back to 1777?

This is to make the sceptics admit that, in addition to humans, animals and plants, minerals too were only 'fluids' at the Origin, emanating from that Light which sprang from the Darkness and which, mathematically, expanded first: one which became two, two which became four, then eight... The Sons of Ogdoade were ready to grow and multiply! Ever since the Negadah discoveries, and the appearance of the Denderah planisphere, this has been apparent to all researchers into Egyptian mythology, proving the perpetuity of the cyclical system of the Eternal Return, in a permanent evolutionary space.

As Leibniz said, "Space is an order of coexistences, just as time is an order of successions". But adding:

"That distance is nothing but a void through interposed voids, where temporal duration is nothing but an illusion!"

For Time, like God, although it is an almost tangible reality, remains impalpable. It is not a substance of any kind that can be felt! It does not modify objects or forms by itself: as Time

"Everything that is something exists!" said Balmès, quite rightly, before adding: "Show me where Time is!

Therein lies the difficulty! In mathematics, time does not catch up with the spatial continuum. It is divided into instants, themselves infinitely divisible, but which succeed one another, incapable as they are of merging into simultaneous acts! Of merging into joint existences!... Time is therefore not a concrete reality. To conceive of an instant existing in time, it must be actualised as a very short whole, without before or after, and be taken as such! For only God can be of the Four Tenses: to be and to have been, as the proud Saïtic motto reminds us!

No criterion seemed impossible to the ancients, who had learned that if nothing is made out of nothing, everything is possible to God, who constantly generates Creation. Space has as its fixed point the duration of the sidereal day, which is invariable.[8] Duration is itself symbolised by Light, the beacon that guides all "Divine-Mathematical-Combinations". And if, in this case, criticism seems

---

[8] Some astronomers do not agree with this postulate, whose absolute truth cannot be rigorously demonstrated. But their protests, if they are valid, do establish a Principle: that this postulate is necessary to demonstrate the measure of Time!...

easy, it's worth taking inspiration from certain possibilities that seemed impossible just a short time ago!

We have already seen how Laplace 'corrected' Newton's nonsense, but do we know that the latter had previously attacked Descartes himself? In his twenties, Newton was already very interested in physics, and although he was a fervent Cartesian, he nonetheless furiously scratched out the French author's writings, with continuous annotations that always began with: "Error...

Thanks to the third law, brought back into use by Kepler and of which Descartes had been unaware, geometers had succeeded in bringing this tendency towards the centre out of the vagueness in which Cartesianism had left it. Huygens, by improving this conception of gravity, was soon to deduce the real shape of the Earth and determine its flatness. It was therefore quite natural that Newton should conceive the idea of comparing the Moon's tendency to be attracted to the Earth with the analogous tendency of heavy bodies on our globe. In 1666, there was no difficulty in making this comparison, and there was no risk of the same repercussions that Copernicus had suffered fifty years earlier! Especially as the end of the "Principles" is strictly in line with the ancient texts: "This admirable arrangement of the Sun and planets can only be the work of an Almighty and intelligent Being. And if each fixed star is the centre of a system similar to ours, it is certain that, since everything bears the imprint of the same design, it must all be subject to one and the same Being: for the light that the Sun and the fixed stars send back to each other is of the same nature. Moreover, we see that He who arranged this universe placed the fixed stars at an immense distance from one another, lest these globes fall from one another by the force of their gravity.

"This infinite Being governs everything, not as the soul of the world, but as the Lord of all things."

Newton continues a few paragraphs later:

"As each particle of space exists, and as each indivisible moment of duration lasts everywhere, it cannot be said that He who made all things and who is their Lord, is never or nowhere. Every soul that feels at different times, through different senses, and through the movement of different organs, is always one and the same indivisible person."

The same is true of our solar system, which is totally isolated in space - on our human scale, that is! It is surrounded by these twelve constellations, some one hundred light years away, whose smallest Suns are thousands of times bigger than our own! Which is to say that if one of them, instead of being located billions of kilometres away, replaced ours at the centre of the solar system: the solar system would be reduced to ashes!

Fortunately, our planets are subject only to the mutual gravitational actions of their various components, and only to the heat of our daytime star! But the intense rays coming from the twelve constellations of the celestial equator bombard our planet without interruption, crossing it from one side to the other! What can we say about our carnal envelope, which is the first to suffer the effects, whether beneficial or harmful, depending on the 'combinations' and the measures taken to avoid certain consequences!

Quite happy to counter the ancient and Newtonian theories, both astronomical and divine, and certainly because they were "divine", Laplace, who prided himself on being an atheist, liked to write: "God is a nice hypothesis that explains a lot of things! In other words, God is a Force that Science cannot reach and that explains all the forces without which Science would explain nothing!"

This caused the very Catholic and very learned Barthélemy-Saint-Hilaire to literally jump to his feet, commenting shortly afterwards on these words in the preface to his translation of Aristotle's "Treatise on Heaven": "How can it be that astronomy has come to ignore God to such an extent? Is this not the blindest and strangest of contradictions? Was it worth denying everything to the senses and giving everything to reason, only to deprive reason of the only foundation on which it and the rest of the universe rest?

For my part, I have quite the opposite opinion of astronomy, and, full of gratitude for the teachings it gives us, I thank it for having taught us so much about the works of God. However, I believe that to this first lesson it can add another, no less valuable. It teaches us to know ourselves better, at the same time as we learn more about our relationship with all that is infinite and eternal.

Although I am in complete agreement with M. Saint-Hilaire, his opponent, M. Laplace, the famous author of "La Mécanique Céleste", apart from his atheism, and placed very high by the five volumes of his work, agrees with him! That's why we shouldn't hold a grudge against his astronomical mind alone, which is completely devoid of any celestial soul! Why should we? Because he provides scientific proof that, despite the "Great Cataclysm" and the Earth's rotation, the upheaval did not become a "general catastrophe":

"The truth is that the absolute motion of the molecules of a planet must be directed in the same direction as the motion of its centre of gravity. But it does not follow that the rotational motion of the planet is directed in the same direction. Thus, the Earth could rotate from east to west, and yet the absolute motion of each of its molecules would be directed from west to east, which must apply to the revolutionary motion of satellites whose direction, in the hypothesis in question, is not necessarily the same as that of the planets' projective motion."

The end of this passage, as we understand it, is crucial! There could be another 'Great Cataclysm' in the times to come, with the Earth pivoting axis to axis, so that the Sun resumes its apparent course in a direct line, i.e. it once again appears to rise in the West, and the survivors will re-establish their roots somewhere, in a territory that will have escaped the upheaval!

Copernicus, moreover, in his work condemned by the declaration of 1616 of the theologians of the Holy Office, demonstrated numerically the theory that the aforementioned Laplace would later adopt! Here is the passage: "Long and often repeated observation has taught me that the phenomena relating to each of the other wandering stars of our solar system, derived from a calculation by which the movements of the stars of the various orbs and of the sky itself were related to the Earth and were thus so closely linked together that it became impossible in any of the parts of the sky to move anything without causing confusion in each of the other parts and in their entirety.:.

This extract from the book "On the revolution of the celestial orbs" caused quite a stir at the Holy Office!

This is why the Church, going against the grain of its detractors, and responding to Catholic scholars who did not know how to express their deep convictions about a "different" historical chronology of the Old Testament, advised its exegetes to take a more moderate stance on the Holy Scriptures. In 1943, His Holiness Pius XII warned his listeners in an encyclical about certain chapters of the Old Testament: "The Bible is not a single book, but a group of works of very different literary genres: some exhort, others tell; and even those that tell are not necessarily historical in the modern sense of the word.

On this significant note, in January 1948, the Biblical Commission clearly stated its position on the problem posed by Genesis:

"The first duty of the scientific exegete is to make a careful study of all the literary, scientific, historical, cultural and religious problems connected with the chapters of Genesis. It would then be necessary to examine closely the literary processes of the ancient Eastern peoples, their psychology, their way of expressing themselves, and their very notion of historical truth. In a word, all the material from palaeontology, history, epigraphy and literature should be brought together without any prejudice. It is only in this way that we can hope to see more clearly into the true nature of certain accounts in the first chapters of Genesis. In the meantime, we must practise patience, which is the prudence and wisdom of life".

Which is our case here; being able to decipher the ancient texts of 'MathematicalCombinations' more easily than many of the scholars who have previously studied the problem. If so many scholars have been "condemned" by the Past, it is because Man is automatically against his fellow man as soon as he does not understand him, and that consequently, it is beyond his comprehension!

CHAPTER THREE

CREATION

In the beginning was Nou, in whom floated the seeds of all things present in Ptah.
　　　　　　　　　　　　　Temple of the Lady of Heaven
　　　　　　　　　　　　　　　　　　　　Denderah

In the beginning God created Heaven and Earth.
But the land was deserted and empty,
darkness covered the abyss,
and the spirit of God hovered over the waters.
　　　　　　　　　　　　　　　　　Old Testament
　　　　　　　　　　　　　　　　　Genesis, I. 2.

In the phonetic Egyptian language of the early dynasties, Creation was pronounced NOU, which was written as described briefly in the previous chapter.

Naturally, much later, the Greeks made her a goddess: Nut. But she was no more than a pale imitation of the "Lady of Heaven", the very human and good Queen whose admirable story made her much more than a goddess! Better still, as the millennia passed, the Pontiffs of Denderah confused her with her own daughter Iset, whom the Hellenes named Isis!

Before explaining this in more detail, let's delve a little deeper into the hieroglyphic understanding that animated the Priests and Hierogrammatists, both in their religious thoughts and in their everyday lives.

The first alphabet, which was more nuanced, was more conducive to popular writing. It was only later that a form appeared that assigned different values to different groups of characters, so that their meaning could only be perceived by the initiated. In this way, certain additive signs appeared in various numerically determined spaces, completely changing the meaning!

This spiritually advanced language, which was in danger of being lost forever when Aha-Men-Ptah was swallowed up, along with all its written archives, was the first concern of the surviving Pontiff when he arrived on dry land in the company of a few novices, including his own son. He set up an "Oral House of Life" for them, where they were taught a piece of Knowledge by heart, even though they were still incapable of understanding it! Their only task was to preserve intact and pure in their memory the precious extract that the eldest of their own children would in turn have to learn and pass on.

Thus, for several generations, the Original Tradition of the Sacred Texts was preserved, including that of the "Mathematical Combinations". And little by little, the written transmission procedures of the Ancestors were re-established: *hieroglyphics*. These were developed during the long period of the Exodus across Africa, during which all kinds of rock engravings flourished along the continuous line followed by the reformed people, and multiplied over hundreds of metres in width. Thus, from southern Morocco to Nubia, passing through southern Algeria and northern Chad, Tripolitania and Libya, first tools, then writing itself on skins, reappeared where deserts had not yet been created and where the wadis were still rushing rivers gnawing away at steep cliffs, as is still very easy to see today.

This is why the arrival in Ath-Ka-Ptah was accompanied by an astonishing display of an entire civilisation, well developed and very old, of which hieroglyphs were the last link to be reconstituted.

Since Champollion, Egyptologists from all over the world on both sides of the Nile have been examining these "bizarre" characters, which baffled them quite a bit, and which derived from the knowledge of the predynastic monarchies, well before the reign of Menes, forming a false idea of the civilisation they were discovering.

In this way, a parallel interpretation of ancient Egyptian life was forged, based on multiple animal worships and "abominable tales", whereas this was founded solely on the cult of a single God who, having created man in His own image, demanded that he live in complete harmony with Him. All the rest was popular literature, embellished with inferior spirits and genies created by High Priests in need of constant supervision of their flocks in order to preserve their original purity.

If the scholars who "translated", or rather "interpreted", the ancient texts did not solve anything about the various "combinatorial" sciences, this is essentially due to four causes:

1) A definite lack of study, and therefore competence, in ancient Divine theology, the reason for the imperative dogmas, and the various cults that were included in them. This is why the metaphysics spread out without any scruples by innumerable authors, provides incomprehensible "abstract" translations! The only concrete example of this would be the idea, found everywhere, of the Sun being elevated to the rank of Divinity... if it were not also false! This mythological fabrication is unthinkable from a race whose intelligence cannot be doubted, and whose 'Mathematical Combinations', based on precessional cycles of 25,920 years, amply proved that they knew the solar mechanism as well as we do, devoid of Divinity, but not of creative power.

2) Secondly, the ignorance of the learned translators of the phonetic origin of the words making up the Ritual of Priestly Science, which formed the exclusive heritage of the "An-Nu", the Pontiffs teaching the future High Priests!

3) Ignorance, above all, of the fact that these "An-Nu" transmitted their spiritualised language only among themselves, personalising it as it were within the hieroglyphs in an "anaglyphic" language dating back to the most remote antiquity of Aha-Men-

Ptah, communicating to their Ritual: the Word, the primary cause of their temporal as well as spiritual powers.

4) Ignorance, which stems doubly from this, namely the hidden and sacred meaning of the hieroglyphic anaglyph, which used the vehicle of the "vulgar language"! (sic, Plutarch). It was in this way that Pythagoras began his studies at the Temple of Sais, learning popular hieroglyphics, i.e. the everyday reading of characters, before beginning to learn the dotted consonance symbolising anaglyphics. And to pronounce it correctly, he had to be truly initiated into the specific phonetisation itself, in other words... the opposite of the system advocated by Egyptologists.

It is therefore absurd to continue to try to translate or, at the very least, interpret the hieroglyphs using Champollion's method for the Sacred, which is still hidden in the modern Coptic language of the early Christian era! The fact is that the existence of a language that also conveys Number and Measurement, along with Divine Law, is clearly disturbing to Egyptologists, especially if they are atheists! For others, it seems that everything is clear, and that there is no need to explain the inexplicable any further!

Yet modern Coptic is made up of nothing but scriptural conventions, whereas ancient hieroglyphics were nothing but symbolism! The Greeks were the first to set the sad example of simplified and very approximate interpretations of texts that were already very ancient for them! Pierre Benoit's book is undoubtedly thousands of times more 'true' than Plutarch's 'Isis and Osiris', which has nevertheless served as a reference for Egyptologists for two thousand years! No one questions this hodgepodge of abracadabra texts, because everyone is convinced that this is the only way it can be, given the insurmountable wall of protection used to conceal the original context! The most insane of these imbroglios was when one scholar tried to point out that the Crab was indeed officially accepted, since it was engraved on the zodiacal planisphere of Denderah, in the place reserved for this constellation. But the learned "defenders of the tradition emanating from the works of Plutarch" retorted that there was nothing incompatible with the ban, since this zodiac was of Greek origin and already known to the author!

These researchers, who are highly erudite, patient and very honest, undeniably lack the opportunity to immerse themselves in the Ancient Spirit, directly and not through the Greeks! This would enable them to understand, along with the ancient Egyptian soul, the true nature of the Faith that animated these genial builders of monuments to the glory of their God, who themselves lived only in brick houses, and therefore destructible, because Eternity belongs only to the Eternal. Man, as a mere mortal image, did not represent the Creator with a human face because of the respect he had for his Divinity, but built a Dwelling for him in his own size, and placed a symbolic animal in it: a bull, then a ram, in order to remain in harmony with heaven, linking the creature to the Almighty. This was the general idea of ancient Thought, determining the action and reaction that flowed harmoniously from Origin and Creation.

This ideological penetration, which will be carried out step by step to make it easier to understand, will in a way be the oxygen coming from that distant era and which will bring Life back to resting minds, thus bringing back to us many learned presences, both spiritually and mathematically.

From now on, therefore, we should identify with them, by thinking like them, in other words, by using an identical style of associating ideas. The sterile war that has pitted several different conceptions of Egyptology against each other and has held back the work of many scholars in this field for more than a century should have no place in this book, whose sole aim is to enable everyone to make their own contribution to the edifice, by modifying it, so as to give it an unshakeable structure: the one that was its own 7,000 years ago!

Finally, and this is where the comical - naive - side our contemporaries lies, all the ancient Greek authors admit that not only did they give their own interpretation of the Egyptian writings that they did not read in any way, but that there was also a symbolic script that was incomprehensible to them!...

Diodorus of Sicily speaks of "sacred discourses heard, but which are words without continuation". Jamblicus "understood nothing of the entire language of the order of priests". Plutarch, for his part, says more suavely that "the language of the Priests remained obtuse to him!" Porphyry does the same, but speaking of the "hereditary language" of the Priests, which is more interesting, proving that there were two. Tacitus wrote that "the language of the Fathers was insoluble". The same was true of Lucian, Lucanus, Origen, Philo, Synesius and hundreds of others who tried in vain to solve the enigma. Not to mention Clement of Alexandria, who had all the information and could have provided clear instructions, but probably didn't want to!

But the problem of understanding the sacred language was clearly posed because, even in the so-called "vulgar" language, the greatest source of error came from the total uncertainty as to the nature and quantity of the hieroglyphic symbols. One well-known Egyptologist made a certain drawing into a crown, while another made it into an eyelid! But the classic case, often cited, is that of the differences between Champollion's dictionary and that of Birch, an equally famous Englishman: in a typical sign, the former sees a crenellated parallelogram (?), whereas the latter indicates that it is in fact a chess game! (This game was all the rage among the elite six thousand years ago).

How, under such conditions, can we not be tempted to give new meanings to symbols that the ancient spiritual understanding makes obvious? For, as Clement of Alexandria wrote in his "Stromata" (quoted as the epigraph to the preface of this book), hieroglyphics have always retained their three symbolic meanings, namely:

-the *value of a thing*, in a popular idiom;
-the *value of an idea* in a concrete sentence ;
-the *value of a reason in a sacred text*.

In addition, the various Pontiffs who succeeded one another in Ath-Ka-Ptah included in it a hidden, occult value, in order to protect from possible invaders the Knowledge that would enable them to change the face of the world and thus put it at odds with God. The 'common' use of the word was perpetuated only in the 'Houses of Life' attached to a few Temples, where the future High Priests were trained. But the same phonetisation could be written symbolically in three different hieroglyphs, which allowed for nuances that were much more gradual than ours, almost to infinity!

Creation, for example, phonetised as NOU, was written as N:  and the "OR":  . But there are countless 'other' variants, since with the three signs of each, there are three different interpretations! Either:

N = the wave at rest 

1) *Thing-wave*: inert water ;
2) *Idea-wave:* primordial water (containing potential Life) ;
3) *Wave-reason*: water containing the Origin of all things.

N = a vase (or empty container) 

1) *Vase-chose:* an empty container;
2) *Vase-idea:* an empty carnal envelope ;
3) *Vase-raison:* a container for soulless content.

N = a germ 

1) *Thing-germ:* a food seed ;
2) *Idea germ*: the origin of the earth ;
3) *Germ-Reason:* the creative Origin of the Universe. The occult meaning of the three "N's" is: the Uncreated; it is the Divine germ which contains within itself all the creations of the Universe.

For "OR", the three ancient versions are:

OR = a spiral ☺

1) *Spiral-thing:* the image of a multitude ;
2) *Spiral-idea:* an idea of grandeur ;
3) *Spiral of Reason* Cosmic Force in the Uncreated.

OR = an empty skin

1) *skin-thing:* envelope without soul ;
2) *idea-skin:* no consistency;
3) *reason-skin:* empty space.

OR = a chick

1) *chick-chose:* containing the newborn ;
2) *idea-chick*: containing a potential life ;
3) *reason-chick*: containing the potential soul.

The occult meaning of the three "ORs" is: the Soul that comes from the Uncreated. It is the complement of the Divine seed that gives access to Knowledge.

This brief overview of the hieroglyphic language as it was learned in the Living House of the Temple of the "Lady of Heaven" at Denderah, six thousand years ago, provides an excellent insight into the subtlety, as well as the intelligence, of the Sages of the First Hour.

The phonetics of "NOU" will therefore have a hundred different interpretations, depending on its place in the context, depending on the reason or idea leading to its use in a sentence. Not to mention creative occultation.

Inside the western wall of the Great Temple of Denderah, which is more than two metres wide, a staircase leads up to the terrace twenty metres higher up, where the observatories for the "Mathematical Combinations" were located. On the inner eastern wall, the story of Creation is inscribed in relief: "In the beginning, NOU was the celestial envelope containing Ptah, GodGreat-in-Numbers, in which floated, merged, the germs of all things and all beings present in Ptah, who rested before starting Creation again according to the eternal cycles".

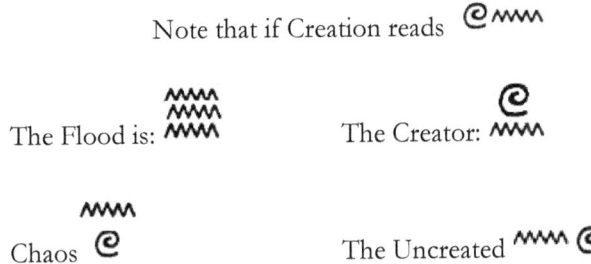

An extremely precise and comprehensible storyline emerges for those who follow the initiatory cycles. The very origin of the hieroglyphs is then revealed, borrowed from the Original History of the "Elder" people: that of Aha-Men-Ptah.

From this "NOU" derived the nickname of the last Queen of the Sunken Kingdom, for she gave birth to the one who would soon enter into Glory: Ousir, or Osiris in Greek. In memory of the Queen - not a goddess - whose children took on the onerous task of leading all the survivors, even though they were divided into two enemy clans, towards their new common destiny, which only the Great Cataclysm had been able to bring together: In this second homeland of Ath-Ka-Ptah, Nut became the "Lady of Heaven", the Protector of the Living, while Usir became the Protector of the Dead, given the miraculous way in which he was resurrected after being murdered by his own half-brother!

This is what determined the primitive symbolism of the eye, which means: "He gives Life". This meaning, in the present and therefore still relevant for centuries and centuries, must be taken literally, in all its expressive beauty.

In the many fragments of mathematical papyrus found here and there, there are extracts from a treatise on fractions, which provide all the possible fractional operations that, one day or another, an inhabitant of this second homeland might encounter. While looking through them with interest, I chanced upon the key that opens the mathematical doors to the calculation of the days born of Divine Creation! And it was only possible to do this by adding the guesswork of another 'coincidence': that revealed by knowledge of the symbolism of the 'oudjet' eye.

Aristotle, intuitively aware of the harmonic flow that flowed from all the constructions that struck the sight of visitors to Egypt, exclaimed on leaving the Temple of Denderah: "The continuity of Time and that of Space are indeed correlative here! Mathematics inspired this eminent philosopher with some fairly abstract thoughts, but they also left him perplexed!

Einstein was more rigorous and pragmatic in his assertions, declaring much later, without having been to Egypt: "The mind cannot bear the idea that there are two structures of space independent of each other; one of metric gravitation, the other electromagnetic. We must be convinced that these two types of field must correspond to a unitary structure of Space.

The worthy 'Masters' of Measurement and Number had, however, integrated the key to this unitary structure into their cosmogonic writings, thanks to Numbers, and precisely through this 'Treatise on Fractions', where they were well protected from prying eyes!

To penetrate still further into the thought processes of the "Great-of-True-Science", we need to take up their reasoning which, while occultly addressing initiates and novices in hieroglyphic to inculcate in them the symbolism of Knowledge, wished to include a turn of phrase which could nevertheless make it understood by all future generations for whom this language would have become hermetic!... Prescience or Conscience? Both at the same time, most certainly, in the desire pass on their setbacks as a warning of what they themselves had experienced, and which should not be repeated a second time! And to be comprehensible, this symbolism should only be dictated by Divine Law and its 'Mathematical Combinations'.

It was therefore logical to assume that the Key to Understanding could only be symbolised numerically at that time! It was the only way to be understood by future generations. Calculus is, and always will be, the same process of numerical understanding at every level of scientific discipline that will follow, both on Earth and anywhere else! For the Pontiffs, like our present-day scientists, also thought that other interstellar systems might possess a planet, where another Divine Image of the same development as ours through the Divine particle that is the Soul, could in the Future come to Earth and try to understand them!

In December 1974, American scientists from the N.A.S.A. used the same symbolic digital key to try and make themselves understood by a people from "another Universe". They sent an Atlas rocket, christened Pioneer X, to photograph the planet Jupiter and then sent it far away, out of our system, to get lost in infinity, in Space... Get lost? Who knows? Perhaps a civilisation similar to ours, elsewhere... The chances of that are so slim that there isn't even one in a hundred million when you calculate the probabilities! But who knows? So the rocket carried a golden aluminium plate, 150 mm × 230 mm, on which were engraved the symbols of its terrestrial origin, as well as those of the trajectory it is following.

The very principle of ancient figurative hieroglyphs has been employed for this purpose. It will be easy to read for any intelligent person with a basic understanding of astronomy and calculus, in other words: "Celestial-Mathematical-Combinations"!

To the left of the engraving, a sort of explosion represents the positions of fourteen Pulsars[9] in relation to our Sun, represented by intersecting lines, obviously of different dimensions, but to scale.

---

[9] *Pulsating stars*, whose diameter is around ten km, but whose mass is greater than one million tonnes per cm² /... This is why they emit regular and easily identifiable radio sources.

Above, schematically reproduced, are the two states of the most abundant element in the entire universe, and therefore easily perceptible 'elsewhere': the neutral hydrogen atom. The transition from one to the other is accompanied by a very characteristic emission at a wavelength of 21 cm. At the end of each of the lines representing the trajectories of the Pulsars, small lines give the frequencies of the emissions of each of them in relation to the 21 cm band.

As the frequency of Pulsar emissions decreases over time, intelligent beings intercepting Pioneer X would determine the time elapsed since the launch of the device. The scale for the size of the man and woman is provided by the spacecraft itself, stylised in the background, and very characteristic in its shape. The final motif at the bottom of the plaque represents the solar system itself and the planets that move within it, including the Earth, from which the rocket's trajectory originates.

So this numerical symbolism is the easiest thing in the world to explain, whatever the intellectual baggage and language of the "person" likely to find one day - or millions of years from now! - this golden aluminium plate! So the Pontiffs had done the same when they engraved their texts: introducing a digital transmission code to obtain both the Key and the Knowledge worthy of those who wish to live in harmony and communion with Ptah: the God-Great-in-One, the Eternal Almighty.

The tombs uncovered over the last century, and more precisely since 1820, in the Valley of the Kings opposite Luxor, as well as at Saqqara and Denderah, are edifying in this respect. Most of them have walls and ceilings covered with texts that amply demonstrate the fear of the Soul leaving its carnal envelope of not joining in Amenta those of its "Elders". During their earthly lives, the body *and* soul did everything in their power to live in accordance with the Divine commandments, even if they no longer fully understood the rite, even though the end result was obvious!

So translations, imperfect though they may be in this respect, do no more than illustrate this immemorial theme. Here, for example, is G. Lefébure's translation of the text engraved in the tomb of Petosiris:

> "O living people! If you read my words and listen attentively to them, you will find them useful. The way of the one who is faithful to God is good; the one whose heart directs him to it is blessed. I will tell you what has happened to me; I will make you aware of God's will; I will make you enter into the knowledge of his spirit.
>
> If I have reached this place, the City of Eternity, it is because I have done good on earth, and because my heart has followed God's path, from my childhood until this blessed day when I join my Elders. All night long, the spirit of God was in my soul, and at dawn, I did what He loved. I practised righteousness and hated iniquity. I did not associate with those who ignored the Spirit of God. I did all this thinking that I would reach God after my death, and because I knew that the day of the Lord of Righteousness would come at the weighing, at the division of Souls, at the Judgement.
>
> O living ones! I will make sure that you are instructed in the Divine will; I will guide you towards the path of Eternal Life, the right path for those who obey God, for if their happiness is great on earth, it is even greater in Amenta".

This extract, from the beautiful text inscribed on the walls of the tomb of Petosiris and composed by himself before his death for this purpose, implies a spiritual life that no modern theologian would dare deny, even though it dates back to well before the beginning of the Christian era. And as this Sage did, almost all funerary monuments attempt to instruct the living in the Divine Will. Not only by the strict commandments instituted since the Great Cataclysm, but by proving their earthly necessity by symbolising them in a tangible way. This is why Creation entered into the "Fractional Spiraloids", which by their very essence represent the infinitely divisible multitude, but whose sum cannot be greater than ONE.

This is why the "Treatise on Fractions" brings together the constituent elements of Creation with a subtlety that still leaves you amazed! Because there are so many 'coincidences' here that you can't even begin to fathom!...

Lastly, the "Masters of Measurement and Numbers" taught, and with good reason, that the fractions of a whole were primarily intended to lead their students to conceive in their thoughts the notion that all things are creative, because every hieroglyph thought up and projected after another would be embedded in a word in its rightful place, then in a sentence that took on a precise meaning, to arrive in a text at a conclusion: a unit of a whole, forming a tiny parcel of Knowledge.

CHAPTER FOUR

THE ORIGINAL SYMBOLISM OF CREATION

> *God is the immortal, incomprehensible and universal object, the eye that never closes, the light that penetrates all things.*
>
> EPICTETUS
> *(To the Emperor Adrian)*

> *In addition to this, a considerable number of geometric shapes are included among the elements of Sacred Scripture. Straight, curved and broken lines, angles, triangles, quadrilaterals, parallelograms, circles, spheres and polygons, among others, are frequently reproduced, as are the simplest figures.*
>
> CHAMPOLLION
> *(Précis of the hieroglyphic system)*

In the very conception of the symbolic numerical construction of Creation, in the early stages of the new soul's impulse towards God, everything suggested that the Divine particle that had made Man a carnal envelope could only move towards Knowledge by domesticating its own knowledge acquired through observation.

One having created the many, it was appropriate at the outset to reconstitute the elements of this unit, which could be broken down into infinite numbers. But in what order? And above all, having lost all tangible contact with this first intelligent civilisation, how was one to choose from among the twenty-eight fractional calculation procedures set out in the papyrus, each specifically responding to a particular subject?

Certain very complete categories were complicated as if for fun, such as those concerning the weighing of precious metals: gold, silver, electrum, etc. The study was therefore by no means easy for the researcher with a point of reference! The fractional systems for masses, volumes, liquids, powers and even 'abstract' distances had to be reviewed, each with its own fractional scale!

The same applied to the measurement of grains, which was symbolically linked to notion of duration in Time! This seemingly surprising abstraction, and the fact that it was necessary to 'break down' a unit weight into six of its parts, merited closer study.

The seed being the Germ, and therefore "Creation" in potential, and the six fractions representing the six days of Creation "in Time", all that remained was to take a serious look at the calculation to obtain the Key! The six fractional hieroglyphs of this subtle mathematics are:

$$\frac{1}{2} = \bigcirc \qquad \frac{1}{4} = \triangleleft \qquad \frac{1}{8} = \triangleright$$

$$\frac{1}{16} = \frown \qquad \frac{1}{32} = \smile \qquad \frac{1}{64} = \text{∫}$$

With my logical computer training, the base 16, hexadecimal, appears clearly, immediately evoking the incomplete total of this series! In fact: $\frac{1}{2} + \frac{1}{4} + \frac{1}{8} + \frac{1}{16} + \frac{1}{32} + \frac{1}{64} = \frac{63}{64}$

So there was no doubt that $\frac{1}{64}$ was missing from this sequence, which, in the context in which it was established, seemed illogical. For a fractional set established for a numerical system apparently serving no purpose, but appearing in anaglyphic language as primordial, UNITY. or the entire Divine cycle, had to exist! Unity = Creation: the association of ideas was obvious! But what was missing was the seventh hieroglyph which, numerically, would allow us to calculate Man's Time, and which, symbolically, would be the seventh day: the Lord's Time of Rest.

These six drawings were reminiscent of something important and already defined, which had to be found and completed in order to understand the overall meaning of these graphic representations.

It was then that the admirable story of Iset, during the Great Cataclysm that engulfed his country, reappeared with the meaning of the Sacred Eye - oudjet - which symbolises resurrection: a new Creation.

The six fractional symbols are in fact the six parts of the oudjet: the eye of Iset which, through the tears that flowed from it, resurrected her husband: Ousir.

The occult meaning of this 'oudjet' is Creativity, but there was still no seventh symbol! It was only incidentally, when looking at the various components of the analytical chronology of the "Temple of the Lady of Heaven" at *Denderah*, that the solution, both symbolic and numerical, became apparent.

This religious edifice, often rebuilt, but built on the first predynastic foundations, was dedicated first to Nut, then to her daughter Iset, with whom she eventually became confused. It is for this reason that the Lady of Heaven has a double quality here. A third must not be added, as is often wrongly done, because the name "Hathor" means "Heart of Horus", in other words, the mother of Horus, and therefore Iset, under her real name!

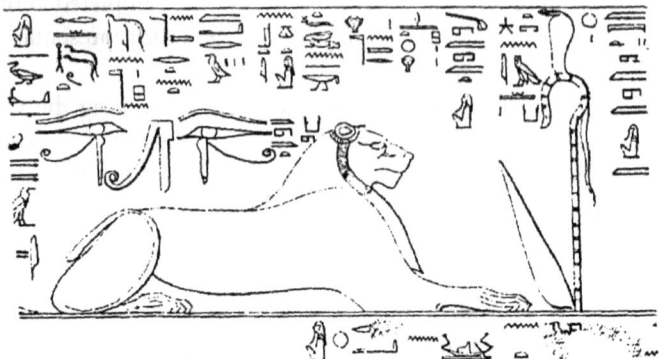

The lion looks to the right, whereas all the faces in the hieroglyphs look to the left. The "oudjet" eye, the sacred eye, is represented in its two positions: the old, on the left, and the new (Creation) on the right.

In this Temple, then, in a very dark back room, the ceiling is entirely engraved with an eye: that of Iset, weeping and reanimating her husband's body through her tears, under the impulse emitted by this reflection of the Divine particle that is the soul, the holder of the processes of creating sight and creating Life.

Tears are symbolised in their triangular form, whose cyclical symbolism has already been explained, and there are sixteen of them, to which were added two angular branches of a seventeenth for the termination on the ground.

The hexadecimal base is still clearly visible in this representation. And this is all the more clear for those initiated into the ancient mathematical sciences, because a whole philosophical page of the "Combinaisons-Mathématiques-Divines" (Divine Mathematical

Combinations), taken up again by Pythagoras in his "Golden Numbers", explains "Human Time" by the occult Number 16: the Phoenix Number 0588235294117647.

The eye of the new Creation leads the boat "Mandjit" to its new destination, watched over from heaven by Osiris, son of God.

That's right! That's right! It's a number that starts all over again, spinning endlessly on itself: a Phoenix Wheel with a base of 16...

Man's Time is divided into 16 cycles, the seventeenth being the end *of a* time, not *of* Times! Apart from the philosophical considerations of each of the eras determined by this 16-digit Number, multiplied 16 times by itself, always gives a result with the same arrangement of the 16 digits!

Or: × 2 = 1176470588235294

× 3 = 1764705882352941

$$\times\ 4 = 2352941176470588$$

$$\times\ 7 = 4117647058823529$$

$$\times\ 13 = 7647058823529411$$

$$\times\ 16 = 9411764705882352$$

And the end of *the cycle* comes on the seventeenth beat:

$$\times\ 058823529411764717 = 9999999999999999$$

The Eye of Iset, reconstituted in its entirety, in its "*Oudjet*" symbolism, thus takes on its full meaning of creativity: Creation.

The tears here represent the vital fluid in full creative conception. We must see in them the whole of the Trinitarian rhythm impregnating humanity, just as, according to the same Law, the Sun physically impregnates the Earth.

The sun rises in the sky to reach its zenith at noon, then descends towards the West, where it is touched by night as it disappears over the horizon. Night is symbolised by the horizontal line joining the angle formed by the day, thus aptly representing the "Underworld": the Amenta, the double, the "Ka" of the engulfed Aha-Men-Ptah, which has become the "Kingdom of the Beyond Life", wrongly translated as the "Kingdom of the Dead": "Kingdom of the Dead".

The tears of Iset are human; the rays of the sun are the celestial transmitters; and the cosmic souls follow the same triangulation cycle with a similar rhythm, which eternally revives in this Kingdom those who have been able to navigate the Great River of the Douat, i.e. those who have been decreed pure and without sin at the weighing of Souls.

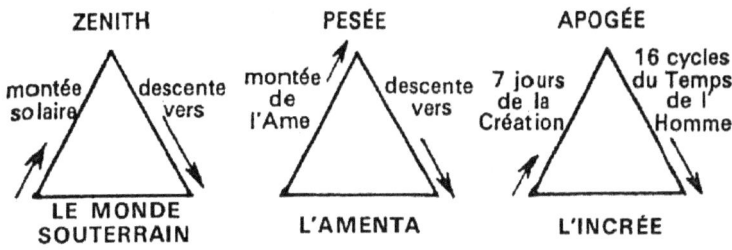

(Divine Triangulation, or: from the Uncreated to the Created)

These three triple cycles, punctuated by the current of the same "Great River" with its three names: the Nile, which is terrestrial; the Milky Way, which is celestial; and the Douat, which is cosmic; augmented by the fourth Time, that which belongs to God alone, are strictly identical in their numerical and geometrical formulation, but in times - or days - of increasing mathematical fractional duration, which will be explained later. Let us confine ourselves here to that of Creation.

Coming from the Uncreated, the apogee of Divine Time is reached on the seventh Day, when the Creator rests from His work. It was on this Day that the Time of Man was established, meaning that it was from this moment that the Divine particle reached the already-formed hominid, forging the Soul that would enable him to become Man, the image of the Eternal, who would have free will and the free choice to create his own future.

Each of the sixteen human cycles is therefore broken down into three celestial triangulations which are the precessional "Great Years", and which thus occupy a duration of: $25{,}920 \times 3 = 77{,}760$ years; or, for the duration of the sixteen human cycles in this triad: $77{,}760 \times 16 = 1{,}244{,}160$ years. To obtain the complete Time of this 7th Day of Creation, we need to add the part of the 17th cycle symbolised by the unfinished triangle touching the ground, which will be explained in "its time", and which is the Historical Time of Humanity, in a way: 38,505 years. They are the Time of growth: of intelligence!

The Time of the 7th th Day is therefore:

1,244,160 + 38,505 = 1,282,665 years,
or: $\frac{1}{64}$ *of the Total Time of Creation.*

The various calculations for the other six days are therefore easy, and the accounts are simple:

Time on Day 6th: $\frac{1}{64}$ of Total Time

Time of 5thth Day $\frac{1}{32}$ of Total Time (or) $\frac{2}{64}$

Time on Day 4th: $\frac{1}{16}$ of Total Time (or) $\frac{4}{64}$

Time on Day 3th: $\frac{1}{8}$ of Total Time (or) $\frac{8}{64}$

Time on Day 2th: $\frac{1}{4}$ of Total Time (or) $\frac{16}{64}$

Time on Day 1: $\frac{1}{2}$ of Total Time (or) $\frac{32}{64}$

The Spiral, the hieroglyph for Creation in SIX DAYS, is expressed as follows:

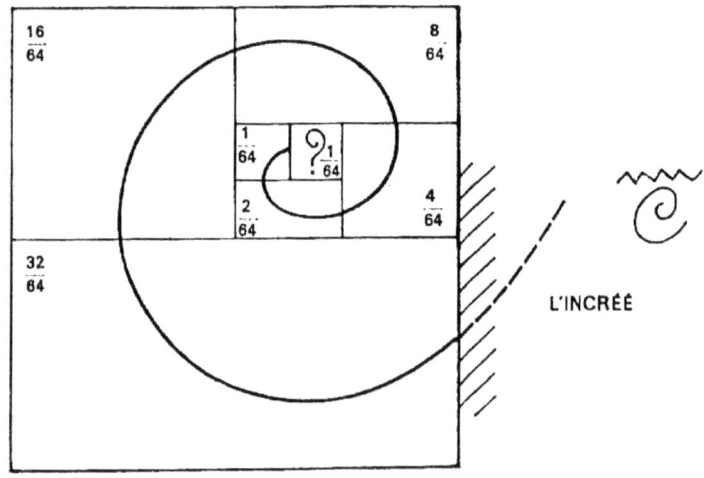

L'INCRÉÉ

In this basic square of the "Sea", the Beloved, or the Pyramid, is inscribed the spiraloid of Creation, sor so much of the Uncreated, providing in this half of Time, the calculation of the half-perimeter and the half-surface, as well as the location of the exact entrance to the "Sea" - which is the hieroglyphic contraction of: Seqt-Ben-Mer-Shoum, "the Beloved to whom the Light descends", which has become "Pyramid"!... And its symbolism is Unity: the ALL. For from God comes all the multitude: ONE drawn from Nothingness, like Man, to create the multitude, or $\frac{64}{64}$.

In order to set out the mathematics of the Law of Creation without further ado, an anticipation will precede the proofs that will be provided by a few pages, and will be presented in a sort of apodictic manner, so that the threads of the skein can be untangled as we go along.

The four Tenses, of which we have already spoken at length, the Past, the Present, the Future and "the Other", are interwoven and entangled with those of Creativity, which are: Human Time, Terrestrial Time, Solar Time and "the Other".

Each was created in six days, according to the same Law:

1) Divine Time, or "the Other", is that of the expansion of the Cosmos and the regularisation of its movements, down to the tiniest solar systems comprising tiny planets such as our Earth; but this Time is incalculable in our mathematics, with billions of centuries added to billions of millennia of years!

2) Solar Time is that of the expansion of the planetary system that is our own, and of the regularisation of the Earth's movements within this Space, as well as the stabilisation of all the particles and molecules forming Matter, which allowed the first elements of plant and animal life to take root.

3) Terrestrial Time is that of the slow but continuous expansion of Life into plant matter and the first invertebrates, before transforming into animals.

4) Human Time is the time when Souls impregnated the brains of human carnal envelopes, the only ones to have supported this Divine parcel, and to have chosen, as a result, to stand on their two legs and use their two hands to live intelligently: to work, eat and write.

The Origin of Cosmic Creation, forming a new "Great Cycle" and equivalent to Divine Time, represents a pulse of: 168,121,466,880 years.

- *From this Origin, to the creation of the Earth,* that is to say from the moment when the implantation in space of our planetary globe became definitive $\frac{63}{64}$ of the duration of Divine Time elapsed. In other words, the duration of the 7thth Day is $\frac{1}{64}$. It is the Time allotted to the Earth to ensure its survival in another cycle of: 5 253 795 840 years.

- *From the Origin of the Earth, to the appearance of quadruped mammals,* i.e. from the moment of implantation in the terrestrial environment predestined for them, of those that have endured the continuous evolution of species, and are still able to survive today, even in an imperfect form at the time, $\frac{63}{64}$ of the duration of Solar Time has elapsed. This means that the duration of the 7thth Day, which represents $\frac{1}{64}$, and which is the Time allotted to the most robust animals to ensure their survival in another cycle, is: 82 090 560 years.

- *From the origin of quadruped mammals to the appearance of biped Man,* that is to say from moment of the appearance of the Divine particle, the Soul, when the hominid, touched by grace, raised his body towards Heaven and began to use, however imperfectly, the intelligence granted to him, to improve his human condition, there has elapsed $\frac{63}{64}$ the duration of Terrestrial Time. This means that the duration of the 7thth Day, which represents $\frac{1}{64}$, and which is the Time allotted to Humanity in its infancy to ensure its multiplication and survival in another cycle, is: 1,282,665 years.

- From the Origin of biped Man, to his blossoming as an intelligent Man, that is to say from the moment when the Soul turns the carnal envelope into a Divine image, and allows Man to be the true Master of all the terrestrial environment that was predestined for him, whether mineral, vegetable or animal, $\frac{63}{64}$ of the duration of Human Time has elapsed, which is not defined in the absolute since Man has the free choice of his destiny in the free will of his states of mind, the last $\frac{1}{64}$ being mathematically almost $\frac{17}{16}$, i.e. the 7thth Day, Man's Time, will depend for its duration on the balance that he will ensure in Good. What is certain is that the $\frac{16}{16}$ make: 1,244,160 years, as seen previously, and that the remainder, that is to say the part of the 17th sixteenth, is 38,505 years. But this is "Other" Time: God's Time...

This date is fundamental, because it is consistent with the annals and chronologies that have come down to us. Herodotus, and above all the historian-priest Manetho, speak of the beginning of Time 36,000 years ago; and as they lived more than 2,000 years ago, it all adds up!

That's why, in the next chapter, the History of Mankind will begin on this date in Aha-Men-Ptah...

First, let's clearly break down this process of "Divine-Mathematical Combinations": starting again from the origin of the Origin!...

"Let there be Light! ... And the Light was! At that instant, EVERYTHING began again, and from the Uncreated, God made Light spring forth. Seeing that it was good, he separated it from the Darkness. The impetus was there! One became two; two became four, then eight... and so the process continued, generating Space and Time, as well as the raw material for the multitudes of celestial bodies, for half the Time of this cycle, i.e. $\frac{1}{2}$, represented by the fractional hieroglyph: ⭕ which makes $\frac{32}{64}$, i.e. the 168,121,464,880 years, the same duration being the Lifetime of the remaining Cosmos.

This was the Universe's first Cosmic Day.

The most distant Quasars are therefore in place, boiling titanically, and under phenomenal pressure; from this multitude of gigantic complexes at their critical point of explosion, certain supernovae will explode to form the most distant galaxies, imparting from that moment on the gyratory movements of various spiraloid forms, during the quarter of the Time of this cycle, that is to say: $\frac{1}{4}$, and represented by the fractional hieroglyph: ◁ which makes $\frac{16}{64}$, or half the remaining time, i.e. 84,060,733,440 years, the same remaining cosmic time, being the Cosmic Lifetime of this cycle.

This was the Universe's second Cosmic Day.

Galactic supercentres continued to develop, releasing spiral arms around central nuclei, whose uniform centrifugal movements gave rise here and there to the explosion of novae, enormous stars still in fusion that became, in their parts, the giant Suns of very high-magnitude stellar groups. Such as the enormous fireball called Regulus in Leo, which stabilised some one hundred light-years away from us, to become the centre of a major system whose energetic and radiant power is so powerful as to be inconceivable to the human mind! Let's just say that if this star had been propelled a little closer to our Sun, our Earth, like all the other planets in our solar system, would have been instantly reduced to impalpable ashes, and we would therefore not exist! The process that put each star in its assigned place during this eighth of Time of this cycle, i.e. $\frac{1}{8}$, represented by the hieroglyphic fractional phe: ◁ which makes $\frac{8}{64}$, or half of the remaining cosmic time, i.e.: 42,030,366,720 years, the same duration being the remaining Lifetime of the Cosmos.

This was the third Cosmic Day of the Universe. Other huge blocks of molten rock then swirled around at a respectful distance from the giant stars, of the order of several hundred light years or so, to form large stellar groups. Within our Milky Way, a dozen or so of these formations have been inserted: the constellations that were propelled in this way, initially by their Suns, such as Regulus of Leo, which we have already mentioned, around a gigantic space that was still empty! From that moment on, the radiation began to be sent into this spherical volume where nothing yet existed, but at the centre of which they would all meet! It was the culmination of this sixteenth of Time in this cycle, $\frac{1}{16}$, represented by the hieroglyph which makes $\frac{4}{64}$, or half the remaining time, that is: 21,015,183,360 years, the same length of time remaining for the Lifetime of the Cosmos.

This was the fourth Cosmic Day of the Universe.

The smallest solar systems were then created by the billions within these enormous masses. First there were the Suns, constantly effervescent blocks of molten matter, which stabilised in this way, like our own, held in this position by this Force R which centralised the twelve rays coming from the Suns of the constellations. Surrounded in this way by a photosphere, and receiving no external input of matter or energy, it was this Force that not only preserved its power of regeneration, but has been renewing it ever since, according to well-defined laws of physics. As this chain-like process placed ever-smaller masses - our Sun is fourteen thousand times smaller in diameter than Regulus! -required a much shorter "creation" Time, so the thirty-second Time of this cycle is more than sufficient for this work, i.e.: $\frac{1}{32}$ represented by the fractional hieroglyph: , which makes $\frac{2}{64}$, or half the remaining cosmic Time, i.e.: 10,507,591,680 years, the same length of time remaining for the Lifetime of the Cosmos.

This was the fifth Cosmic Day of the Universe.

For the last Day of Cosmic Creation, all that remained was to complete the formation of the environment of the Universe: in other words, to bring to certain appropriate places the possibilities of creating Life, through the ideal conditions that would prevail there.

On that day, then, the Suns that had been in place "the day before" suffered the after-effects of the strong nuclear pressures that shook them. Some exploded, creating apocalyptic conditions in certain 'corners' of the Cosmos, while others simply exhaled, projecting more or less voluminous balls into space where they were already exerting a strong attraction, the matter still being in fusion.

The smallest masses, such as Mercury and Mars, stopped fairly close the parent star and began to spin rapidly around, remaining in permanent gravitation around the solar star. The larger 'chunks' continued to 'fall' at distances of several hundred million kilometres, such as Jupiter, Saturn, Neptune and Uranus, gravitating and spinning in the same direction and in the same plane as the others, perfectly demonstrating the continuity of the same Law.

One of these balls, neither too small nor too large, stabilised itself neither too close nor too far, so as to be ideally neither too hot nor too cold, and to become capable, in time, at the rhythm of the cycles and the Law of Creation, of generating Life.

And this is essential for anyone seeking to understand this "phenomenon"! For billions of years, there has been a continuity of Creation to bring about the optimum conditions for procreation! And this cannot be the effect of one or more "coincidences", because it would have taken thousands and thousands of "coincidences" for this continuous Law to be the work of God, with each creation bringing a new element to the environment so that when the time comes, and in the place foreseen, Life appears!

Since there is no humanity in place, and, in any case, since men are still incapable of ordering such work, who, or what, could have done it? For, if the atheist does not want to admit Divine intervention..., who is responsible?

The problem is the same, albeit proportionately, for a car travelling on a busy main road in front of yours. From the sixth onwards, the probabilities are clear: if there is no accident after the sixth junction, there must also be a driver in the vehicle in front of yours! It's an absolute certainty, even if he remains hidden from view!

So, as far as Creation is concerned, why not admit what is an identical certainty? There is a driver, a pilot: a Guide, even if He too is hidden from our eyes, which are only a reflection of those of His image.

The Earth - let's give it its name already - has finally reached its rightful place, and the Sun, having cooled down a little, has caused the extinction of its photosphere, ensuring at the same time that the movements of all the planets in the solar system are regularised.

The acceleration of the process of Creation completes the Cosmic scale, and passes the baton to the scale of Solar Time and duration. So once sixty fourth of the time of this Cosmic cycle has just elapsed, completing $\frac{63}{64}$ of total Time, and leaving the last $\frac{1}{64}$ to the life in time of the solar star! It therefore took 5,253,795,840 years for our terrestrial globe to come into being, and it still has as much Life Time left in this cycle.

This was the sixth Cosmic Day of the Universe.

As the Egyptian Annals statereferring to their ancient texts: "Mut is now the container of all the 'out' in the Cosmos, just as Nut was to become the container of all the 'out' on Earth.

It was the great work of the scholars of the "Double Houses of Life" of the ancient Aha-Men-Ptah to draw up sky maps, some fragments of which, copied from figures on leather scrolls, can be found at Denderah, on the tomb of Seti Ier and at the Ramesseum, among other places, and which fixed important configurations marked for specific dates when serious events had occurred, thus explaining that forces other than mere human forces combined the movements of the stars and their mathematical combinations with terrestrial events.

The Creator therefore still has 5,253,795,840 years to organise the Earth and bring to life the image that He will have engendered there as His final work. Time will be solar and, by coincidence, it will be the Sun that will be the radiant vehicle of the Creative Force that will first bring the plant and animal worlds to life.

CHAPTER FIVE

SYMBOLIC DIGITAL TERRESTRIAL

The only
who daily reaches the ends of the earth
and looks upon those who walk in them;
who ascends into heaven in his solar form
so that from the months he can bring forth the seasons,
heat when he wills it,
cold when he wishes,
every day when he rises:
the whole country sings his praise!

HYMN TO THE SUN
(Ancient Empire stele)

To the Lord belongs the earth and all that is in it, the world
and those who dwell in it;
for it was He who founded it on the seas
and established it on the rivers.

OLD TESTAMENT
(Psalm 24)

So, more than five billion years ago, the Earth was still a partially liquefied, partially molten mass, with various metalliferous layers beginning to form internally in order of density. Above the outer crust that was forming, a vast and very dense atmosphere held in suspension all the vapour given off by the various gases, which was totally unbreathable!

The earth's crust, thickening as it slowly cooled, split open. Through these openings, these giant cracks, under the immense internal pressure, molten matter escaped from all sides. And so the heat released led to a high surface temperature, even though the sun's rays were not yet able to penetrate the thick layer of clouds.

But that didn't stop the torrential rains from falling non-stop on the waterlogged land! And all over the Earth, the poles, ice and snow still unknown in the stingy, diffuse and clammy light that reigned here below.

And then, at the propitious moment foreseen: a cone of light pierced the cloudy vault, reaching out with its healing rays to the high ground...

"In the beginning God created the heavens and the earth. And the earth was desolate and empty, and darkness covered the deep, and the Spirit of God was upon the waters. God said, "Let there be light", and there was light. God saw that the light was good, and God separated the light from the darkness. God called the light Day, and the darkness Night.

This took half of the total Solar Time, i.e. $\frac{1}{2}$ or the $\frac{32}{64}$ of: 5,253,795,840 years; therefore: 2,626,897,920 years. There was therefore as much Life Time left in this cycle, to come on Earth.

This was the first Day of Creation on Earth.

Near the Temple of Ath-Mer, "the beloved Elder", the capital of Aha-Men-Ptah, stood the hill of sycamores; and near the Temple of the Sun in the city of Heliopolis, in Ath-Ka-Ptah, stood the hill of sand. Both had the same original meaning: "the Primordial Hill". It was the representation, both physical and symbolic, of the first earth touched by sunlight, creating the firm ground around which the earth solidified to the rhythm of the days and nights.

Geologically, the very dense cloud layers at the equator, which were practically boiling, condensed into vapour and fell back into the already less torrid regions in vast expanses of water that hardened the earth's crust a little more, on which they stagnated, except in the highest places: the mountains of those early days.

Little by little, the Sun enlarged its field of vision through the window opened in the middle of the clouds, a veritable eye through which the beneficial rays seeped in, allowing the mounds surrounding the mountains to dry out and the first unicellular organisms to be born, adopting the Earth's rhythm of life, made up of alternating solar day and stellar night...

"God said, 'Let there be a firmament in the midst of the waters, and let it separate the waters from the waters'; and it was so. God made the firmament, which separated the waters under the firmament from the waters above the firmament; and God called the firmament heaven.

This took half of the remaining Solar Time, i.e. $\frac{1}{4}$ of Solar Time, or $\frac{16}{64}$, i.e. 1,313,448,960 years. So there was still as much Life Time left in this cycle, to come on Earth.

This was the second Day of Creation on earth.

While the atmosphere gradually took on its current proportions, the reactions coming from the still molten central magma were cruelly felt when the enormous pressures supported by the Earth's thin crust exploded through the cracks caused in the meantime by the internal upheavals that continually deformed the land.

The more rapid cooling of the seabed also caused excess steam to build up under the submarine crust, resulting in chemical reactions in the internal mass, which was still very fluid and gaseous, and literally overturning the cartography that could have been made at that time!

Gradual heightening, in successive stages, and like so many gigantic blows, caused entire continents to emerge from the waters, topped by giant mountain ranges all along the fracture zones. Eternal snows then appeared on these snowdrifts.

Other regions dried out completely; between these two extremes, humid but temperate regions favoured the growth of a whole range of immense plants, with forms that appear to us today to be the most hallucinating: aquatic algae with tortured, stretched forms; enormous sponges; schools of tentacular corals. This same water gave rise to the first animalcules: amoebas, which became brachiopods, pelecypods and other biozoans of this sublacustrine kingdom.

In the twilight of that day, the volcanic phenomena redoubled in violence, driven by the injection of water into the igneous layers of the magma, rushing through the fracture lines and propelling itself further and further towards the magma as it was transformed into steam under pressure. While the regions affected were turned upside down, other, more tranquil areas saw their soil become more fertile. Fruit and vegetables grew from the surrounding greenery and orchards.

Finally, on the shores of warm seas, on fine sandy beaches such as Erfoud, on the edge of what is now the Moroccan Sahara, which was a sea "on that day", nautiluses were born, commonly known as ammonites, still invertebrates, but shaped like a perfect spiral, the symbol of multitude!

And if the Creation of "that day" does not mention animals, it is because it is very difficult to assimilate these invertebrates fossilised some six hundred million years ago by the disappearance in a few moments of the sea that occupied the Moroccan Sahara. *Billions of* these ammonites fossilised at that time, forming a blue or brown marble today, depending on the area, in which the spiraloids have kept their perfect shape...

God said: "Let the waters under the firmament gather into one mass and let the dry land appear"; and it was so. God called the dry land earth and the body of water the sea, and God saw that it was good.

God said: "Let the earth bring forth vegetation, herbs bearing seed and fruit trees bearing seed"; and it was so. And the earth brought forth vegetation, herbs yielding seed according to their kind, and trees yielding fruit according to their kind, containing their seed; and God saw that it was good."

One 'curious' remark concerns the mountain ranges, the lands that emerged from the waters. At the very tip of Cameroon, just at the equator, there was an isolated mountain whose peak exceeded 10,000 metres, according to the writings of ancient navigators and the sayings of old 'wise' Cameroonians. It was called the "*Chariot of the Gods*" and was considered to be the Original Land. It was Henon who, witnessing the upheaval that lowered it by half its height, wrote about its various adventures in his "African Journey".

Having had the opportunity to climb all the way to the summit, which is still 4,150 metres above sea level, which it dominates, there was no shortage of food for thought! The place is Dantesque at first glance, even though this summit is still that of "the Gods": Fako, in dialect. It is still a volcano, and fumaroles were escaping from it when I was there in 1947.

The old local man who had advised me to go on this pilgrimage, and who had agreed to accompany me, knew intuitively the enormous benefit I would derive from it. We bivouacked there for four nights, in the cave where the lava had erupted some fifty years earlier, levelling the former capital of what was then British Cameroon! Many things are easier to understand on the spot. It was there that I learned the meaning of the Egyptian 'Mer', the pyramids that resemble the primordial mountain of the 'Beloved-Who-Descends-Light'.

But half the remaining time passed, i.e. $\frac{1}{8}$: 656,724,480 years. And all that remained was an identical Time of Life for the duration of the entire cycle on Earth.

This was the third Day of Creation on earth.

The general cooling accelerated, following the square progression of the Law of Creation. Finally, it brought stability to the dimensions of the Earth's geological layers, as well as the harmony of planetary rhythms in the solar system; normal and continuous emission of stellar rays, as well as the constitution of the atmosphere; finally, balanced rotation of the Earth in relation to the Sun, the Moon and the other planets. Only the ground itself on our globe continues to jiggle here and there, with changes due to the precession of the equinoxes, which makes its appearance on "that day", as do vertebrates...

God said: "Let there be lights in the firmament of the sky to separate the day from the night; let them be signs for the seasons, the days and the years; let them be lights in the firmament of the sky to illuminate the Earth"; and so it was. God made the two major luminaries: the great luminary as the power of the day; and the lesser luminary as the power of the night; and the stars. God placed them in the firmament of heaven to shine on the earth, to control the day and the night; to separate the light from the darkness, and God saw that it was good."

The most important question resolved by the scholars of the "Double-Houses of Life" in Aha-MenPtah, is that of this fourth Day, on which the days and years appeared, that is to say the "MathematicalCombinations": the NUMBERS, with the Divine Law that they imply through the introduction of the notion of the TWO luminaries, but that they automatically imply through the combinations that they trigger, and about which the text leaves no doubt: "*so that they may serve as signs*".

This took half of the remaining Solar Time, i.e. $\frac{1}{16}$ of Solar Time, or $\frac{4}{64}$, i.e. 328,362,240 years. So there was still the same amount of Life Time to come in this cycle on Earth.

This was the fourth Day of Creation on earth.

The environment was now perfectly in place on land, in the air and in the water, to accommodate vertebrates: those that fly, those that swim, and those that walk and run more or less heavily on their feet. The evolutionary progression, now shorter in Time, nevertheless remains constant and in accordance with the Law, especially in terrestrial Nature, where races that could not adapt to the conditions of life, and therefore not likely to survive, appeared and disappeared. But that was the day of gigantism! It was the day of enormous birds, such as the Pterodactyls; of mammals of proportions that we can scarcely imagine today, such as the Brontosaurus, some twenty metres long, with four massive legs that supported some thirty tonnes and a flexible tail five metres long that swept everything away; of the Ichthyosaurus, whose very prominent fins enabled them to move through the water at astonishing speeds despite weighing between ten and fifteen tonnes!

God said, "Let the waters swarm with living creatures and let birds fly above the earth against the firmament of heaven," and it was so. God created the sea monsters and all the living creatures that glide and swarm in the waters according to their kind, and all the winged creatures according to their kind, and God saw that it was good. God blessed them and said to them: 'Be fruitful and multiply, and fill the waters of the seas, and let birds multiply on the earth.

This express growth took up half of the remaining Solar Time, i.e. $\frac{1}{32}$, or $\frac{2}{64}$ of the total Time, i.e. 164,181,120 years. So there was still the same amount of Life Time to come in this cycle on Earth.

This was the fifth Day of Creation on earth.

At the dawn of the new day of creativity, it was time to give impetus to the rays finally reaching the planet, which came from the distant suns of the twelve constellations encircling the solar system, so that Divine Power could engender other animal races that would be better able to take advantage of the constantly evolving conditions of Life. The rays of this Force caused mammals, birds and enormous fish to fight titanic battles! Entire races were wiped out, allowing others to evolve for the better. This led to the emergence of better-adapted living races, whether they remained wild or could be domesticated, seeded as they were with an embryonic soul during that day...

God said, "Let the earth bring forth living creatures after their kind, cattle, creeping things, wild beasts, after every kind," and it was so. God made the wild beasts after their kind, and every creeping thing of the ground after its kind, and God saw that it was good."

The biblical text concerning the sixth day does not stop here, encroaching on the Time of Man, which, as the Ancient Annals demonstrate, is part of the very Time of God, dedicated to rest and to His own image, which does not require any additional creation. The Creator creates him once the whole environment has been created, i.e. after the sixth Day!

As we saw earlier, the text of Genesis had been somewhat interpreted and brought up to date, for the time, and that it had "appealed to the literary processes of the ancient Eastern peoples, with their psychology, their way of expressing themselves, and their very notion of historical truth".

The compilers of Genesis under Ezra were obviously faced with a major difficulty, impossible to overcome for the mortals of this century, who were not familiar with the mathematical sciences and their "combinations".

The Creation of the Sixth Day is written, as we have seen, using the hieroglyph: ⎎ which represents the Word Creator within creation itself: the "oudjet" eye (God said... and did it). The important thing is to know that this sixth symbol is unpronounceable, and must not be pronounced under any circumstances, representing the Word Creator; moreover, as it is written "qd" it is indeed unpronounceable!

From a purely occult point of view, the symbolism is made very clear by the statement itself: "qd", or "what is above is similar to what is below", which is equivalent to saying: "everything comes from God". This sixth symbol is also found in the creative "Great Principle", which means the Breath that shapes the Soul.

It is the double of the carnal heart which becomes the true impalpable heart of any envelope made of raw flesh, and not yet fertilised beforehand, but which will be thanks to God; which gives in hieroglyphic: Ath-Ka-Ptah.

Ath-Ka-Ptah, being the name given by Menes, King of the 1st Dynasty, to the first Temple consecrated to the Almighty God, in conjuration of the swallowing up of the "First Heart": the Elder, so that this "Second Heart" would eternally remain that of the Descendants of God, it is easy to see all the symbolism attached to this sixth unpronounceable hieroglyph, far beyond its mere meaning.

What is also clear from this interpretation of creativity is that God, at the end of the sixth Day, had already set His sights on the "animal" category likely to see fertilised within it the Divine particle that would become the Soul, and capable of becoming His perfect image. Of course, it couldn't have been the latest creature to emerge from the twilight of that day: the mammoth, which, at three metres tall and with fifty centimetres of hair, had only a small brain...

But this progression in the evolution of the various animal species had still taken up half of the remaining Solar Time, i.e. $\frac{1}{64}$ of Time, i.e. 82,090,560 years. At that moment, there was still the same amount of Life Time to come in this cycle on Earth, where Human Time would replace the previous ones.

This was the sixth day of earthly creation.

Let us now do as the Biblical Commission recommended in 1948, and apply the second part of the text of Genesis, still relating to the sixth Day, to the third part of Universal Creation: that which brought about the Time of Man. As for this second part, let's use the duration of the seventh Day and its complementary Time to establish the third. Since there are 82,090,560 years left,

the first Day of this Time will last   41,045,280 years,

the second Day of Creation					20,522,640 years,
the third day	"	"	"		10,261,320 years,
the fourth day	"	"	"	5,130,660 years,	
the fifth day	"	"	"	2,565,330 years,	
the sixth day		"	"	"	1,282,665 years.

Everyone can try to model this third cycle of Time, like Ptah, who was often represented as a potter modelling shapes, in all the animals, wild or otherwise, that preceded Man. Just remember:

"God said: "Let us make Man in our image, after our likeness, and let him have dominion over the fish of the sea, and over the fowl of the air, and over the cattle, and over every beast of the field, and over every creeping thing that creepeth upon the earth.

So let's say that at the end of this sixth Day of the third part, there were still 1,282,665 years left in this "Great Divine Cycle", which represents ONE pulse 168,121,466,880 years. What an infinitesimal duration for Humanity compared to Eternity! But it's the one devoted to Man! It was from this date, more than a million years ago, that the hominid was transformed, and that "God made Man in His own image". The brain, engendered from the Divine parcel, would mature over the millennia. Human Time began on that Day, as the texts make clear:

"So heaven and earth were finished, with all their host. And on the seventh day God finished the work which he had made."

As this is the Day for Human Time, the fractional system as applied by the six symbols of the creative eye is no longer appropriate, as we saw in a previous chapter. Here, it is the triangular symbolic 'tears' that will enable the calculations to be made. Moreover, the mathematical proof of the impossibility of using the other formulation is provided very simply! If, since the first number of the first Trinitarian part of Creation, it has been continuously possible to divide Time by two at each operation, this has been impossible since the last Number relating to Human Time:

1,282,665, for the good reason that, for the first time, it ends with an odd number!...

This Day will therefore be divided according to the cyclic hexadecimal form defined above. And Man, who has just received the elements that will constitute his Soul at a later date, will do with his body what he decides over the next million years! For Humanity, as a whole, will be the completion and culmination of this end of the Divine Cycle.

The "Divine-Mathematical-Combinations" regulating this last slice of Time will obviously be calculated according to the harmonic trinitarian rhythm of the precessional "Great Years", i.e.: 25,920 years $\times$ 3 = 77,760 years.

The sixteen cycles that have elapsed since the beginning of this seventh Last Day, as described the archives of the "Four Times" of the Temple Denderah, represent an ultra-fast human evolution in cosmic time, but a relatively slow one in human time of: 77,760 $\times$ 16 = 1,244,160 years.

In the end, Man came to understand what he is, and what he must be in relation to God, to whom he owes everything, starting with himself! In this gradual evolution, he passed from the bestial biped to the caveman, then to the beginning of civilisation, which brought him to:

1,282,665 - 1,244,160 = 38,505 years.

This very precise date agrees with that given by the Egyptian historian-priest Manetho for the beginning of the History of the Ancestors of the Inhabitants of Egypt; and it coincides admirably with that given by the Annals of Aha-Men-Ptah for the beginning of the historical times of this country, which will be the subject of the next chapter.

For the Past, therefore, we will retain the very concept of calculating dates, provided by the "Mathematical Combinations".

It is up to the reader to see for himself the possible concordances for the completion of the cycle, because Man will always have his free will; and he will have the freedom to choose between the Golden Age and the Apocalypse right up to the final moment!..

CHAPTER SIX

AHA-MEN-PTA
("THE ELDER-HEART-OF-GOD")

> *I can see nothing physically to prevent there having once been a very large expanse of land between Europe and America, of which the Canary Islands and the Azores are the surviving remnants.*
> MENTELLE
> *(Ancient geography,* at the word: Atlantica)

> *O superb land, which, through your great sea trade, has showered so many different nations with goods!*
> *By the multitude of your riches and the of your peoples of your people, have enriched the kings of the earth!*
> *Now the sea has broken you!*
> *Your riches are at the bottom of the waters, and all the multitude of peoples who were among you,*
> *have fallen and perished by your fall!*
> *You have become a source of surprise and astonishment to all the inhabitants of the isles!*
> *And the kings changed their faces when they saw this cataclysm!*
> OLD TESTAMENT
> (*Ezekiel:* XXVII, 33 to 35)

There is no question, in the context of this work, of demonstrating certain analogies, certain "coincidences", between other cataclysms, such as the one cited by Ezekiel, which related to the engulfment of Tyre in Phoenicia, and the "Great Cataclysm" which literally wiped the continent of the earliest historical times, Aha-Men-Ptah, off the Earth.

But it's a good idea to make a few quotations, like the ones in the epigraph, and ponder them another day, *a-parte*.

In his chronology, Manetho lists, after God the Creator, the demigods, then the "Heroes", the "Manes", before arriving at the "Masters", the descendants of the Elder, the "Son of God", who had only the Soul as the link uniting them to God.

It was after the demigods; the Ogdoade, or the EIGHT, that humanity in this country developed, around 38,000 years ago. And over a great number of millennia, humanity grew and multiplied for a good thousand generations, at the centre of a perfect harmonious agreement with heaven and God, for the best of all worlds at the time.

But the scientists of this country, who combined Knowledge with the Knowledge of the Priests, already knew the main possible hazards of the entire globe, and this was amply demonstrated to them by the "Mathematical Combinations".

The Earth itself, as it cooled from the outside, shaped its overheated interior differently. Titanic seismic and telluric phenomena had shaken the solid crust on which the temples were built enough for them to understand the reason for the instantaneous jolts that agitated the 'central core', still in fusion, and whose shock waves, under the pressure of the gases that wanted to free themselves, caused these explosive bursts, disintegrating atomic elements still contained on all sides inside.

The memories left behind by the ancestors of these first civilised people 38,000 years ago were full of cataclysms that were scarcely imaginable to their humanised minds: huge mountain ranges rising up where before there had been only peaceful plains or even a calm ocean! Others, spitting fire and spewing huge blocks of stone, sank into the earth itself, only to be suffocated when they disappeared...

And if these spasms occurred less and less frequently, if these convulsions calmed down, it appeared to the learned observers, according to the sayings of the oldest living beings, that the movements driving the planet in space were becoming cyclical, arriving regularly in Time, at the rhythm of the evolution of the solar and stellar system governed by a single Law.

Let's stop for a moment to consider these notions before going any further, in order to explain them in terms of our modern conception of geology. But what is certain is that these ancients had the exact formulation and calculation of what we call the precession of the equinoxes.

In its translational movement around the Sun over the course of a year, the Earth maintains the same apparent position in relation to the stars; in other words, the axis of the terrestrial globe always points at the same time to the same region of the sky, which is to say that in fact its axis of rotation maintains its parallelism in space, despite its inclination of 23°5 on an imaginary perpendicular to the plane of the Earth's annual orbit. But this, too, is true only in appearance, and the Ancients of Aha-Men-Ptah knew it!

While the plane of our orbit remains the same, the axis shifts very slightly, by fifty arcseconds, plus a few dust particles, per year: this is known as the "precession of the equinoxes". This phenomenon has a major impact on the Earth's equatorial bulge. This sort of bulge, or belt, is subject to a stronger pull than at the poles, thus slightly slowing down the Earth's rotational movement, but still disrupting it.

The resulting tiny backward movement retrogrades the Earth's axis, taking it backwards in space, as it were, along a vast circumference with the North Star at its centre, which would take 25,920 years to cover, since fifty seconds of arc give 360° years.

As far as Time is concerned, there is no particular problem in catching up. Ever since the calendar was put back into use by King Athothis, the second pharaoh of the very first dynasty, some 4200 years before the start of the Christian era, a day has been added every four years so as not to fall behind the exact time. But the ancient scholars had taken this decision, not in relation to the movement of the Sun, but by the "Combinations" caused by the movement of the star Sirius, the Greek Sothis, or Sep'ti in hieroglyphic phonetisation.

And what about in space?... Because the Earth was moving backwards - and still is! - in Space too! And yet it is indissolubly linked to Time: so what? In this case, there's nothing to do but record the 'Combinations' and their effects! Arithmetic and its calculations are of no use whatsoever. Only an Atlas-type supergiant could be capable of keeping the Earth's axis in the same place, but there is no one who is remotely likely to accomplish this feat! So the fifty seconds of arc reversal on the circumference of space is unattainable!

According to the beautiful mathematical theory, it will therefore take 25,920 years for the Earth to return to its initial point of departure in space, having thus covered a complete circumference in a regular Time that Plato already called the Great Year, to which he assigned a duration of 26,000 years, which was not bad for a Greek who had spent five years in Egypt! Perhaps, moreover, in his gloom at seeing his people surpassed and surpassed in every respect, he felt that the figure of 25,920 put forward by the Egyptian priests could only be the result of a miscalculation!

However, if the 'Combinations' and their results were correct, this was only valid in theory, because one very important factor was bound to upset these fine assumptions! It even caused confusion, to say the least, until more precise observations made it possible to pinpoint the causes, if not the effects!

This is the famous 'Magma', our central core, which may have cooled somewhat since Origin, but has not yet solidified... Now, this indeterminate, imprecise mass, both in shape and in consistency, has a lesser weight, but it is nonetheless a determining factor in the precessional retrograde evolution of the Earth's outer crust alone; approximately, the internal weight would be: fifteen billion tonnes!

However, everything here is still unknown! At depth, certain agents, in particular those known as thermodynamics, create movements and states of 'magmatic' matter that are still virtually unverifiable from the surface, especially in terms of the pressure exerted and the temperature. As for the duration of these sudden changes, they are brief reflections - the order of a few seconds - the pressure exerted on the outer layer by the mass itself as it breaks free of gravity.

As it cools, its internal volume diminishes, albeit insensitively, but on a daily basis over the last few billion years! What happens inside the 'fluid' zones that are created?

If we are to believe our mathematical colleagues, however, it has been shown that this random vacuum exist[10] ! So what do you think?

However, since it is impossible to accept that the earth's crust can support itself without any support, there must be a "buffer" zone made up at least of gas pressure!

It is this perpetually evolving contraction that cracks the crust when the incandescent mass, out of internal equilibrium, presses against it, causing earthquakes and volcanic eruptions, or on the contrary, engulfs the earth and causes tidal waves and floods when the cracks occur at the bottom of the oceans.

This weight - unthinkable, even! - of the magma, is the overriding factor in determining the actual length of a cycle, which would be very difficult to complete in 25,920 years!

For thousands of years, the precessional retrogradation, with its incessant rocking and retreating, slowly, very slowly, of a gigantic internal mass, will rock it to this external rhythm, so that at a given, precise moment, the shapeless and unstable magma will be in a position of imbalance.

This break, similar to that of the tightrope walker who stands magnificently upright on his legs... until the moment when an

---

[10] Porphyry is the rock with the greatest resistance; it crushes under a pressure of 240 kg/cm². And this rock, in order not to move, would have to be *265 times stronger!*

instability causes him to lose his footing, leading to his fall. The same applies to our globe, with the enormous difference that the general attraction will prevent it from "falling" into the void at the moment of loss of balance, which will only cause the Earth's axis to pivot almost instantaneously, at a point "x", precisely where the fifteen billion billion tonnes will suddenly press down on the weak crust, like a gigantic battering ram!

The resulting cracking will create the fault, which will be all the more imposing because the swivelling on the axis caused by the magma mass will have been more sudden, especially if it is an enormous metal "peak" several kilometres high inside, which pierces the crust!

When the recession is 90°, for example, i.e. after 6,480 years ($\frac{25\,920}{4}$), an earthquake or flood will occur, on a scale greater than those occurring at any time during friction between the inner mass and the outer layer of the Earth, which do not have the same precessional recession, due to the non-uniformity of the gravitation governing their particular recession, will take place along a line of rupture that can be identified according to the planetary "combinations" and the inclination of the Earth's ecliptic.

When the retreat reaches 180°, i.e. after a period of 12,960 years, our globe will tilt 'axis to axis', the main effect of which will be the submersion of a continent, or a series of earthquakes that will lead, on the contrary, to truly apocalyptic elevations from every point of view!

And so the "Great Cataclysm" took place, spoken of in ancient texts with varying degrees of grandiloquence and, above all, fright! Temperate zones became glacial, while others, which were "polar", took on tropical climatic locations. These changes are confirmed by all the geologists specialising in the subject.

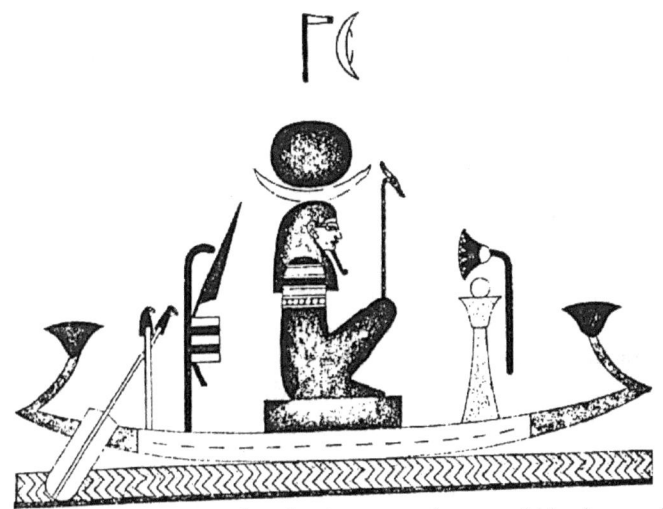

Ever since Osiris returned to the Amenta and resumed his place at the right hand of God, the Sun has been rising in the East and travelling *backwards* through the sky.

For this reason, as the upheavals are cyclical and punctuated by pulses of around 12,000 years, the precession of the equinoxes does not seem to be in a position to complete its retreat along the entire circumference: halfway through its retrograde course, the Earth will tilt, and... "This will cause the Sun to appear in the opposite direction to its usual path, which it had followed for the previous 12,000 years: the daytime star, which used to rise in the east, will now rise in the west, or as during the last 'Great Cataclysm', it will rise from the west in the east, travelling backwards along its path! These radical changes have marked the human period twice in the last four hundred centuries. One, 24,000 years ago, and the other around 12,000 years before our time, which we will define without further ado in this chapter.

In the chronological logic that will follow, the dates recorded with mathematical accuracy tinged with computer rigour will be consistent with the various ancient sources.

The previous upheaval took place on 11 February 21,312 BC, exactly 23,287 years ago, in 1975.

We will therefore start from this precise date in the History of Aha-Men-Ptah, because the preceding 15,000 years saw populations living in peace in these blessed places, where evolution was nevertheless slow, except in the milieu of "scholars" who were concerned with defining life and its movements, and why the man who was born was already dominating animals that were much more powerful than he!

At that time, the northernmost part of the continent of Aha-Men-Ptah was much more temperate than regions such as Greenland are today. Thick forests covered this part of the territory, where ice had yet to appear and snow made only timid appearances. Further south, lush vegetation grew all year round, inhabited not only by peaceful humans living in village-like clearings, but also by great apes of a type that had completely disappeared; they were similar in size to today's gorillas, but without the 'spiked' face. Here and there, there were also enormous mammoths, vegetarians and peaceful; four-metre rhinoceroses with four fingers: the acerotheriums, who wreaked havoc on everything; lions and tigers who were constantly engaged in deadly battles to protect or take over a reserved territory; there were also a few old specimens in the process of total extinction of a bygone gigantism!

Finally, in the very south of the immense continent, there were mountains, of course, but even more so plains, where nature had spread out her most precious treasures: fertile countryside, which practically unassisted produced everything that can delight a tranquil humanity! These vast expanses, ideal for the settlement and meditation of a race eager to ascend towards its Creator, were in return blessed with unrivalled abundance.

On the horizon, the mountain ranges were nothing to be feared, and the pyramidal cones of the few volcanoes that mingled with them had been extinguished so long ago that human memory had lost track of them. All the living could see were slopes covered with evergreen trees, some of which, laden with pulpy, juicy fruit all year round, were a joy to behold!

In these places, veritable cities had been built, using barely squared tree trunks, solid dried mud to fill the holes in the wooden shafts, and thick layers of dried foliage to make the roof watertight.

When the upheaval of 21,312 BC occurred, seismic tremors caused a major subsidence in most of what had become the North Sea, carving out countless breaches as far away as present-day Iceland, as well as in Canada, where a large part of the territory sank to form present-day Hudson Bay, which is very indented. The same happened to the state at the northern tip of Aha-Men-Ptah, which was completely swallowed up!

A period of severe frost set in over the whole of this part of the world, accumulating the ice into a uniform polar cap. Today's Siberia itself, which was a fairly temperate region at the time, saw its verdant vegetation burn to the ground and the mastodons that had been unable to escape the ice cover in time were wiped out.

However, none of this was the result of a total cataclysm, and the Earth's axis did not "pivot". There was no break in equilibrium, but simply a rapid 'sliding' of the globe, in the same plane as the axis, which brought it forward 72° further, apparently, for the Earth observer! Just before the first tremors began, the Sun appeared, precessionally, in the twentieth degree of the Constellation Sagittarius; when the elements had calmed down, i.e. half an hour later, the star of the day was at the end of the Constellation Aquarius!...

But it's quite clear that the star that allows us to see clearly does not move from where it is: it's only the Earth's rotation that is disturbed by this precession! That's why the Earth is under so much pressure from above or below!

From this date, the history of Aha-Men-Ptah really begins, chronology logically using this upheaval, which human memory has endorsed as such, to mark the Annals with a characteristic beginning. The scholars of those early days had a growing understanding of celestial movements and combinations, and of the beneficial and malefic phenomena that resulted from them. From the day that a figurative graphic method was instituted, they carefully observed and meticulously noted the progress of the planets, the Sun and the Moon, their figures and configurations, as well as the more geometric forms of the twelve constellations of the celestial equatorial ecliptic, and the more distant constellations of Orion and Sirius, with their singular characteristics! The repercussions of these "Combinations" on the Earth followed, both in terms of human behaviour and the evolution of Nature.

So 21,312 years ago, before the beginning of the Christian era, Aha-Men-Ptah, despite the removal of its territory from the sunken Great North, still formed a quadrilateral thirty times the size of Europe! Not to mention present-day Greenland, which, having become an island through the disappearance of its territory, and having frozen over, no longer had any inhabitants.

There were few casualties, however, as the inhabitants were evacuated to the south. Only the undisputed leader of the region and a few followers preferred to disappear with what had been their reason for living! But the beautiful wife and four children of the head of state were taken to a neighbouring province, where the chief was a cousin of the family.

Life had therefore regrouped further south, where villages quickly sprang up again, initially with tree-trunk huts, which were soon replaced by mud-brick huts that were much more comfortable and more resistant to the animal invasion that the upheaval had brought to the more hospitable area. Bears suddenly swarmed, as did deer and elephants, not to mention wolves, their howling tearing up the night!

This gave rise to the idea of domesticating other breeds, including reindeer, elk, wolverines and musk oxen.

For hunting, at the same time, throwing flints disappeared to make way for bows and arrows, which were soon fitted with metal points sharpened from flint.

Because the iron was found on the ground, brownish, in more or less large blistered slabs, which led to a real search for similar materials. The surface haematite thus became the real iron, from a mine covering several kilometres of land in the far south, right down to the sea.

The discovery of other ores and minerals, and above all their rational use after some trial and error, completely changed the face of life for the inhabitants of this country. A new age began with the use of tools to cut stones and assemble them, as was the custom with bricks. Henceforth, the dwellings, although made of unpolished stone and still rudimentarily assembled, quickly became very "liveable", and gave rise to the idea of building monumental religious edifices so that God would be pleased to come and find shelter there himself, at least in spirit.

This prelude to philosophico-theological unification led the "Scholars" to a more ardent search for the primary truth... but also to one of the first violent discords in Humanity! For the "Monarch", firmly seated on his throne, wanted to be considered the undisputed successor "begotten by God" to lead the people, whereas the "Priests" implied the primordial benevolence of the Creator who "begotten all men" towards his creatures.

And so fifty centuries passed peacefully by among the people themselves, especially those living in the countryside. For them, the Divinity's intentions were obvious: all His bounties were spread out under their feet! All you have to do is bend down to harvest and enjoy it! Everyone takes what they need, without worrying if someone else takes more than they do!

When travellers passed through, attracted by the "rumoursabout this land of milk and honey, they quenched their thirst at any fresh spring, without any hang-ups, helped by the locals who offered them jugs.

During these long centuries, this gentle nation ignored hatred, war, revenge and, more simply, contempt! They expressed their joy as often as possible through popular festivals where dancing and singing were at their best. They often followed the huge mountains of fruit and vegetables that the frequent harvests caused them to pile up! And where everyone came to draw to their heart's content, without being envied or held to account!

It was at this time, around 16,000 BC, that a lesser cataclysm once again shook this part of the world, this time with little effect on the continent itself, although it did upset the geology! The Sahara appeared, and above all, a tidal wave from the Caspian Sea opened up the Black Sea and the Bosphorus, flooding several Mediterranean islands. It was also this tidal surge that opened up the present-day Straits of Gibraltar, although they were much wider than they are today.

And it was at this moment that Aha was born: "the Elder", who gave his name to the continent. A Queen, widowed and inconsolable at the death of her husband on her wedding day, at the time of this cataclysm, when he was helping buried people, locked herself in her room and never came out. Six months later, however, she reappeared transfigured, saying that she had been touched by Divine grace, and that a Son would be born to her in nine months' time! And so it happened...

Very quickly, the child, named Aha-Men-Geb, or the Elder Master of the Earth, appeared to have superhuman intelligence! It was he who taught the: men to use their intelligence to resemble the image that God had modelled for this purpose, and the leaders of these souls: the Priests, to use the Divine Law of Creation to perfect creativity, and to be its true Guides.

Aha-Men-Geb married a young mortal: Princess Nut, a descendant of the famous chief who had left himself to die in his territory in the Far North five millennia earlier, but who had sent his wife and four children to live with his cousin. Nut was an admirable wife, who also had two sons and two daughters. The eldest, who took over from her, was enthroned as "the direct Elder descendant of God", according to a ritual that became immutable, even later in Pharaonic Egypt: "You become the Master of the

Throne of Geb, and you will give it to your Eldest, as a direct inheritance from Ptah".

Thus was born Aha-Men-Ptah: 'The Eldest-Heart-of-God', from which Plato coined a name so tainted with fantasy and unreality: Atlantis. We won't be keeping it for him, even though it had the good fortune to fire the imagination of the masses! The Latin Posidonius perfectly expresses the opinion of the scholars of his time: "It is necessary to believe that Plato's account is not a fiction, and that there is more than one point that makes the account of Atlantis welcome rather than reject it".

In short, this is what has been done here, at least for the beginning of the story in the 'Timaeus', where Solon is portrayed and transcribed in the preface. For the rest, Atlantis, as an entity, has unfortunately Hellenised too much of the basic geographical and mythological data to be able to re-establish reality on the basis of this text. The Atlantic Ocean, for example, which is of Platonic origin, has replaced the Western Ocean, which was previously its own, since the time of the 'Great Cataclysm'.

In earlier times, the name was even more significant: the Eastern Sea. Quite a programme, since it amply demonstrates the opposition that took place at the time! Despite all the political ups and downs, prosperity reigned in Aha-Men-Ptah. Cereals and crops abounded; metals from the soil, such as copper and lead, were mined in the open air; tin and antimony were mined in galleries at ground level; iron, silver and gold were mined rationally at greater depths. Fine stones were already sought after by women, and were artistically cut after being collected in the hollows of easily accessible valleys. As for the stones known as 'precious', they were not sought after for their financial value, but for their beneficial power: they were carriers of influences emanating, for each of these twelve stones, from one of the twelve suns of the zodiacal constellations, whose emanations they alone captured: the breaths. Most of these stones came from oblique veins, vertically aligned with certain characteristic but arid soils, on which herds of sheep, aurochs and peaceful bison grazed.

Finally, there were certain rare minerals, much sought-after for their symbolic properties, such as aurichalcite, with its shimmering greenish glints, within which glowed the 'Burning Inferno', the symbol of Ath-Mer, where the eternal rejuvenation of the heart was renewed.

The many forests also provided all the types of wood needed for social life. Carpenters and joiners, cabinet-makers and artists used hardwoods as well as rare species, transforming them into delicately shaped furniture or galleys and boats of all kinds.

Only the sycamore, of the 'maple' type, was formally prohibited, both for cutting and for private use, except after a very strict ritual of blessings. The sycamore was the Sacred Tree: the An-Auhi, which could only be approached by a priest who was always pure. He could also 'take its life' after a highly complex ritual in order to extract 'the heart' in its entire length and shape the sixteen Tan-Auhi, which by contraction became the Tau, or the Crosses of Life, also known as 'annealed crosses'. It was common knowledge that the owners of these 'taboos' personifying Life, and which were owned only by people with the 'Right Voice', were endowed with the blessings of the Almighty God!

A special territory, delimited by the obliquity and degree of the sun's rays, was dedicated to the growth of the sycamore tree. This sacred enclosure was called the Nahi, and only the practising Master, apart from the pure Priests, could gain access to it to converse at his leisure face to face with his Father.

Aha-Men-Ptah was therefore still a unique haven of peace in the world *twelve thousand years before Jesus was born*. Wild animals lived there, grew there, and died there after multiplying, the notion of killing for pleasure alone being totally absent; defence alone, and sometimes hunger in the depths of the forest, authorised man to take a life.

The pastures were abundant, the lakes were clear, and the forests were welcoming to the last mammoths nibbling as many young plant shoots as they wanted! So this land bore a strange resemblance to that biblical Eden, if it wasn't Eden itself!...

Only the centre still had a mountain range worthy of the name, as the main peaks exceeded four thousand metres. Among them were a few volcanoes that had fortunately been extinguished since the end of the Tertiary Era, and whose last 'fumaroles' themselves were now no more than vague memories!

From these slopes flowed the springs that made the immense plain green, with only the sea to the south stopping some six hundred kilometres away. As for the clear water cascading from the many streams, it was channelled to the capital, Ath-Mer, as well as to the other major towns in the Princes' States. As for the three mineral springs, as well as the hot water spring, they were tapped on site and used in fountains or pools, where their more or less sulphurous, more or less radioactive action was used for the greater good of the country's sick, who came to take cures at the Thermes to treat their ailments by regenerating defective cell tissue without any financial constraints, as everything was available free of charge to all those who came there.

Aha-Men-Ptah thus enjoyed seemingly perfect administration within a seemingly ideal way of life! But if this had been a reality from the beginning until a few centuries ago, the evolution towards a cultural revolution in values had changed the face of the country! In the twelfth millennium BC, peace was no more than a false appearance! Envy and jealousy were everywhere! And the 'Master' had to supervise far more carefully the management of the Provinces administered by his great-cousins: the eight Princes, who were marred by a host of irregularities!

For the States that made up the country, expanding their internal autonomy as time went by, were gaining ground in relation to the central power. Each province now had, on a par with the capital, a Council of twelve notables, who administered the territory's assets, and a Regional Court of Justice, who judged offences - minor ones it was true - so as not to encumber the High Court of Ath-Mer, at least that was the official version of the Princes.

The reality, however, quickly became very different! And all the more so because events were happening so fast! Such as the fact that the Master's Privy Councillor, who attended the deliberations of the Regional Councils in order to report to the Monarch, had had to temporarily cease his travels due to the nameless 'hassles' he was becoming the object of during his trips to the Provinces.

The population, generally quite lymphatic and at ease with itself, paid little attention to the internal dissensions between the Master and his vassals, who, as a descendant of God, was great enough to re-establish the situation if it was disturbed, which, incidentally, was hardly the case in everyday life for ordinary mortals! The latter even tended to laugh heartily at this opposition, without realising that he would be the first to suffer when the time came to settle scores!

It was during this troubled period, when Power was losing more and more of its authority and power, that the "Scientists" in the "Mathematical Towers", where "Mathematical Combinations" were studied, brought terrible news: the exact date of a "Great Cataclysm" which was to occur, and which would be likely to completely wipe out the continent of Aha-Men-Ptah!...

Despite the secrecy of this discovery, announced only at the Palais Royal, the news spread around the capital like wildfire! There was irrational panic for a few hours, culminating in a gigantic burst of laughter when the "Master", himself, announced that the upheaval would only occur... in 2,000 years!

Once calm had returned, unconsciousness and selfishness cast doubt on the mathematical veracity of the event. Other centuries passed, denying the possibility of the cataclysm, and then others, simply denying it! And the State itself suffered the consequences! Three states had seceded, proclaiming their independence in the face of the inability of the powers that be to manage the interests of all properly, preferring instead to contemplate the eventual demise of the country and its abandonment!...

The last millennium before the end of Aha-Men-Ptah came to an end! It was the year 10000 BC: the continent had just two hundred and eight years left to survive! And An-Nu, the Great Pontiff, knew this when he came to the Great Council that day!...

CHAPTER SEVEN

A MEETING OF THE GRAND COUNCIL

> *Ask the generations of the past,*
> *Listen to the wisdom of their fathers;*
> *For we are of yesterday and know nothing,*
> *Our days pass like shadows on the earth:*
> *But they will speak to you and teach you,*
> *They will draw these lessons from their hearts.*
>
> OLD TESTAMENT
> *(Job, VIII, 8-10)*

> *Human beings are created in the image of God.*
> *Everyone has the ability to hear*
> *He who provides all the answers.*
> *It is not the scholar alone who is His image!*
>
> PAPYRUS OF ANI
> *(Maxime 62)*

Texts abound with accounts of this kind of meeting, especially when the Grand Council is renewed! The An-Nu, the Pontiff of the College of High Priests, alone, could not be changed, since he was Pontiff for life by virtue of the Knowledge he possessed in its entirety and only bequeathed to his successor when he had taken the decision to do so, after mature reflection in solitary retreat. He had deserved this first place, being at the pinnacle of perfection[11],

---

[11] A full bibliography is appended at the end of this volume, but the main papyri reporting meetings of this kind can be found in the collections of BRUGSCH, MASPERO and PIERRET; BERGMANN's *Hieroglyphische Inschriften*; PIEHL'S and ROUGE's *Inscriptions hiéroglyphiques*; the *Annales du Livre des quatre Temps*, from the temple of Dendérah, etc.

and this recognition was not disputed, even among the highest figures of Aha-Men-Ptah!

Only the current 'Master' could have raised his voice, but the man who presided over the country's destiny at the time was morose and timid in the face of the scale of the disaster that was about to unfold, constantly dithering with his conscience about what to do. His new central administration had only forty-five Venerables left, instead of the usual seventy-two, due to the defection of members from the three states that had openly rebelled and seceded.

So as not to be put off by original quotations whose grandiloquent phrases, frequently repeated, would be tedious, this memorable meeting of the Grand Council is reported in a contemporary dialogue form, but which is totally accurate in its content, if not in its form...

The "Master" having arrived at the same time as the Pontiff, the opening of this session took place without further delay, at the appointed time. After welcoming the new members and bidding farewell to those who had joined their ancestors, the "Descendant of the Elder", in a sombre tone, gave way to the Pontiff. Without further ado, the Pontiff addressed the assembled Venerables with intense emotion:

- Wise men, my brothers, the ritual formula of blessing that I should make: "May the Peace of God be upon you and your work during this Assembly", is clearly insufficient this year! It would even be hypocritical, given the terrible events that will put an end not to your work, but to that of your grandchildren! Now is not the time for politeness, but for warning! You must start organising the Exodus of all our people to other lands, as this will require a long-term effort on everyone's part!

The initial murmurs and whispers soon gave way to protests and then howls! The younger new members were not yet used to this kind of jousting, and on one of the left benches, a Venerable who had just reached the number of years required to obtain a seat, leapt to his feet, waving his purple surplice around him. As he reached the centre of the hemicycle, sensing that silence was settling in without difficulty and that he would have his audience well in hand, he took a deep breath. He could see himself at the pinnacle of glory, and he slowly looked at his colleagues, just as he had seen practised by the Ancients, all fine strategists, who had preceded him! Then he turned back to face the An-Nu, to whom he spoke in a tone that he intended to be condescending:

- Venerable Pontiff! Our deep and sincere respect for you, all of us gathered here today to deliberate on serious matters, is in no way called into question by my questioning. Your Wisdom is legendary far beyond our territorial limits; and your Knowledge in all matters alone places your superior intelligence on a much higher plane than those contained in all the other brains gathered here... apart from that of our venerated Master of course, who is even higher!"

This last part of the emphatic sentence had been added quickly, the mentor having realised to his horror, slightly late, that the 'descendant of God' was also present! A few smiles and laughs were quickly stifled. But very quickly, the questioner picked himself up and continued:

- It's true that this is the first meeting I've attended, and I apologise to this learned assembly for my slip of the tongue. But I know that I'm speaking on behalf of everyone, not only here, but also those who are waiting outside, and above all the young people who are concerned, by asking you this question: "How can you be sure that this cataclysm is coming, and when?

A light murmur ran through the pink marble benches, as everyone took the opportunity to move around and try to find a more comfortable position to hear the An-Nu's answer. The An-Nu thoughtfully stroked his long white beard, thinking that he had been wrong to come and prophesy after all, and that this fight he wanted to wage to preserve the race of his forefathers - and theirs! - was ultimately pointless! The men who were doubting God at this moment were even doubting themselves! The old Pontiff sighed, hoping against hope that many humans, at the last moment, would attempt the great adventure of leaving their homes before it was too late, to escape final annihilation.

Standing alone, stiff in his immaculate white linen tunic, he faced the four rows of pews of members. In silence, he raised a gaunt hand, the bones showing through the skin, towards the Cross of Life that stood above his head, a giant symbol of Universal Harmonic Life, carved into the very heart of a very old sycamore tree, whose two arms measured one metre sixty from one end to the other!

After the short silence that followed this gesture, the Pontiff's voice rang out, much firmer and more vibrant:

- O you: Remenhep, whom I held together on my two hands during the initiation ceremony, in order to force you to drink the Living Water, which you vigorously refused! You were already screaming!"

A good-natured laugh broke the dramatic atmosphere of the place, shaking the manes of the Venerables and creating several whitish waves, which served as a beneficial outlet. The An-Nu continued:

- A soul, sent by God whose existence you all seem to forget, had barely taken possession of your carnal envelope as a newborn human, when you rebelled against the Divine ritual! However, all the celestial blessings have been gathered in you; you are rich, esteemed and respected by all, for if only in Ath-Mer: you are fair of voice and kind to anyone who finds themselves in any kind of trouble. That's why today you sit on the Great Council, in the company of the wisest of the wisest! Among the 'Elders of God' who made this country, shaping it according to Divine Law, Elder after Elder!... So why do you unconditionally echo the shameful doubts of those who, by doubting the Power of our Creator, call into question the very Principles that made Aha-Men-Ptah great?....

A murmur, not particularly disapproving, ran through the great hall and reached the young questioner, who pretended to rise to reply. But the Pontiff, who still had one hand raised towards the Tau, imperatively raised the other, making it clear to everyone that he had not finished speaking and did not want to be interrupted:

- It's true that the greyness of your hair is nowhere near the whiteness of mine! You represent youth to all the elders here, but there are several points where you are no less mature in spirit than they are... because they have forgotten what you failed to learn, and which is our direct inheritance from God! Namely, the extraordinarily life-giving value of what now appear to everyone as nothing more than mystical symbols! Like this Tau, above my head and yours! Does it still represent Justice and Peace hovering over Aha-Men-Ptah? No one will contradict me if I answer a resounding no to that question! But if the general situation has become so critical, it's because no one is trying to understand the profound meaning of the constituent elements of the very foundation of our Homeland! This Tau, if not a prayer to God, should inspire you and give you the strength you need to set your hearts once again on the path of understanding and Truth!... The lies and impostures that are breaking in ever closer waves across the continent are reaching our venerable Grand Council! The capital is being eaten away, and it won't be long before the country destroys itself: before the Great Cataclysm has nothing but ruins to sweep away!... And the foreigners who sail past in their ships, built according to our plans, will laugh and say: "In the bosom of this vast sea was a people of profound Wisdom, who ruled the Universe, rich and fertile under a sky that was always pure and serene!... And yet no trace of them remains! All gone!:. Do you want, all of you, venerable Fathers of this Great Council, to hear these sinister words, when you are in the Kingdom that will welcome us all when we are beyond earthly Life?... I don't think so, knowing you very well! That is why you would do well to reread, as I have done, the annals of our archives of the "Houses of Life", to which you have access at all times, don't forget that, given your high responsibilities, and you will thus learn to resolve the problems that haunt you!

- Does this mean, O Venerable One, that we could understand the sacred texts? It seemed to me that this was impossible for the uninitiated...

- These are not religious texts, but those relating to the calculations of the Mathematical Combinations themselves, whose current practical uses should be learnt by heart by all those who can! And you would all understand that in this case no arbitrary use is being made to define the Great Cataclysm and its probable date. Each movement of the stars and planets generates a whole series of harmonious movements between them, which have a very precise meaning, willed by God who has defined the Law. It is this agreement between Heaven and Earth, God and Man, that is already in the process of breaking down, and that will break down when the time comes!

Another Venerable, straightening up, said, while leaning heavily with both hands on the gnarled cane:

- Do you want us to understand, Pontiff, that this Great Cataclysm, which we have been hearing about for ages, is a punishment sent by God, willed by Him to annihilate us and thus prove that we humans are nothing compared to His omnipotence! But in that case, who is He going to prove it to, since there won't be anyone left?...

- You are translating quite spiritually, O Sage Perhitsou, the Divine alternative of a cause that was very good in the beginning, but which Man has been doing his utmost to destroy for centuries! The fact that remains certain, however, is that all our knowledge of God and His Universe cannot foresee, let alone prevent, this Great Cataclysm from happening! What we do know for certain is that the "Divine-Mathematical-Combinations" influence all the organisms living on earth, through the influences that these figurations represent. And observation and experience show that the geometric patterns formed are the exact reflections of the Divine influences breathed into the parcels generated by the Creator, which are our souls. Their directives are infallible to those who wish to be inspired by them when they are beneficial. Our poor envelopes of flesh live only by the subtle thoughts that emanate from them! They are the generating organs that act on the sensations we feel, and which we should be able to tame when they turn into bestial passions! Because there is nothing human about what is happening in our souls at the moment, in this denial of Divine Power! And that's why I shout it out loud to you: our Beloved Homeland has become a heartless land, and it will be swept away by the fury of the heavenly movements, if nothing is done to calm God down!

There was an awkward silence for a few seconds in the face of this threatening diatribe. Just long enough for Sage Perhitsou to ask, in a lower but distinct voice:

- What would it take, O venerable Pontiff, to calm God?

The answer came immediately:

- First of all, calm the human spirits themselves, by giving them back Faith in their leader: their Master! In this way, God will regain his place, which he has just lost. For the bond of Peace, which so strongly united God and His earthly image, and which seemed so solid even four or five centuries ago, has become strained over the years, and is becoming so strained today that it will soon be broken! The soul is no longer the common receptor, but a mere container, a vessel, which absorbs all the heresies elucidated by human carnal envelopes alone! The spirit of the Creator no longer inhabits them!...

- We readily admit your criticisms, O Pontiff! And we are aware of our weaknesses. So why don't you give us the details of this cataclysm yourself, since you know them better than we would learn them from the archives!

- The calculations of my predecessors, the Wise Pontiffs, as well as those of the scholars of our 'Double House of Life' of Septa-Rerep, whom I have just consulted on the spot, and who, generation after generation, are also repeating the calculations of the 'combinations in oppositions', in order to see if their elders had not made a mistake somewhere in their supputations, all, all are formal! A dreadful catastrophe, a disaster far worse than the one recorded by our Ancestors, which in its time ravaged the whole of the north of our country and many other parts of the world, a

'Great Cataclysm' will occur and will mainly affect our land, this primordial land: the God-born!... I've done the calculations again, and they confirm those of the scientists: the "evil combinations" of this Great Year are such that our country will literally be swallowed up by the waters, in its entirety! Nothing will remain of it, and if you do not intervene immediately, O my venerable children of God, and also Members of this Great Council, there will be neither you nor anyone left to tell the story of our admirable country, for it will have become the Kingdom of the Dead!..."

Murmurs and a few protests greeted this long diatribe. But the majority of the Venerables remained silent, frozen in astonishment in their benches, for, knowing the Wisdom of the An-Nu and his lack of taste for ostentation and the vanity of grandiloquence, they had been struck by the vehement and persuasive tone, unusual indeed, of the Great Pontiff. A long-term plan was undoubtedly necessary, and it would have to be put in place as quickly as possible. This was the subject of the Silent Ones' meditations, and one of the oldest Members, in the restored silence, expressed the general anxiety:

- No one here is questioning the slightest of your words, O our Wise Spiritual Guide, and above all their implications! On the other hand, it is obvious that if we all accept this Great Cataclysm to come as a certainty, the Exodus that will have to take place must be pre prepared as of now in the calm of this Assembly, so that everything can be ready when the time comes. But that will mean building tens of thousands of boats! Not to mention the food for millions of people, and all the other vital things that need to be taken along, including the books of our Knowledge!... The tools and the whole humanitarian process that would promote the rebirth of our lives, elsewhere!... It's clearly a long-term plan, which will extend beyond our generation and even the next! So, and this is the vital problem for the moment, we need not only to be convinced ourselves of the veracity of this Great Cataclysm, but also to persuade the rest of our People! How do you expect to prove the reality of the facts to come, let alone the date... a question which is on the lips of every Member of this venerable Assembly!...

The An-Nu shook his head doubtfully, as his predictions had once again proved correct! If he lost himself in mathematical explanations that none of them were capable of understanding, nothing concrete would come out of this meeting:

- You have always been one of the most active and reasonable Members of this Great Council, Khaankton, and your experience in this matter will be most valuable. I shall try to answer all of you at once, after which I shall retire and never speak again in public. My great age will bring me to the end of my earthly sojourn, and my eldest son, already High Priest of Ath-Mer, will become Pontiff of Aha-Men-Ptah before long

Ignoring the sympathetic, pitying... or already hypocritical murmurs, the An-Nu continued:

- To all of you I make a threefold appeal: to your intelligence, because it is the holder of the Wisdom that creates the various mental states that animate you; to your intuition, which beyond your rational thought process, is the clairvoyance that combines your Wisdom with your Intelligence; finally, I also, and above all, appeal to your Soul, that Divine particle that alone until the end of Time links your carnal envelope to God, because it is the canvas of all human sensations and on which your bodily as well as emotional acts are based. Good and evil spring from it, from your soul! Now, depending on whether you decide to think in one way or another, the destiny of our entire people, who have lived in peace and happiness for so long, will be totally turned upside down in one way or another! Indeed, since envy, discord, slander and perfidy have taken root in several parts of our Homeland; since our priests have had to leave their temples on pain of abjuring the one Faith; since cruelty, imposture and vengeance have made their appearance in these places that have already become accursed, fear is taking hold everywhere! From now on, no temporal order alone can restore the Justice and Peace that have made our reputation and our tranquillity for two hundred centuries!... God and His Son, our Blessed "Master", are no longer heard in several Provinces, as you know as well as I do. His orders and prayers are not respected! And doubt penetrates through slander and flattery even within our walls... And you, O venerable ones! What are you doing? You doubt and ask for proof! Proof! You need the certainty, in advance, that your entrails will be torn apart by the rocks that will tumble from the mountains onto you! You need the horrible spectacle of your ruin and the knowledge that if you don't make a decision now, the only thing left to do is to kill yourself when the time comes, as there is no way of saving you and you don't want to prolong your agony!...

Several Members rose to their feet, gesticulating wildly. Such a sermon had never been heard in this hemicycle and protests arose from all sides. The "Master", seeing that the word of the An-Nu was being challenged, stood up, waving a hand. Immediately there was silence and everyone sat down again:

- Dear venerable Members of this House: I had no intention of speaking again, but it is important! As our An-Nu so aptly put it, to whom I pay tribute here for his loyalty and extreme frankness, while wishing him a very long life in our service, for centuries a hypocritical perversion has crept surreptitiously into our morals as much as into our institutions. One day, it discovered our fortunate country, which God had endowed with all the bounties of nature, invading some of our territories, camouflaging itself in a thousand different forms, and spreading the poisonous breath of the first slanders! This country, blessed by God, suffers as a whole from the subtle and all the more pernicious contagion of wanting something other than what had from all eternity made it happy! It wasn't long before the first seeds of this derision were sown in the population so dear to our hearts! The son cherished his parents less tenderly; the wife her husband; the general love of the common good against one's own, much more contemptible; harmony weakened more and more in our society, each one beginning to apologise to his neighbour for the work he no longer wanted to do, whereas before he would willingly help him in return, which was the pretext for the songs and celebrations now banished from customs! Mutual duties disappeared; so did friendly help; even family help! And the watchword became: "Why should I undertake hard work for which I will get nothing? And this misconception gave rise to something that had never happened in our country for twenty millennia: hatred of our neighbours! Three Provinces, one after the other, decided that they would live more freely without Divine tutelage: they are now in complete chaos! Without faith or law, they make a very particular use of yours and mine, in fact imprisoning them in bonds that a fatal bloody knife can no longer even cut! The corruption of the Law has only brought confusion and disorder! And now the murmurs and groans have reached our capital! They emanate from the fools who, no longer listening to the voice of God, and of his representation, nature, which allows us all to live free from want, cry out and weep in mock indignation against our councils and our decisions! Fools! They will become the architects of their own evils and their own demise! And I see the finger of God in the approach of this Great Cataclysm! It's coming at the right time, and if it doesn't happen, mankind will take it upon itself to create it!

This long harangue was suspended for a few moments, the Master catching his breath after the uninterrupted flow of words that had escaped from his mouth, where he had been blocked for too long. The Venerables took the opportunity to express their opinions amongst themselves on the scabrous subject of the people losing their understanding with God. The Master raised his hand, and the An-Nu, who was about to speak again, remained silent, because the "Voice" was right:

- I understand your murmurings, but you cannot ignore why peace no longer reigns anywhere in this country, and why God wants to put things right in his own way, since ours is no good! Because peace no longer reigns in people's hearts, not even in yours, dear and venerated Members of this Assembly, which is still so close to the happy state we all used to be in! And if I see, like our very Wise An-Nu, the way to restore Order, Peace and Happiness everywhere, it seems just as surely that nobody wants to think about it any more, or try to do what needs to be done to return to those happy times!

Hypostyle hall of the Temple of the "Lady of Heaven" at Denderah.

The same room in the Temple of Denderah as seen by the scientific commission accompanying General Bonaparte to Egypt in 1797.
(Drawing taken from the "Description of Egypt").

Pectoral of All-Ank-Amon, Cairo Museum.
The Eye, which symbolises all creation and navigates the divine boat, is found on the chest of every Pharaoh (or Pêr-Ahâ), the "Descendant of the Eldest", or Son-of-God.

Enlargement of the Eye of the Pectoral of Seti 1er. *(Ph. of the author.)*

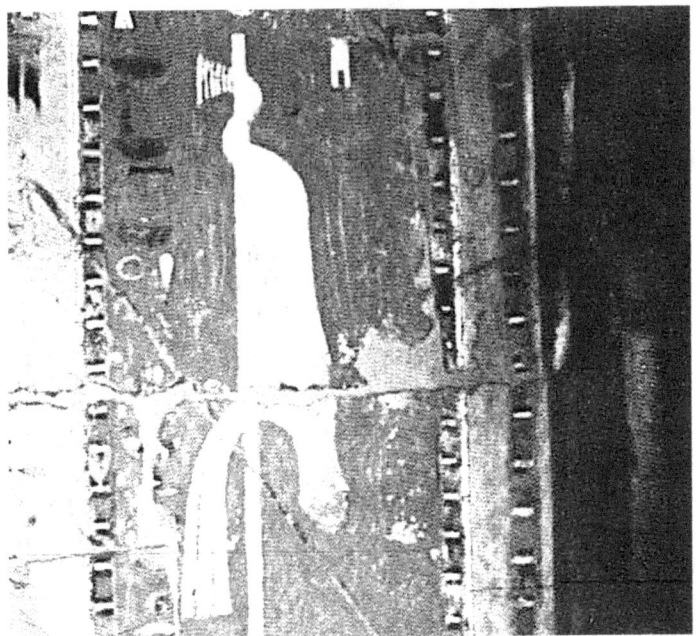

The symbol of the Holy of Holies of Denderah, the skin of the bull that enclosed the body of Osiris. *(Photo taken by the author in the basement room adjoining the 1976 archive room).*

Planisphere of Denderah, showing the exact position of the sky at the time of the Great Cataclysm on 19 July 9792 BC.

These few bitter words, full of common sense though they were, penetrated people's hearts, but they did not have time to be studied in depth, for the Pontiff, having risen, had taken up the same theme:

- How happy our humanity would be, O Master of Aha-Men-Ptah, if it understood what it losing by not understanding your words!

If the false, which has become habitual in this day and age, has so much power over the soul, the Divine particle: what can we do, when the time comes, to try to thwart the 'Mathematical Combinations' that will act on both the minds and the Earth?

Some of the Members, having recovered their senses, became agitated at this question, and it was a noble figure with a beard that was still black who spoke up:

- To answer this question, O Venerated Pontiff, we would need to know officially, that is to say through you, the date foreseen for the beginning of this cataclysm, and also how certain it is that it will strike our earth? As far as I'm concerned, I must confess that I've been hearing about it for some time now...

-We have all reached this point, O Khaontou; but you have always been among the most active Members of this Council, and as such, you will understand: the Divine Law which regulates celestial harmony, and which was revealed to our Ancestor Aha, gives rhythm to the movement of the Earth in the Mathematics of Time, as much as in that of Space. It was therefore easy for the Ancient "Masters of Numbers" to determine the exact date and place of the upheaval: it will take place with maximum intensity on 27th July 9792, i.e. two hundred and eight years from now! The Time is at hand when all souls will render their accounts!

This last sentence had been uttered in a much more powerful voice, the hubbub having risen at the mention of the date, which was so close. And the Pontiff resumed in the higher tone he knew how to use from time to time, in a hurry to finish this harangue, which he knew would change nothing!

- And this is inevitable! For although our ancient ancestral traditions predicted that God, in his infinite goodness, could restore balance to the Earth without the Great Cataclysm occurring if humans returned to the ancient understanding of Happiness and Peace, it now appears that this has not been the case!... So, Members of this Council, hurry up and take all the necessary decisions so that, in two centuries' time, we can save those who will be able to set off on the Exodus and found a second Homeland, with the help of God and rediscovered Faith. The warning signs of growing impiety are already piling up below the horizon of our sky, where the Sun becomes redder and redder as it rises in the West! Truly, I say to you solemnly in conclusion: the West is turning so red that when it has taken on the colour of our blood, it will be no more than a synonym for Aha-Men-Ptah, the Kingdom of the Dead!

And the An-Nu, without further ado, after bowing first to the Monarch, then to the Members of the learned Assembly still reeling from the latest and very dark prophecy, walked out slowly and majestically.

CHAPTER EIGHT

GEB THE LAST MASTER!

The Earth is waiting in terror for something terrible!
An atrocity that our children will never understand,
for these high-pitched whistles are unbearable!
It seems as if the sea is rolling into the abyss,
mingling with the lightning and the hurricane,
searching for living bones!
And over there, in Ath-Mer, a swirling crimson pool
covers with blood the Golden Circle
of the God-Temple that was nothing but idolatry!

CHIBET D'AHOU
(Annals of the Ahou Scribe)

There were only seventy-two years and sixty-four days left before Aha-Men-Ptah would be invaded by the waters! But the majority of its inhabitants continued to live unaware and unconcerned about the event that would engulf them!

On this day, 13 May 9864 BC, large crowds were gathered all around the forecourt of the TempleGod, curious to witness the presentation of the eldest son of the reigning "Master": the "Monarch of the Righteous Voice, Abu", who had been born a few days earlier. The An-Nu was to name him "Men-Geb" during the blessing, thus drawing Divine attention to the fact that he should not lie down and perpetuate the race. This name, borne by the one who was to be the last "Descendant of the Elder", would perhaps draw down upon his head the indulgence of the Creator, which he would certainly need most!

So thought Ahou sadly, as he reached the forecourt with his slow, majestic step, followed one step behind by the Pontiff, in the still dark dawn of the new day. The College of Priests followed in files of eight, preceding Queen Petsout, who had not wished to leave it to any of her successors to carry her baby, and whose haughty bearing was much admired by the people. The Annals describe the ancient tradition of this ceremony in detail. The ritual process began when the first rays of sunlight appeared over the Golden Circle. This was an obvious first sign of good fortune, ensuring a long life of Justice, Peace and Goodness for those who benefited from it. This circumference was inlaid with pure, solid gold, making the white marble covering the esplanade even more immaculate, if that were possible. It was arranged in such a way that, every morning, the first rays of the daytime sun were reflected directly onto just one part of it. Due to the phenomenon of the Earth's rotation, each day they varied slightly from their positions of the previous day, always within the circle, thus touching, one after the other throughout the year, the twelve monolithic blocks of black granite covered with a very specific crystalline material. Each one symbolised one of the twelve constellations that encircled the celestial equator along the Milky Way, harmonising the Earth with the heavens.

After stripping him of his finely plaited linen garment, the Queen placed her first-born child gently on the crystal corresponding to the beneficial influences of the day he was born. The mineral, in fact, having absorbed over thousands of centuries certain rays that only its Creator allowed it to capture, was able to retransmit them to their beneficiaries, themselves only tuned to the same wavelength, and enlivened to the maximum by the first rays of the Sun.

As at dawn, the star was the first to appear directly on the block facing the east, on which the newborn child was standing gently, everyone waited anxiously for the daily apparition, announced by a very clear dew on the western horizon.

Joyful cries were soon heard, the baby's flesh quickly lighting up in the surrounding half-light, taking on a lovely golden hue, similar to that of the circle, which now seemed like a huge Divine halo!

The An-Nu and Ahou were satisfied with the beneficial omens: God would certainly help Men-Geb to accomplish the heavy task that would be his ! And while thinking about this, the Pontiff "saw" the Golden Circle sink beneath the waters and become stained with the blood of those present! He shook himself energetically, for he had already had similar visions on several occasions! But this was hardly the time for catastrophic prescience!...

The High Priest slowly raised his two arms towards this ball which had become dazzling, and in the restored silence, chanted:

"O you, Sun resplendent with your beneficent powers, Great Fruitful River of the Original Source, deign to imbue this young body with your Divine mark, to develop in it the being who will become Men-Geb, and who will guide Your people, the only ones descended from the Elder, according to Your commandments."

The ceremony continued with its normal ritual, despite the exceptional nature of this blessing of the last 'Master'. One of the rooms in the south wing, with its excellent exposure, had always been the flat where the 'Elders' took their first steps in life. Men-Geb grew up there, year after year, until the age of twelve. He acquired an innate sense of harmony, with beauty in everything around him and his every desire satisfied. His father wanted him to have at least one wonderful memory of his early years, before he went straight into the distress that was engulfing the world!

But the day came, all too quickly, when he was transferred to the flat of the Master's heir. And the first thing he learned from his father was the purpose assigned to him: to prepare his people to leave - in spite of themselves - this land that would become cursed! Without further ado, he began the long education that would make him the next - and last - Master! On his fifteenth birthday, he also learned that a Princess of the North was already destined for him by the An-Nu, to give them children who would be the 'Elders' of the future survivors of the Exodus! Which would not prevent him from being very happy with this wife...

Men-Geb had quickly entered a life full of lessons that were difficult for even the most intelligent young brain to assimilate. To give him a rest, An-Nu kept him company by telling him about the ancient history of their beautiful country. The Pontiff had befriended this very dark-haired boy, whose intelligence was becoming increasingly open to metaphysical questions. To try and relax him completely, he also explained to him, in great detail, the story of the young Princess who would one day be his wife. Her name was Nut, just like the first mortal who had married the 'Elder' with the same name as his. She was still only ten years old, and lived in the far north of the country, where her ancestors had taken refuge after their state had been swallowed up so long ago.

Apart from these brief moments of relaxation, Men-Geb was hardly free to think or act as he wished. He got to know his cousins, who were still loyal and governed the Princes' States, but who saw him more as the Master 'assigned' to them in the future than as a real ruler. Subtly, the mentality was evolving here too, and the An-Nu made the young man understand that the Destiny planned by God was being organised precisely in view of these mental changes in His human subjects.

As numerous regulations had been enacted to quickly perfect his Divine education, his every move was more strictly organised. He hardly saw his mother any more, and his governesses had been replaced not by servants, but by four sons of the first Priests, including the eldest son of the Pontiff, who were all over twenty years old and had been trained for this role.

The future 'Master' therefore had models of virtue and austerity to serve him, day and night, who would not allow him the slightest action that was reprehensible or simply outside the limits defined by the special protocol. This taught him many things, such as the fact that no Monarch could be unkind to such wise advisors.

When he reached the age of sixteen, his father took him with him to teach him the duties of monarchy that would await him when his turn came to reign. Every hour of the day, and even of the night, was marked by an action to be carried out, laid down in immutable codes that could only be waived with great difficulty.

As soon as he woke up, the Crown Prince would rush to his father's study, where he would find the Monarch already going through the various letters that had arrived during the night from the distant faithful provinces. The King would then reread all the letters aloud, slowly, so that his son could get to grips with the different turns of phrase. In this way, from the moment they woke up, they both had valuable knowledge of what was happening in the Kingdom. In this way, the day's actions were coordinated with the urgent decisions to be taken.

Only then did the Palace wake up; Men-Geb left his father for a moment to perform his morning ablutions. He took the opportunity to put on an immaculate and purified tunic, before going to the Temple, accompanied by his four aides-de-camp, where the whole family gathered to give thanks to God for the day ahead. The An-Nu issued a few sentences taken from the "Book", recalling various models of ancient justice. This made Abu smile because, as if by chance, a few hours later, the Monarch would have to solve problems similar to those he had heard in the morning! He was thus lending his own authority to that of his Ancestors, the Wise Men, whose effectiveness was very real in those remote times! Each act of the day was part of an intangible but magnificently 'oiled' royal cycle that regulated everything. This is what Men-Geb retained from this long initiation into power!

By the time he was eighteen, accustomed to an ascetic existence, slim in figure for he ate frugally and drank little, although he felt he was becoming a man, he was in no hurry to marry! Princess Nut, who had just turned sixteen, had sent him a pastel-coloured miniature on his coming-of-age day, depicting her in a halo, resplendent in pure beauty, her eyes full of warmth and restrained ardour.

The girl's parents had enclosed a letter to Abu reminding him that Nut was now "old enough" to be married. But, to his great astonishment, the Monarch learned from his son that he was in no more hurry to take a wife than to become King! So the Master flew into a rage that An-Nu, who was fortunately present, found it hard to calm.

After much negotiation with the Pontiff, Men-Geb agreed to be crowned King on his twenty-first birthday, and to marry at the same time - ten days after the coronation ceremonies, as tradition dictated. This solution pleased the father and filled the mother with contentment. As for AnNu, the date chosen suited him admirably, as the celestial configurations were much more favourable at that time!

During these three years, Men-Geb, who became simply Geb, the Heir, worked hard to perfect his education in every discipline, including that of how to make his wife happy, who, by Divine Law, would be his equal in all things and "God's follower".

The people, meanwhile, lived rather passively, taking little interest in the change of "Master", which used to be the occasion for great festivities. During Ahou's reign, twenty thousand boats of all tonnages had been carved out of so many trees that several beautiful forests had only the name of what had once been a splendid collection of nature! This was the only selfish comment made by those who didn't think that nature would disappear anyway in the Cataclysm!

The population of Aha-Men-Ptah had clearly chosen to continue living in the inane ways that would leave only the ultimate choice to the Creator himself, when that became a necessity. There was no doubt about this tragic decision in Geb's mind, any more than there was in the minds of those who both "knew" and feared the Divine Wrath that was about to reach its climax! No counterweight could yet counterbalance the terrible and scandalous events unfolding on this continent, where the total freedom acquired in all areas had become synonymous with the bondage of dissolute morals! This freedom, too dearly paid for, could no longer be thrown back from whence it came! And other upheavals were occurring, spread by this contagion to three new provinces!

It was in the midst of these fantasies that the coronation of the new Master took place. An-Nu was proud to be still here to assist his own son in the role of High Priest, which had just been entrusted to him. His homily had been remarkably well received by all present, particularly this vital passage:

- Each son of man endowed with a carnal envelope and a Divine soul cannot differ from his father, whom he perpetuates in the same conditions as his forebears did, imprinting the family name in the Great Book of Life on Earth, engraving it also in the dwellings of Eternal Ancestral Life, but above all impregnating himself with it as he grows! For the flesh of the one before makes it possible to make the flesh of the one after, and the person of the son is therefore the very person who begat him. The generation of Masters, on the other hand, which is immortal, depends on the only Elder of the Divine Sphere! His descendants are thus the Sons, the sole heirs in turn of this Divine inheritance by Divine right. I therefore solemnly declare today that God has placed you, Geb, as Sovereign Master of AhaMen-Ptah, in order to ensure that His Commandments of Peace, Justice and Goodness reign there and are respected.

These last sacramental words made the young "Master" sit up straight, and he took a deep breath to reply in a deep voice:

- I swear to be a faithful servant of God, my Father; to uphold his Commandments of Peace, Justice and Goodness.

For the last time, Ahou approached to act as Monarch. He held out his royal sceptre to his son:

- With this sceptre that I now hand over to you, Geb, from this moment Master of Aha-Men-Ptah: your reign begins! May it be carried out with the serenity and continuity of the Sun in its eternal cycle.

The choir of priests then chanted loudly:

O You, Lord of the Earth, unique and universal,
Whose mysteries hide and whose goodness reveals,
Bless Master Geb in the name of God,
Supreme Father of a hundred names in all places,
Who sees this crowning from heaven
May this reign be most gracious!

And the An-Nu added alone:

May He also preserve us from the Great Trial,
O Sovereign Guardian of the River!

The silence that suddenly followed was interrupted only by the rustling of the golden threads of Abu's tunic as he took his son by the right elbow and led him to take the place he had previously occupied on the Divine throne, which was now no longer his. When Geb was seated, his father put his hands on his shoulders and said loudly, so that no one would ignore him: "Long live Master Geb", and he repeated it three times, before the crowd did the same and ended in a general ovation.

The Sovereign of Aha-Men-Ptah was now enthroned, reigning over five Provinces and some sixty million souls. But this ceremony had been very different, compared to the splendours of yesteryear! Especially as only three of the Princes had attended the various coronation solemnities. The other two, with their families, had not turned up at the Royal Palace for various reasons, the main one of which was unmentionable! Fear of impeachment during their absence, as there had recently been almost constant unrest in the States.

Whereas at previous similar ceremonies, even for the coronation of Ahu, the crowds from the capital and the eight provinces had still flocked, filling not only the central nave, as for Geb, but also all the side bays, pouring the overflow of attendees onto the esplanade and completely whitening the linen tunics of those who were trampling the grass in the gardens!

As the ex-Monarch withdrew, bringing the ceremony to a close, he admitted that he was not too dissatisfied with the way it had gone. It wasn't very crowded, of course, but the presence of the eight High Priests - those who had not been able to remain in the rebel provinces were there - enhanced the spiritual and mystical reputation of the religious aspect, and augured a long and beneficial life for Geb. He would do all he could to ensure that the succession did not weigh too heavily on young shoulders, especially during the idyllic period coinciding with the wedding!

As for putting down the rebels in the rebel states, a task he had always put off, then put on hold so that his son could take care of it: that would have to wait a little longer, despite the obvious concern of the cousins who were still loyal! Ahu had hesitated too long to found an army; it would be up to Geb to learn to make an effort of will and take command by force of arms! What was written by God would come to pass, but it no longer depended on him!

Behind the old Master who was retiring, majestically all the same, the atmosphere in the Temple relaxed a little, in front of the extreme youth of the new Master, whose lost, not to say distraught, gaze beneath his smiling mask, was searching for a path that was difficult to grasp! He would certainly try to put his country back in order, and his union with the pretty Princess Nut would make things much easier by giving new blood to offspring who would themselves be better able to adapt to the new living conditions that the numerous protesters were advocating for political and social stabilisation throughout the continent of Aha-Men-Ptah, if it remained *above* water *of* course!

This was what was making up most of the murmurs from the crowd as they slowly made their way towards the Palace and its banqueting hall, where the feast awaited the guests.

That day was 22 July 9843 BC, and even the best guesses of the most sceptical did not realise that there was only a survival time of fifty-one years and five days before the swallowing!

It was not for this reason that the agape planned for the whole night ended before dawn for lack of participants! Quite simply, the new 'Master', seized by a sudden inspiration, had asked his father to immediately convene an extraordinary impromptu Council with their three cousins present, who had agreed, as they too were in a hurry to get back to their States! So the banquet quickly came to an end.

With this first official act of authority, the new young Master proved that he was a fine diplomat and that he knew what he wanted! Demonstrating from the outset the great firmness that would be his all his life, and which could not fail to establish his authority, he immediately demanded that his cousins and their families stay at the Palace to await the arrival of his future wife and attend the wedding.

Without giving the Princes time to recriminate, he sent for two royal messengers, to whom he gave imperative missives, ordering the other two cousins to come with their families for the wedding ceremony, and assuring them that a national army had been formed, which they could use if need be!

The former monarch gazed at his son, amazed to see him decide in a matter of minutes what he had hesitated to do all his life! He was now sure he was leaving power in the best possible hands, especially as his forthcoming marriage would only strengthen the balance.

The next three days spent feverishly making the final preparations to ensure a warm welcome for Nut and her retinue. The next day, as soon as the sun rose, the capital was awakened by the joyous sounds of the parade drums and the lively music that accompanied them.

Ath-Mer, quickly out in force and jubilant, learnt that the princely retinue was only two hours away on foot, which suddenly had an unexpected effect: the people felt their interest growing by the minute! As curiosity grew, crowds swarmed along the six-kilometre stretch of road running north-south through the city, which the procession would have to use to reach the Palace.

The royal guards took up positions all along the route, to leave a central passageway free, as the inns, stalls and shops were literally emptied of their occupants, as were the dwellings. An almost unanimous impulse drove the whole town into the streets, in one fell swoop, whereas the procession, which had set out the evening before on a two-hour march, had only raised a few shrugs of the shoulders. The turnaround was as complete as it was sudden! No one had even seen the young King and his escort as they set off to meet the Princely retinue!

Meanwhile, Nut was making her way along the road on horseback, a little weary on the last day of her journey. She had not slept well, as she had secretly sent an emissary to the capital to come back and tell her all about the festive atmosphere in the city, and the result had been very poor, with everything looking very ordinary! For the six nights that the Princess had been living in an encampment with her retinue, with a hundred or so men setting it up every evening and dismantling it in the morning, she had been looking forward to arriving at her destination, but she had had time to dream, perhaps a little too much, as she had hoped for a more enthusiastic welcome!

On that last morning, she had looked sadly at the large buffalo hide tents, spacious with their feather and goose down beddings, before mounting her horse, thinking that her future husband had not bothered to come and pick her up at the last stop, as he had implied in his last letter.

This made her more apprehensive about getting to know the man who ruled the world and who would soon make her his wife. All she knew of him was a small reproduction that had reached her the previous year, in which his eyes were so sad that a warm hope had overwhelmed her at the time. But on that day, she was somewhat disappointed by this solitary arrival, still imagining, in spite of everything, that this union would be the happiness of her life!

So, despite the vehement protests of her attendants and her chief of protocol, she categorically refused to ride in the ceremonial carriage specially gilded and harnessed for her entrance to *Ath-Mer!* Instead, she took one of the crew's four spirited but gentle chestnuts from her father's stud to ride.

Advancing along the road at the head of her troop, she was a remarkable sight against the silky, dark background of the horse, her long yellow scabbard blending beautifully with the gold of her shiny hair, which swirled around her waist to the rhythm of her beast.

But it wasn't a quarter of an hour into the procession before, at a bend in the road, the first stop was made: the royal cavalry was there! In full regalia, paying the honours in total immobility, they stood ready to serve as the traditional escort of honour for the future Bride. Amazed without showing it, the young girl passed, stiff on her horse, in front of the four ranks of two hundred riders each, frozen in impeccable attention, helmeted in gleaming bronze, their great vertical blades raised in one hand, while the other held the famous triangular shield, also in bronze, the upper point of which brushed rigorously against the chin, indicating the respect and submission of the cavalry to the future Queen.

As a connoisseur, the Princess also admired the mounts, no longer regretting, in front of these outstanding riders, that she had shown such audacity in appearing like this in their eyes! This royal escort, so impeccably organised, sent a rush of pride and joy deep down her throat: her future husband was proving to her that he was indeed a powerful King and that his regard for her was no less!

It also proved that the rumours circulating in his distant northern homeland, which had been told to him by his companions that Geb was a Master in name only, were completely unfounded!... Or at the very least, greatly amplified!

The two captains, who alone had swords, raised them as the Princess passed. They then approached her, pressed the blade against the toe of Nut's left boot in turn, as a sign of allegiance, and then took up a position just behind her horse, waiting for her to give them the signal to leave. Which she did without further delay. Not a word had been said, but the future Queen sensed that a silent message had been exchanged, and that she was already admitted among them, better than her title could have made her! However, the light veil that covered her face to protect it from the dust that was rising everywhere in this scorching weather was not doing her any favours! She didn't even think of taking it off, as had been her intention, having gone back almost immediately to her future husband, who was appearing more and more enigmatic to her!

Barely an hour's gallop later, new, hurried heartbeats slowed the troop's pace. A few hundred metres ahead, in what looked like a large clearing, a gathering was raising clouds of dust. As it gathered, the Princess saw a crowd materialise, at the centre of which, standing alone in front of her, was a young man, upright, on foot, dressed all in white. Her chest suddenly tightened, then loosened just as quickly, then tightened even more, and her heart was suddenly racing! Nout felt herself faint, stupidly, without being able to reason, and finally pulled herself together only by calling herself every bird name in the vocabulary of her followers!

Her well-mannered horse stopped where it should, a few dozen metres from the elegant male figure that was so paralysing her! An innumerable crowd roared their greetings, while the two captains, behind her, swooped down to gallop towards their King, pulling up behind him and dismounting to follow him, showing that their mission had been accomplished.

Geb took small steps towards the slender yellow figure, whose veil formed a whitish halo around a divinely beautiful face that made the sovereign's chest swell with joy. With a delicate hand, the Princess gave her stallion a pat on the neck, and he understood perfectly well what was expected of him: he took a few steps forward to meet the biped in white, unaware that it was the tallest and most handsome young Monarch in the world, towards whom his mistress's heart was already soaring! He stopped there, judging that he had done enough, leaving Nout distraught with shame, forgetting what she was supposed to do! Why wasn't she in her golden carriage with her attendants?

Everything that protocol had taught her to ensure that Tradition was respected was swept away in the turmoil that whirled around her and turned inside her into uncontrollable anguish!

As for the King, his feelings were less visible! As he took the last few steps, he thought to himself that the beauty of the thinly veiled face was a thousand times more sensational than the one painted on the miniature he wore under his tunic! But he didn't have time to develop this theme mentally, because he soon realised that Princess was in intense trouble and that she needed his help.

His shyness suddenly left him; he took the last two steps that separated him from the splendid horse's bridle. He took hold of her firmly with one hand, while with the other, raising his arm, he supported the young girl's slender waist, helping her to descend gently towards him. Then, without any further ado, he placed both his hands on Nut's shoulders and gave her a welcoming hug, over the veil, to the delirious ovation of the crowd now massed around them and embracing them ever more tightly, all the barriers having been broken!

Indifferent to the indescribable crowd, the King gazed at his Belle, still under her veil, which she had completely forgotten to remove. Her eyesight had been fogged for some time, so she was unaware of this additional - slight - disturbance! Tradition having been respected by this kiss,:however chaste it may have been, it nevertheless meant that he had taken Nut as his fiancée, and that from now on nothing could break this union that God - and Geb - had accepted and which would be consecrated in a week's time!

What's more, the young King had literally fallen under the spell of this apparition! He could hear nothing around him, entranced by the young girls delicate bearing. He had forgotten to welcome her with the official compliment he had prepared in advance... which in any case seemed completely out of place in the face of this dazzling reality!

All this was literally swept away, moreover, by the thunderbolt which, as suddenly as thunder bursting, had fused their hearts, and in the face of such a phenomenon any words would have been grotesque!

No one cared about the silence that united them alone, given the noise everywhere and the enthusiastic gesticulations of everyone else on the stage! For Geb and Nut, it was all about the gaze that united the two, their faces turning white, then red, almost scarlet, in the shade of the flamboyant flowers that surrounded this popular forum on all sides.

One of the two captains finally broke the spell by approaching the Master and Princess's horses with great difficulty, because it was time to set off again; there already enough delay on the official timetable! Although the Palace was not far away, it meant crossing the capital, and there were reports of such crowds!...

With a heart-rending sigh, Geb shook himself, resuming his role as King with difficulty. As he helped his wife-to-be back onto her horse, he realised with very masculine pride just how slender she was: his two hands went all the way round her! Reluctantly, he mounted his horse and gave the signal for departure.

The horsemen had a hard time making their way through the indescribable crowd, which cheered up the young King who was seeing his popularity soar thanks to Nut! With the crowd finally out of the way, the Airain Gate appeared, like dozens of others! Except that today, the royal guard on foot was waiting there for the procession to precede it into town and clear a path that was proving difficult!

Four hundred men, preceded by drums and music that had been playing for over an hour, led the triumphal march. Geb and Nut, side by side, followed by the Princess's escort, then by the royal cavalry closing the procession. The entry into Ath-Mer, with the four hundred guards with their coats of arm in wide brown chain mail waving from right to left at the rhythm of their footsteps on this magnificent six-kilometre long triumphal road, was enchanting!

The capital suddenly appeared in all its splendour below, the road descending all the way down once through the gate. She gazed in wonder at the thousands of multi-storey houses with flower-filled terraces, temples and palaces, not knowing what else to admire! And suddenly, the crowd was there! Even more numerous, even more enthusiastic! His name was being shouted at the top of their voices, so much so that it must have been heard in the Palace... still ten kilometres away!

This reception filled the Princess with admiration and the King with delight. Both of them, a little anxiously, wondered if they would be worthy of such an honour, for the ovation was beyond belief! And what had to happen, happened! A larger crowd jostled some of the guards, who stepped back and blocked Nut's mount, who grabbed hold of the mane and saw her veil fall off! Only then did she realise that she had had it over her face until then, and that the King had not yet seen her face uncovered, and she straightened up with a huge burst of childish, unquenchable laughter! And what could have been an incident degenerated into a general laugh of delight and an outpouring of enthusiasm at the radiant beauty that appeared to them in this way.

Geb and Nut were surrounded on all sides, and the guards could do nothing about it! It was a race to see who could kiss the boots of one and the tunic of the other! The King leaned his mount against that of the Princess to protect her a little, while the cavalry arriving next to them cleared them off laughing, with a minimum of snubbing. At last, they were able to continue on their way!

The youthful, spontaneous charm of the pretty young girl from the North was doing its miraculous work on everyone, and it was also having a reciprocal effect on the King, the future husband. He even wondered anxiously if this wasn't a marvellous dream in which he was an alas fictitious actor: he pinched himself! Having hurt himself, smiled happily at his foolishness! He was alive, and *truly* the happiest of men!

Every glance he met from these people in effervescence showed him the fervour of each one in particular. So he looked head-on at "his" fairy apparition, who looked like a goddess who had appeared unexpectedly to help him overcome the many difficulties that awaited them on their common journey. And he understood God's mercy towards him, allowing his mortal existence, however eventful it might become, not to be catastrophic in the present! He even briefly regretted having refused to marry her a few years earlier when the opportunity had arisen! It seemed that his all-consuming love had spread instantly throughout the population

It took a good hour more, in the midst of total and moving delirium, continually making their way through the human tide, before reaching the monumental southern gate, dedicated to Ptah because it led to the Temple-God of the Royal Palace, and built entirely of indestructible electrum. Then the procession took the road linking this gate to the entrance to the estate, which was flat and smooth and made entirely of beautiful red laterite, admirable in its design and construction, which made it much easier to maintain. The path was covered all the more quickly, as the foot guards gave way to the horsemen to open the road. As soon as they reached the imposing twelve-metre-high portico, the bronze horsemen lined up along the pathway leading to the gardens in a final, impeccable salute of honour.

Geb and Nut passed through the monumental archway close to each other, the horsemen preventing the crowd from following the princely escort into the Royal Palace before the day set for the nuptial blessing, exactly the eighth day after the wedding.

The Princess gazed out over the gardens, oblivious to everything else, not knowing what to admire amongst the multicoloured trees and plants of every shape and form! Then there was the trickle of countless riches from the buildings that stood side by side, forming the God-Temple! She couldn't believe her eyes!...

The young girl did not yet know, but the Archives would soon tell her, that the name of the capital: "Ath-Mer", had first been that of the place she had reached: "Le-Coeur-Aimé". At the origin of the first building, much smaller at the centre of the current temple complex, was the Home of the Beloved: the Son-of-God. This was where he really lived for as long as he was present to teach the people how to become a humanity capable of governing itself, aided by the Divine Commandments.

But in subsequent generations, the direct descendants of the Elder married mortal women, who soon had only their Divine part, the Soul, to link them to their Creator. As a result, the Temple became no more than a link, and no longer the abode of the Son. They no longer wanted to live there, and had sumptuous palaces built next to the place of meditation. So, as soon as a new "Master" succeeded the previous one, the Palace became more sumptuous and grandiose, *in order to remain the first "Man" of the Kingdom after God!* This also required successive embellishments to the God-Temple! It was their way of proving their Divine filiation, and perhaps a way of making amends for their luxurious lifestyle...

Over the centuries, more than three hundred "Masters" began their reigns with this primary thought: to have a more beautiful Palace than that of their predecessors! And at the same time, more than three hundred Pontiffs inspired the Masters on the best way to make God's Dwelling even more admirable than before!

The result, ten millennia later, was this immense cathedral, a collective work that was constantly being enlarged, embellished and enhanced with jewels of all kinds! This God-Temple, the Marvel of Splendours, was surrounded on all sides by imposing buildings, a succession of gleaming constructions of the rarest Aha-Men-Ptah possessed, the whole of which formed a veritable city under the sole name of the Royal Palace, to the south of the capital, and separated from it by a wood and gardens that eighty specialists in "Earth and Measure" tended with an Art inspired by Harmony, on the three possible sides: to the east and west, as well as to the north, towards your capital.

The area to the south sloped gently down to the sea inlet. Here, the evergreen lawn was regularly maintained with a pruning knife, which was longer and more oval than the one used to cut barley or wheat. In fine weather, which was almost a daily occurrence, from the various terraces of the flats located in this wing, it was possible to admire, beyond the Gaddir Arm and the "Mouth of the Slit", the Eastern Sea, greener than in the Strait. It was in this part of the palace that Nut finally arrived, accompanied by her retinue.

CHAPTER NINE

LA REINE NOUT

> *Heaven is already blushing for the sins committed in the overflow of morals! This is the prelude to the blaze of the celestial game. Nothing is sane or wise in Aha-Men-Ptah! All his states are infected by impiety and blasphemy!... Alas! The Time of the Great Cataclysm is very near! Terrible time: O suspend thy flight! Your roar from the Lion will break even the lion's strength!*
>
> LES QUATRE TEMPS
> *(Temple of the Lady of Heaven, Denderah)*

During the week that followed, nervousness prevailed over enthusiasm; the King worked non-stop, feverishly, well supported by his father Ahou. The only time he allowed himself to relax was the mid-day break. There, while eating, Geb had the leisure to contemplate his beautiful fiancée, but this too short lapse of time was hardly conducive to the little verbal outpourings that make it possible to get to know each other better. Nonetheless, the young Monarch noticed that the beautiful and wise young princess was also highly intelligent.

This perfection would not have surprised him if he had known that the eldest daughter of the Pontiff had herself instilled in her friend Nut valuable diplomatic notions! Having been brought up with her brother, even though she was not eligible for the priesthood, she had acquired certain solid precepts, which she had been quick to teach the future Queen. One of these was to remain slightly inferior to her husband at all times and in all circumstances. Being not only the 'Master', but also a 'Son of God', his wife should never challenge him head-on, being the Arbiter, the Judge of everything and everyone.

But that doesn't mean that, in private, the best solution to a problem could be demonstrated to him, with a smile, and in such a way as to appear to come from him, especially if the result obtained was fairer!

In her Far North, this concept of equality had not shocked her very much, especially as she considered herself a mere mortal compared to this deified future husband. Since he had appeared to her and she had found that look of wonder and fire in his eyes, he had become her god, and hers alone! And there was no longer any question of competing with him for any kind of primacy! With only two days to go before the wedding, the religious climax of the ceremony had a multitude of specialists swirling around her!

On that day, Geb decreed that there would be four full days of festivities and popular jubilation following the nuptial blessing, which led to almost general euphoria among the population on the eve of the ceremony.

On that very day, a momentous event took place, one that is recounted in all the Annals, and which constituted the Origin of the new chronology of the future "Elders" who populated Egypt: AthKa-Ptah!

It concerns Princess Nut, who every day, after lunch and her short conversation with Geb, went out for a digestive walk in the company of some of her attendants. A few royal guards and an officer followed the group from a distance.

On the day before the wedding, the bride-to-be walked for longer, going deep into the woods that followed the gardens, until, followed by her maids and the group of guards, she came to a small wooden bridge that gave access to the Nahi: the Sacred Island of the Sycamores, where only the 'Master' could enter, for it was that he conversed with God. The Princess knew the instructions, of course, but she was so irritated by the anticipation of the next day's event, and perhaps tired of the long walk as much as she was curious to see the place, that she felt as if driven by a demon!

And then came the Extraordinary Adventure that would profoundly change not only the religious and political history of the continent, but also the love story of Nut and Geb! The Extraordinary obviously seemed incredible *afterwards!* And yet, incredible as it was, this extraordinary event enabled Ancient Times to cross the critical threshold after the Great Cataclysm, to survive in spite of everything, and then to repopulate a second Homeland loved by God. The Princess, knowing nothing of what was about to happen, was about to step onto the wooden bridge that spanned the river, when the officer, out of breath from his race to arrive before the sacrilege, stepped in as respectfully as he could, trying to explain what this Nahi was, this island of Sycamores, the Sacred Trees, the oldest of which, the Pontiff said, was at the top of the hill, the oldest tree in the world, the An-Nahi. It was in its shade that successive 'Masters' had conversed with God.

A splendid smile spread across Nut's lips, and she gave the embarrassed soldier a look as warm as it was innocent! The poor man blushed with shame, cursing his audacity, which showed him afterwards that he was nothing but dust! He had no right to interfere with the desires of a goddess... The goddess nonetheless took a playful tone to point out to her interlocutor that, in any case, she would be Queen the very next day, in other words the equal of her husband, thus adding to her personal titles that of: "Divine Successor". So there was nothing to stop her going to meditate in peace on the eve of her official union with God. She would go alone, without her attendants, and everyone would wait there for her return!

Unfortunately for him, the poor officer had never learnt what to do when faced with such a dilemma! This Cornelian situation before its time was way beyond him! As the first thing that jumped out at him was the obvious fact that the Princess was in no danger on the Nahi, where no human being would ever have dared to venture, he shook his head in helplessness. He took a step back to leave her free to decide for herself what to do with God, if He saw no obstacle to this intrusion.

The officer felt himself being torn apart as he watched the young girl walk away alone. He thought, resignedly in advance, of the repercussions when the Master learned of this escapade! His command at the Palace would certainly be taken away from him! The maids of honour calmed him with their carefree laughter and chivalry took over again.

As her steps carried her forward, Nut felt a strange calm come over her. As she crossed the bridge, she knew that it was not just her will that was at fault: it was like a premonitory dream come true! Something 'already' experienced, something terrible, but something that was bound to happen...

She moved forward mechanically, putting one leg in front of the other as she watched them go, as if she had nothing to do with it! She sank into the Nahi, heading for the end of *her* road, the end of a journey...

The path climbed, winding around a central hill, a huge mound, encircled by a gently sloping yaw. When she reached the top, the enormous sycamore tree, far more gigantic than any maple tree she had ever seen, struck her eyes with a strange glow! The tree was so imposing in its dominance that it emanated an undeniable Divine majesty from the solitude that surrounded it! There could be no doubt about the serenity that the 'Masters' must have found under its leaves when they wished to 'dialogue' with God.

Invincibly, this tree was drawing her towards it, and she couldn't have stopped herself from crossing the few metres that still separated her from it, even if she'd wanted to! There was nothing she could do to turn back, and thus thwart the new course that the history of the Earth was about to take!...

Nut no longer had any doubts about the Force that was driving her there, but that did nothing to help her solve the "Mystery", because she was alone, and the silence was total. Fear suddenly seized her, and her body trembled, for she did not understand what the Divinity wanted from her, this insignificant little mortal, despite her role as the King's wife. For she had indeed come "for something"!

She straightened up as best she could, like a proud Nordic Princess, but deep down she was distraught at not seeing anything, not hearing anything, *not knowing anything!* To reassure herself, she whispered: "Here I am, God of the Universe...". But no sound came in reply! She told herself that, as she was too young to have sinned much in any way, it couldn't have been that afternoon's little infraction that had brought her there, and against her will, that was preventing God from talking to her. Or it could be that she had been foolishly imaginative, and that there was nothing and no one!...

A little weary, and stunned by her lack of understanding of events, the young girl let herself fall onto the thick, tender grass that grew thickly under the trunk of the enormous sycamore tree. No matter how hard she listened, and how receptive her soul, "nothing" communicated with her tense mind!

Out of tiredness, she leaned her hair against the bark of the magnificent trunk, so old and so welcoming. At the same time, her whole head rested against the tree, and all of her body and soul were instantly at peace with the outside world; her eyes closed without her realising it!

Sinking into an unreal sleep, Nut had no time to analyse what was happening, for her astonishment turned to fright as a blinding, radiant light enveloped her, penetrating her from all sides at once. Feeling as if she were being consumed, the most intense fear seized her, but she couldn't open her mouth to scream! She was being reduced to ashes, liquefied, while living in spite of herself the most radiant day that the Earth had known since its Origin!...

She tried to open her eyelids, despite the calm that curiously inhabited her, but she couldn't even move her eyelashes! Frightened at being paralysed, she felt herself sinking into unconsciousness, when a Voice deep inside her, very firm but infinitely gentle and reassuring, said to her "distinctly": "My son Usir is now in your womb; have no fear about this, for you are the daughter of my first child: you are the one I have chosen to help me save mankind once again in spite of themselves! Usir will be the sign of my Power and Goodness. You, Nut, will be his revered mother; you will teach Usir, through the words you speak, that my Heart is within him, and that my Soul will always be with him so that he can exercise his sovereign power... So be it!"

Unable to utter the slightest sound, let alone coordinate even a coherent thought, the Princess could only record what was said, without making any response: the "Voice" was telling her that she would have a Divine child! Good!

One question, however, dawned on her so acutely that it literally chilled her, despite the heat that continued to bathe her: what would become of her, who was to become Geb's wife the next day?... What would the "Master" say when he learned of the reality that she could not hide, and yet could not tell?...

The Lord heard this silent and desperate appeal, full of infinite distress but no rebellion! God decided to come to his aid immediately. A broad ray of sunlight filtered down from the top of the gigantic sycamore to the lowest branches, flooding the distraught young Princess with a soothing luminosity. And the "Voice" spoke again, in the silent aura that surrounded her: "Fear not, Nut; rise in peace and return to the one destined for you. He will receive my Word; after Usir, the descendants of both of you will still provide the first branches of Good and Evil that are inseparable on Earth. It will once again be up to Humanity to make its choice freely! In the meantime, go back to Geb who is already running to you!

Her eyes flew open: all around her, darkness had taken over the low foliage of the sycamore tree. Nout, a little dizzy, stood up and took an unsteady step before regaining her balance. She set off back towards the little wooden bridge, very anxious about what lay ahead, now that reality was taking over again!

In the meantime, Geb, who had just signed the many acts promulgating, by official and divine decree, that from the following day his wife would be his equal, as soon as the public wedding had taken place, and his "Following", as soon as the blessing of the An-Nu had been celebrated, found himself alone for a short while, before going to his last meal as a bachelor, to which he had invited a few young notables from his entourage.

With a blissful sense of accomplishment, slid back into his wide, carved ebony armchair, embellished with ivory inlays of mammoth tusks, tucking the fluffy cushions under him. He closed his eyes to think about the next day, when, at the same time, Nut would be his wife before God and man, and nothing would separate them!

It was at this precise moment that the "Voice" penetrated the young King's soul, disrupting the cheerful rhythm of his thoughts, before changing the Monarch's life itself! "Geb! Listen to my words, which are the Truth! The time has passed when mankind could be saved. I have chosen you to raise my Son! He will become the Guide who will give birth to the Saviour of the survivors of the Great Cataclysm when the Time comes!"

The young Monarch, unable to open his eyelids, felt himself startle several times during this bewildering monologue, having "recognised" the Voice of God, and anxiously wondering if he had understood the meaning of the phrase "of the Son"! The Voice confirmed this with a precision that deeply angered him! "I led Nut's footsteps to the Nahi, under the Sycamore tree, so that Usir might take his place in the movement of Souls in his own time, for nothing can now be changed by Man in the face of the Eternal, except the face of the Eternal! This is why Nut has been touched by my grace, and why you must become her husband, in order to ensure that the Earth has a human offspring: a second Soul!"

While trying to convince himself that it was just a bad nightmare, Geb was unable to open his eyes! As time was running out, the "Voice" concluded: "Do not torment yourself any longer; you who will become the Wisest and will be considered as born of the earth and having given birth to the whole Earth, undergo what you think is a trial, like the necessity that it has become. Nut will then return to you, just as loving! And to give you a sign of Usir's Divinity, he will be born seventy-two days before the normal term of birth. You will then be absolutely certain that your wife is entirely worthy of your love. Get up and run to meet the blessed woman, who is very upset. Bring her back to the living and reassure her of your intentions. She is terribly afraid of having to tell you about a fault she did not commit! Run to her! Truly I say to you: never has a wife been so worthy of your love!

Instantly, the young Master opened his eyes and was free to move again. He rushed out of the room, jostling guests who were gaily chatting in the Palace corridors about the next day's festivities; despite the heat, his face was as white as his tunic! He ran as fast as he could along the path leading to the wood and the Nahi, without even thinking about whether the Princess was there! Geb was convinced that the facts were true, even though they were extraordinary! And Wisdom enjoined him to see for himself, alone!

He reached the little bridge, dishevelled and panting from his run, just as the attendants, worried about their Princess's long absence, asked the officer to send word to the Master. He was spared the fear of committing another blunder. The sight of the Monarch calmed them all, all the more so as he, regaining a bearing worthy of his rank, nonetheless retained an ominous rigidity of expression!

At the same moment, Nut also appeared at the bend in the path coming from the Nahi, walking slowly and hesitantly, looking very troubled. Seeing her like this from a distance, Geb immediately understood the "reality" of the dream he had had in the Palace, and it was imperative that he sent the guards and attendants away before they realised anything. He wanted to be alone with Nut when she crossed the little bridge and came to him.

Without asking for a second thought, they all left, not to witness what they thought would be a strong royal reprimand for their disobedience in going to the Sacred Isle. It was thus in a dramatic tête-à-tête that Nut and Geb met again!

The Annals that have come down to us, in fact, give few details of the painful dialogue that took place during this painful return to the Palace.

Perhaps after the first cries had died down, the two young men drew parallels between their case and that of their very ancient cousins, who, millennia before, had already been called like them, and whose first-born had been Usir, the Elder of God!... In a way, then, they were the new Nut and Geb, prisoners of the Traditions, who would be the parents of the "*Second Soul of Aha-Men-Ptah*"! These were not coincidences: the facts had long been written in the 'combinations' of the stars, and were predestined for them! So they were the unwitting and unfortunate victims, albeit blessed ones... This is what they must have said to each other during their sad return.

As soon as they arrived at the castle, the Princess confined herself to her room, asking her maid not to disturb her; she wanted to be alone to weep at her ease, for she had clearly seen that Geb was not convinced of the need to marry her after what had happened. His good faith was not in question in the young King's mind, but he had thought of living with his wife the very next day, and the cruel suffering he was experiencing made him bitter and unjust! But what could he do but leave her in her solitude? He may have had the heaviest responsibilities, and the care of tens of millions of souls, but he was only twenty-one years old, and he loved Nut madly, like a mere mortal! Yet she was expecting a Divine Son, and it would be very difficult for her to give him her blessing!

The 'Master' had apologised to his friends for his absence at the meal he should have presided over with such enthusiasm and gaiety! He had just fallen ill as a result of his recent overwork, which had led the AnNu to prescribe total rest until the following day's ceremony. The Pontiff, having been informed of the facts, seemed neither worried about what was to come nor surprised by what had happened. However, here too, the Annals give no details of the dialogue between these two supermen concerning God.

All night long, solitary and awake, Geb soliloquised with his conscience on the conduct that would be his the next day, which varied according to the hour! When he thought he had reached the decision to divorce and repudiate her, he would 'see' superimposed on his retinas the young and pretty Nut stretching out her begging hands towards him, her face flooded with the tears of innocence!... And when he was about to give in to this call, he 'saw' this Son who was not his own!...

Endless ovations filled his ears, jolting him from the heavy, restless sleep that had finally overcome his doubts at the first light of dawn. It was now broad daylight and he rose briskly to his feet. There was little joy in his heart on what should have been the brightest morning of his life!

To think that at the eighth hour, when the gates of the Palace were wide open for the jubilant people to come and shout out their vitality and allegiance, as was the custom, under the terrace where Geb and Nut were to appear together the first time, the Monarch still didn't know what decision to take!

The royal guards, meanwhile, were all smiles as the crowds did not trample too much on the flower borders, although they were prepared to remain clustered for hours in order to be the first to enter the Temple-Dieu. But the curious continued to arrive and, at the beginning of the ninth hour, as the young bride and groom had not yet appeared, the people invaded not only the aisles, but also the lawns and gardens! The human tide settled in every available spot. After the royal presentation, which was not long in coming, there would still be three hours to wait before the ceremony took place.

The evil hold that was preventing the King from acting suddenly ceased. He realised that it was impossible for him to refuse this long-planned union, simply because he loved Nut! He shrugged his shoulders, defeated by himself, to become once again the proud Monarch who would endure this additional ordeal because it was necessary. It was long overdue. So he called his advisor, who arrived at once, having been up all night in the antechamber!

The concern reflected on the man's features showed the extent to which those close to him, who had witnessed his return and noted his defection at the meal he had proposed, had marked the night. The old monarch Ahou, who had been warned that evening, had gone to bed only reluctantly, without daring to disturb his son to clarify the drama that seemed to have occurred.

It was not until morning that An-Nu informed Geb's father, shortly before Geb decided to call. So the adviser became the vital messenger, and his exit was watched with great concern.

God had decided to overcome the young Sovereign with sleep, so that when he woke up he would not be able to turn back! And so it happened, as the crowd waited, shouting their joy at the event they had waited so long for! The people even shouted for the two future spouses to appear immediately. And Geb, caught up in a process that he could no longer stop, and in fact had no desire to stop at all, bowed his head! It was with infinite relief that he took this decision, believing with the youthful ardour of his youth that the fate that had been bent on ruining his marriage and making them the instruments of Divine power was unjust but inevitable!

So he ordered the trembling Councillor to warn the Princess to get ready in her ceremonial dress as quickly as possible, as he would be collecting her before the hour was out.

With intense relief, the counsellor withdrew backwards, and gave the good news as he passed through the antechamber to the former Monarch and his wife, who had rushed in. The four priests serving the young "Master" had already entered the room to dress him for the ceremony and immerse him in a mineral and aromatic bath beforehand. The young law immersed himself in it with delight.

Cleared of his impurities, his beard neatly trimmed, he let himself be dressed in the ceremonial garb of the "Masters": the same garb that his father and grandfather before him had worn when they married, and many other generations of Monarchs! The tunic, woven from silky linen and interwoven threads of gold and purple, looked as good as new! On the front, resplendent in brilliant luminosity, at chest level, was the symbol of Aha-Men-Ptah, embroidered by artists: the Cross of Life in gold thread emerging from a purple Heart.

By donning it, Geb became the 588th successor to the Elder, because only his wife would allow him to give this Tunic a new wearer. He smiled bitterly at the thought that this time, it would not be his son who would become the next Master! He quickly got to his feet, as his servants were waiting to precede him to the Princess's flat.

The An-Nu, the former Monarch and his wife, waited outside the door, and it was a small, solemn and somewhat stilted procession that followed the corridor leading to the south terrace. The future Queen was resplendent with a sad, infinitely poignant beauty, enhanced by her diaphanous dress, so pure in line. Nut was leaning on the right elbow of the man who would very soon be her husband. God wanted this ordeal, but she was strengthening her love and hoping with all her soul that the rest would work itself out in time!

When they appeared on the balcony overlooking the lawns and gardens, on the terrace known as the "Quatre Temps", the whole place went wild! A magnificent sun shone blindingly, the golden rays playing in the Princess's blonde hair and creating a kind of aura that surrounded her beautiful face. This divinity-like appearance was perceptible to the four hundred thousand or so people gathered over several hectares, all of whom perceived the phenomenon and shouted with astonishment and admiration! Their ovations were heard as far away as the capital, where large crowds were just preparing to come to the Palace for the blessing.

As he contemplated the colourful multitude spread out at his feet, Geb understood, hearing the increasingly loud and powerful cheers, that the future that was beginning for them both could really begin when "what was to be, would be"! He promised himself, before his people and before God, that after the "event", he would try to win back his wife!

This time, the ceremony took place in the Temple, which was packed to the rafters, as it had been in the best of days, the likes of which the Annals counted only two! More than a million souls, nine-tenths of whom were trampling around outside, were nonetheless communicating with the various rites of the Pontifical Benediction, because the sound had been studied so that the words pronounced in a certain place in the central nave were echoed in certain other places, where the voice was amplified in various architectural axes, and could be heard far enough outside.

Shortly before the end of the twelfth hour, the nuptial ceremony was completed on 2 August 9843 BC. "Geb and Nut were united for eternity, and no one could ever undo what God had blessed.

What the people still didn't want to admit was that the end of the continent was near! And An-Nu thought bitterly that the time had come to an end! Barely fifty-one years of survival for this marvellous country that was Aha-Men-Ptah!

Those who, selfishly, sometimes reflected on the validity of this "ancestral belief" did not feel in the least concerned by the "overwork" and excitement of the ancient "Wise Men" who, having seen a small flood in the north, envisaged a greater one for the mists of time! This was 'priesthood' imagery, to give credence to the belief and observance of the commandments that flowed from it. And the many "atheists" of that period considered what was valid in the past to be inane! In the present, everyone was free to behave as he or she saw fit, but they didn't realise that they were chaining themselves to ideas that would lead to their downfall!

So nothing was going according to the Divine ethic any more, but was in accordance with human needs alone, whose best law was irrevocably that of the strongest! Looking at all those faces, Geb anxiously wondered if he could bring them back to a better frame of mind. But it was a bitter failure, and one that would leave its mark on the rest of his life. Once the festivities were over, the blinders came back on and the unconsciousness became incurable!

However, the young Monarch had had ample opportunity to meditate, for although life at the Royal Palace was apparently normal, life between the master and his wife was non-existent! Except on the rarest of official occasions, the King considered it preferable to let his wife have 'that' son outside his presence. What's more, with the political situation worsening in other provinces, Geb had plenty of pretexts for showing off his bad temper! But Nut, who was becoming more of a woman by the day, suffered from this estrangement, which left her distraught and infinitely sad.

However, the young woman realised that their situation was embarrassing for her young husband, and she confided in the only true friend who could be her confidant: An-Nu. He consoled her all the more, because for him, the Pontiff, it was obvious that this time the Queen was not just a "follower" but one of God's "chosen ones"! So, in order to divert his attention from the life of Aha-Men-Ptah, he told him about the vicissitudes of the Princes who, back in their States, had had many worries! One of them had even imitated the Master by raising an army! For the first time, a military regiment existed, trained to fight against men!... Elsewhere, other Councils were disobeying in other ways, undermining the Central Authority! Geb could well have been morose!

Since the day before, in Ath-Mer, clans of bourgeois had been loudly recriminating against the government in the Court of Justice! These were the very people who had originally shown the greatest attachment to the Throne! Taxes had been raised to speed up the construction of a new batch of "Mandjit", unsinkable boats, thousands of which would enable people to escape at the last moment from ports still under government control! But this Exodus was becoming more and more odious to the 'cultivated' stratum of the population: the very idea was as unbearable as it was indefensible! The very word, with its image of a compulsory departure in all haste to a land that was becoming a second homeland: a Second Heart, no longer made people laugh at all, but stirred their hearts with indignation!

More than ten millennia had passed since the small flood - a veridical one at that - which had ravaged the northern territories of what is now Queen Nut; but why was it necessary, a hundred centuries later, for the entire life of the Kingdom to come to a complete standstill, and for its foreign trade to be totally blocked?...

If it was because the 'scientists', in their contemplative action, had predicted at the time that the cataclysm would strike the country so long afterwards, what faith could be placed in such nonsense? Today's scientists would do better to hide underground themselves so as not to succumb to shame the day after the famous day...

The rumours were all about mental aberrations, and it was unacceptable that such a young King should allow himself to be led by senile old men - as the 'Wise Men' were openly called - on the pretext that the Great Royal Architect swore that his new boat was unsinkable! Why bother? Even if there was a storm, the current boats wouldn't capsize!

One thing was certain, in this psychosis of the end of the world, a growing stalemate was being created, inspired by a few emissaries who had come clandestinely from the rebel states, and who saw a way to put an end to power by starting a kind of civil war!

And slander was rife! Was the young Sovereign really up to the task of his forebears? Especially as it was common knowledge that his young and gracious wife was living as a recluse, still as she had been on the day she arrived! She stayed in the south wing, with only her bored attendants for company! What was this Master made of, who had received so many standing ovations, and from whom we expected so much more than to learn that he lived alone! The royal flat had never been occupied, and what was certain was that if there was an end somewhere, it would be the end of Kings, because there would be no heir!

Gossip was rife, fanned by all those who had a vested interest in seeing the confusion spread from strength to strength, and they were becoming a multitude! An-Nu, much more distressed than he let on in public, or even in front of Geb, realised that very soon, even God would no longer recognise his own people in this miserable caravanserai of bad feelings, made up of impiety and ignominy that were being displayed more and more in public every day!

Few of the faithful came to the Temples, and the novices themselves came only when obliged to do so by their Elders! Spiritual meetings were becoming literary curio sities subject to dispute and denial! The end of a Time was becoming clearer anyway, and it was highly likely that it would 'coincide' with the Great Cataclysm.

But then a new rumour from the Palace spread like wildfire! It was astonishing, unbelievable, incredible!... And yet it was the subject of all the gossip: the gracious Queen was expecting a child!

When no denial was forthcoming, tongues dropped, and there was total incomprehension after what had been said about the reports, or rather the lack of reports, from Geb and his Lady! But the tongues wagged again after just a few days, with no confirmation coming through either, and consequently no one announcing the date of the Heir's arrival!

But six months after the nuptial blessing, the Palace briefly but very officially announced the expectation of a happy event! It was An-Nu himself who, three days later, at the end of his homily dedicated to the day of God, announced that on the fortieth day following, the Gracious Queen Nut would be the Divine Mother!

Those present were stunned beyond words! And then all hell broke loose! And who was counting on his fingers!... And who was trying to interpret the term "Divine Mother"? And who were they kidding? How was it possible to be sure of the exact date of birth, especially when it was so far from the normal time! And also: what did God have to do with this event?

Passion ran through everyone's hearts, as did indignation at not being told the truth! What was really going on? Either their kind Queen was already expecting her baby before the wedding, or something was being hidden!

As the people waited, the 204th day arrived, just as the "Voice" had predicted and just as the Pontiff had announced! A little boy appeared before the eyes of the matrons who had come to help the Queen with this premature birth. But all went admirably well! Usir was born, a little sickly and weighing barely three quarters of a kilo! But that didn't stop him from smiling from the very first moment of his life! As for the rest, he'd have plenty of time to grow strong and shout!

Extract from the History of Isis and Osiris (Iset et Ousir) from one of the many stelae discovered at the end of the 19th century.

CHAPTER TEN

OUSIR AND ISET

> *O Almighty God, of yesterday, today and tomorrow: here is Usir, Your living image, just as You willed, in the image of mankind. He is Thine, Thine: protect him during his life, which only Thou canst take back.*
>
> AM HATI NOUTER
(Prayer of the Lady of Heaven, Denderah)

> *O Nut, Beloved Mother, so weak but indestructible, stretch out your arms over me to protect me!*
> *Keep death away from me;*
> *Grant that I may begin the Divine Work.*
>
> LES QUATRE TEMPS
(Prayer of Usir)

On learning that the new-born child would be presented to God for baptism under the sacred name of Usir, the unanimous indignation of the people eventually spread to the College of Priests. For the An-Nu, psychologically, had judged it preferable not to reveal the Divine essence of this Son, the state of permanent dispute engendering interminable dialogues, from which all respect for God was excluded!

This is why blasphemy, for once, no longer appeared on the side of the crowd, and made the Pontiff, this High Priest head of all God's domains on the entire continent, smile good-naturedly! For if no one understood the insane act blessing a mortal with a Divine name, even if he was destined, like this one, to become the Master of Aha-Men-Ptah, the An-Nu was acting with full knowledge of the facts!

Diplomatically turning the tables, in the sermon he gave on the eve of the ceremony, he reminded the many attendees who had come to listen to him out of curiosity, that the first ancient couple, Geb and Nut, direct descendants of God, had named their firstborn Uzir. Why would the present Master and his wife, who both bore the same names as their Divine predecessors, do otherwise by not naming their first-born Usir?

This ceremony was therefore to take on a solemn form, and would be the occasion for a return to the rite commanded by God.

So, well before dawn began to turn pink on the earth surrounding the Temples, a good hour before the announcement of the appearance of the star of the Day was made by the "Master-of-Measurement", the four officiants designated by the An-Nu as "Baptismal Priests", accompanied by the "Scribedes-Rites" and the "Lector of the Ritual", followed the "First Prophet of the Most Pure Hands", who were responsible for preparing the "Pontiff of Aha-MenPtah" for the Great Ceremony of Baptism.

All night long, An-Nu had remained prostrate, face down on the paved floor of the Divine sanctuary, where he often came to meditate alone. Various expiatory prayers had prepared him for the purification that was about to take place, purifying his spirit before washing his body. After which he would be ready to give the baptismal blessing at sunrise, on the western horizon, which was the best indication of a long life. The ceremony would not be completed until he had received his name of Man, and it had been proclaimed in the four corners of the "Four Times", allowing him to keep it for Eternity. But it was time, and the An-Nu stood up, moved by a sixth sense, and left the sanctuary just as the small group of priests reached the entrance. Despite the pontiff's stance, which was unacceptable to the old man, he appeared fresh and ready in the half-light of the immense courtyard that separated the dwellings of the servants of God from the Temple. No one could have suspected the fervour that had kept him awake all night and his pleas for the *human* happiness of the newborn child!

They all met in front of the enormous bronze double leaf of the eastern portico, supported by four wide colonnades with bas-reliefs painted in red and black on a white marble background, all praising and glorifying the Divine Works of Creation.

The officiants pushed the heavy, half-open bat a little further, which slid silently open, after which they bowed deeply, with signs of the most profound respect, leaving the "First Prophet" to advance in his turn to guide the Pontiff's steps towards the ascending causeway giving access to the "*Heart*", the Holy of Holies of Seqt'b N'MerShoum: "*L'Aimé-vers-qu'-descend-la-Lumière*", that enormous block with its four triangular faces, tending towards a single summit point, and which, despite the night, was resplendent in white.

It took them twenty minutes to climb up this causeway, which rested on the sixteenth height of boulders and onto which the path to the Sacred Hall opened. As it would take the same amount of time to go back down, they had half an hour to ask Divine intercession against the elements that were about to be unleashed. The place had been built according to extremely precise mathematical data, and the very geometry of the architectural complex made it possible to receive the twelve interstellar radiation emissions, which were concentrated in this Sacred Hall, where they arrived through special ducts with cleverly calculated angles of inclination! Only the First Prophet was able to follow the An-Nu. The officiants and the two scribes waited in the corridor for a few moments. Then, hearing the ritual call to God, they bowed in respect to their Creator, before descending and heading towards the Sacred Lake to purify themselves.

At the bottom of the wide carriageway, they took a moment to walk along the wall of the outer enclosure, twelve metres thick and made of mud bricks, which surrounded the Temple outbuildings, isolating them from the Palais Royal, and encircling the gardens and part of the woods in an immense quadrilateral measuring approximately twenty-eight kilometres by twenty-two...

It was only on this day that the priests revived the ancestral tradition of going to the Sacred Lake, which was fed directly by a very pure spring, rather than merely performing a symbolic purification before any important ceremony.

Once the washing ritual was complete, they put on their unbleached linen tunics, which the priest-weavers had specially prepared for this kind of ceremony. Without missing a beat, they made their way to the Well of the Pure Source, where jugs holding around four litres each were waiting, ritually purified the day before. The contents were to be used to fill a reservoir in the shape of a small bathtub, consecrated and kept away from any possible touching in the "Pure Sacristy", to await baptism.

This last room formed a small vestibule, communicating on the west side with the path leading to the Well, and on the south side with the centre of the choir of the Temple-Dieu. Thus, the full bath would only be brought in by the four pure officiants, just as the newborn child was about to be immersed in it three times before being presented to the 'Four Times'.

Everything was so well ordered in the course of the preliminary operations that the purified priests carrying the jugs, even without having practised before, acted like well-oiled automatons! They had poured the precious contents into the consecrated tank the moment the "Priest-Chief of Scribes" arrived at the Holy Place, as the highest priest in the Temple hierarchy, in order to consecrate the Sacristy once again for greater safety, as well as the "Pure Water" so that the Creator could grant the new living being his human name, on this blessed day of all that was about to dawn.

With all defilement thus removed, the Water of Life was ready to perform its complementary Divine function, bringing the new soul into harmonious harmony with God and His Eternity.

After carefully closing the door of the sacristy, the officiants and the Priest, head of the Scribes, then entered the choir, where the altar was also being purified by the "Priest-Grand Conductor-of-Rites": the HamenoutSisinchês, who was shaking a small utensil all around, from which a purifying smoke was escaping with a heady odour. Two other priests, those in charge of the 'Tradition Scrolls', were waiting, their precious manuscripts in hand, ready to give the ritual responses when the time came.

With everything ready, the doors were opened wide, so that the guests could observe that "God was now waiting for His hour". But no one would enter this consecrated enclosure until the presentation to the Rising Sun had been completed in the "Golden Circle of Divine Mathematical Movements", above which, on the terraces redesigned for the purpose, in superimposed terraces, a good hundred thousand privileged guests were seated waiting for the first rays of sunlight to appear.

The sky was just beginning to lighten, in a carefully measured progression. A golden phosphorescence seemed to emanate from the Golden Circle, and the twelve blocks of the zodiacal constellations lit up with a strange glow. It was an unforgettable sight that always drew a storm of exclamations and applause. The influences of the "Mathematical Combinations" were demonstrating their Divine power here, influencing the receiving part of the human envelope, which would be the Soul of the newborn child.

The violet of the sky had turned purple, then light red and pink. Any moment now, the top of the solar circle would appear, casting its first rays on the Golden Circle. At that moment, Geb and Nut, the Queen having insisted on carrying her son herself even though she had barely recovered from childbirth, appeared at the top of the staircase in the eastern wall, which gave access from the Royal Palace to the Temple forecourt via the basement.

The An-Nu, who had just arrived with the First Prophet near the Sacristy, in his turn advanced to the other side of the circle, dressed in his splendid "Sunrise" outfit woven from threads of Gold! He immediately led the Royal couple to the monolithic block intended for the native Leonines, on which the Queen placed her precious burden after removing her short white tunic.

As if waiting for that final second, a short arc of sunlight appeared, dazzling the eyes of those present with its gold; and the first rays appeared, encompassing the crystalline block and the baby in the same aura, quickly caressing the Master and his wife, as well as the An-Nu, who seemed to explode in the golden shimmer of his garment, before spreading over the entire Golden Circle, then conquering the entire territory of AhaMen-Ptah in a matter of minutes!

The Pontiff moved towards the centre of the Circle, satisfied with the celestial "Combinations". Standing firmly on his legs, he raised both arms towards the shining star and uttered the original prayer in a loud voice:

- O Sun, who rises eternally above the Earth to fertilise it in the same way throughout the Four Eras, you are the blessing of the matchless God: the Almighty Creator, our God! From the West, you appear radiant with Divine light! You cross the Great White Celestial River on your golden bark, sailing tirelessly, day after day, towards the East, where, as the Earth slumbers at night, you illuminate its Beyond: Eternal Life. Hail to You, O Rising Sun, God's blessing!

The College of Priests repeated the last sentence in one voice:

"Hail to Thee, O Rising Sun, blessing of God!" The Queen, who had in the meantime given the garment to her son, raised it and presented it to the four horizons. The whole crowd then repeated the salute to the Sun for the third time. And the First Prophet continued, chanting:

- You are the one who, thanks to God, the Eternal Creator, shines on the fields with your best brilliance, so that flowers and trees grow; so that beings and men multiply. You are the essential tool of the One who created the Earth when it began to exist.

The priests intoned a responsory, which was then taken up by the crowd:

"Glory be to You, Almighty God,
Creator of the Sun and the Earth!

The day globe was now fully above the horizon, where, although it had apparently taken a step back, it was still blinding people - quite the contrary! Its golden yellow was impossible to stare at, on pain of blindness; this was what God wanted to demonstrate: under no circumstances should Divine Power be defied, on pain of exemplary punishment!

An-Nu, who had watched impassively as the son was presented to the Four Times, this time pointed his ten elongated fingers at them, near which Geb had come:

- O You, Sun-All-Powerful, in your golden radiance, you flooded with your beneficial Light the crystal that supported the little fleshly envelope that this fortunate mother carries by Divine Will and Grace. All of us here, before imploring God to strengthen the Soul in this young body, ask that you make the Happy Power of your rays shine on her head, and on ours, eternally. -

All chanted the last phrase of the preliminary ritual of presentation to the Sun:

"Glory to You, Creator of Eternity, living and non-living,
in all times: that of earthly Life,
and that of Life in the Eternal Beyond."

As soon as the sentence was finished, with enthusiastic roars, the crowd scattered, running in all directions, some to rush to the other side of the main Temple, in order to enter it and deposit the traditional offerings he had taken care of; others to go directly into the great nave through the eight doors giving access to it, in order to have a place as close as possible to the altar where the baptism would take place, three hours later!

The Master and his wife, still carrying their newborn child, had gone back through the same underground passage towards the

Royal Palace. As for the smiling An-Nu, he shouted to the First Prophet so that he could be heard, even though he was close to him:

- God, too, should be rejoicing! He has faithfully sent us the Sun, the begetter of Life! ... And the "Master of Measurement" has calculated his "Combinations" with extreme precision! May Divine Peace extend to us later, during the Baptism!

- So be it, O Pontiff, God willing! And the harvest having been very good, the offerings seem to have reached our cellars very generously!"

-That's certainly good news! Let's go and check it out! But does it mean a renewed respect for the Creator?... That's the whole point!

Skirting the Temple, the two High Priests made their way towards the adjoining shops and stables, in front of which a great deal of activity was taking place, with the cackling and chirping of the various birds and cattle, as they moved slowly past several openings where the most varied offerings of the "Offering Clerks" were deposited: about forty clerics and scribes carried, annotated on scrolls, and marked with the Seal of the Great Pontificate of Aha-Men-Ptah, the objects and animals handed over to them. They were then divided into categories and sent to the appropriate premises!

These ranged from foodstuffs of all kinds to the most diverse beverages; from plump poultry to hairy pigs; from beautiful fabrics and luxurious furnishings to sought-after perfumes and expensive jewellery!

The An-Nu remarked, as the queues respectfully moved aside to let them pass, but this time half-voiced:

-Once again you are right, O Prophet of good omens! The offerings are very generous, and very important as far as we can see!

But I fear, without wishing to upset you, that the good harvest of the past is not the primary cause!

-Why is that, O Pontiff?

-It's the fear of the Great Cataclysm! Everyone is crying out against it; but the cries are only the tiny unconscious parts of a Truth that is fast approaching! These people perhaps imagine that their gifts will ward off evil, and that in any case they will mitigate their past impiety... By sowing a tiny seed here in relation to what they possess, they think they'll get a free pass when the time comes! But in the end, you are right, O Prophet of good omen: they are thanking God, quite simply, for the birth of a future 589^e Master! Perhaps he will be their Guide when disaster strikes! Let's go and pray before the ceremony, so that they may be heard; it's time... "

Half an hour before the start of the Divine blessing, the Temple was full, as was the surrounding area. The officiants were already in their ritual positions, stiff and silent. Only the occasional whisper from the guests could be heard.

An Nu entered the central nave, which he had reached just a few minutes before the royal couple and *their* son, via a staircase cut into the central pillar, nearly three metres thick, which led directly from his flats via an underground tunnel that opened out beside the altar through the interior of this column, one of the eight that supported the vault.

A priest immediately passed him a censer, which a second officiant then proceeded to light at a nearby brandon. While the Pontiff carried out the final purification of the altar, the four officiants left to fetch the "bath". The total silence that had prevailed before these preparations seemed even more profound with the entrance of Geb and Nut, carrying her son, which coincided with the bringing of the vessel containing the "pure water".

The First Prophet emerged on the pedestal to the left of the altar, while the King, his wife and their son took their places in armchairs arranged for them near the Sacred Table on which the bathtub was placed. The speaker, seeing that the An-Nu had finished his service and was waiting standing, beckoned the assembly to rise, which they did, as did Geb, and, without further ado, the First Prophet intoned the opening prayer:

- Great Eternal God, may your blessing accompany the rite that is going to give a new Soul to Your people here in Your Abode, so that this newborn child may be not only a man, but Your faithful servant.

The priest reading the ritual took over, intoning with both hands raised above his head:

- O You, Great Eternal God, may this newborn child become Your faithful servant, as are all things and all beings here below if they wish to live in Your Peace. You are the Creator who modelled and fashioned the Great Luminary which this morning generated a new day with its rays. We pray that it will be so, day after day, so that the little being who is about to receive his name of Man may make use of it for a very long Life.

The An-Nu approached the altar and faced the crowd of "faithful", in the front row of whom were the King, standing like the audience, and his wife, seated alone and holding her son tenderly, but much more moved than she would have liked!

Raising his spread arms to shoulder height, the Pontiff began to recite the ritual, his voice trembling slightly at first, but quickly becoming stronger:

- Glory to the Father of us all: God ...

The phrases were repeated one by one, in chorus. The long litany, however, ended in an unusual way:

- Eternity is Yours, Almighty God, for the Origin of life is in Your spirit alone for all things and all beings, wherever they may be, including the Blessed, Your benevolent guard extending to the whole of Heaven. There is no protection more powerful than Yours, O You: the One-God of men of good will.

The First Prophet paused for a moment, waving to the crowd to return to their seats, which they did a slight hubbub, some on granite benches, some on wooden seats, some in the front rows on armchairs like Geb, who gazed sadly at the baby that was not his! The speaker, after a satisfied glance at his audience, and certain of sustained attention, resumed by pointing an accusing index finger at an indefinite point above the heads:

- Anyone who has entered this Sacred Place in a state of impurity will suffer death by not going to the Beyond of the Blessed Life! For God loves purity far better than the thousands of offerings you have so generously brought to His feet today; the best food you can give the Creator is your purity! It is this alone, which I pray with all my wretched strength will be introduced into the Divine parcel, that will make the new carnal envelope held by our most Gracious First Lady of Aha-Men-Ptah, the next conductor of our "Elder-of-God" people. This pure and upright Soul will be our satisfaction, as it will be Her satisfaction!

The four officiants then hurried around the altar, unfolding rolls of fine, specially woven linen, to complete the preparation of the ceremonial baptismal service. Meanwhile, eight harpists sang a chorus of praise in honour of the baby, drawing harmonious accompaniment from their instruments. The crowd, which had been humming the tune for several days, took up every refrain.

With everything ready, An-Nu approached the table:

- May it please God to preside over this blessing, for this is His Home! And in the arms of this blessed bride is a Son-Beloved, whom Divine Grace must shower with its blessings!

A reproachful murmur ran through the assembly at what they considered to be blasphemous words! But the First Prophet, still standing on his pedestal, imperatively signalled to everyone to get up, while he articulated in a loud voice:

- Let Geb, from the Earth, Master of Aha-MenPtah, come forward; let Nut, Lady of Heaven, God's follower, approach. Together, before this altar, we will present your son to his Creator, the Eternal!

The Queen raised her baby above the bath as soon as the An-Nu reached her side, and handed it to her after removing the beautiful little silky tunic. The Pontiff held him carefully, saying:

- Blessed is the one who lives good and just, for he will gaze upon Your face, O You, God of all generosity! Grant that this little being, Your Son, may grow in righteousness and goodness, so that he too may be able to contemplate You! Let us raise our voices in a common prayer to intercede for the fulfilment of this wish.

All the throats uttered the prayer, learnt long ago but somewhat forgotten, while the Pontiff, turning towards those present, presented them with a smiling new-born baby. And the crowd, forgetting for a moment the prayer and the holy place, shouted their delight! But the An-Nu turned round again and raised the baby above the pure water, and silence returned:

- Into this liquid, coming directly from the Sacred Source, itself emanating from the Great Celestial River, you are going to be immersed three times, O young carnal envelope! First, so that your path follows the same path towards the zenith as our solar star, and so that it illuminates the sky of Aha-Men-Ptah as the Sun shines in the middle of the day...

Immersing the whole body in water for the first , the Pontiff supported the baby's tiny, fragile head in the face of the instinctive defensive movement that had arched the Queen's body, *and* that of the King, very visibly.

The Pontiff smiled inwardly, before continuing:

- A second time, so that your mortal soul may follow the same path to the horizon, and set down without faltering, in all the radiance of spotless fairness and fullness equal to that of the eternal Sun...

And the Pontiff plunged the baby back into the water; this time it let out a resounding "aâ-rê", but did not cry! Picking up the pace, he continued:

- The third time, so that your immortal soul pursues the same invisible road in the immaterial Beyond of the non-living, who are in eternity reborn in the rhythmic cycles of the Great Years.

The third immersion produced no cry, and two of the officiants hastened to present a thick cloth to the Queen, who wrapped it around her son's body to wipe it dry. Then the An-Nu helped her to put the tunic back on him, before raising it again above all the heads, towards the Cross of Life carved into the heart of an enormous sycamore tree, which the Sun, already at its zenith, was illuminating completely:

- You! Lord of Life: here is this little man; you have the life of each and every one of us. Here's another one: from now on, his name is Ousir for Eternity!

The four officiants repeated:

- His name is Ousir for Eternity!...

The crowd, won over by the ceremony, finally calmed by its anxieties, repeated the same to all the echoes:

"Ousir! Ousir! Ousir!"

It wasn't long before the ceremony came to a close in a general atmosphere of gaiety. Nut had taken back her son with the name of Man! The bride and groom, as one, walked down the great central aisle through the crowd without leaving via the underground passage. A tremendous ovation greeted this innovation, which shook the building, but did not prevent Usir from smiling.

Geb squeezed his wife's arm a little tighter as she held the frail burden, to support her through the human tide that was trying to ease their passage down the aisle. This reassuring image pleased the Pontiff, who saw in it the first Divine sign of a future resumption of the much more human relations of a well-understood married life!

In seventy-two days, the baby regained a normal appearance; an accelerated rate of growth seemed to have been breathed into him. To celebrate this happy day, which fell on what is now the first of May, the Master decreed that this date would be well suited to a beneficial action concerning childhood, and more specifically the babies born that year. As a result, the Palace presented a superb gift to Usir's cadets, and the day was spent in festivities for their parents.

This is why the people were once again admitted to the Palace that day, where they could admire the physical transformation of the man everyone called by his name. Ousir had become as handsome "as a God", and his wide-open eyes were constantly observing his surroundings, with a welcoming smile that never left his lips!

The certainty took root in people's minds that God had certainly intervened in one way or another to make him "Divine". This is why the term "Elder" would certainly suit him later on, as the prediction made by *the An-Nu* had made clear.

The College of Priests also forgot their vehement protests and cried miracle at the harmony now radiating from such a pretty little body! The reception at the end of this memorable day was unanimous: Usir deserved the name he had been given! And the Pontiff, who was assisting the royal couple, smiled good-humouredly at the praise, for he knew!... There really had been a miracle from God!

As the royal flat had finally "opened" for a good month, all was well at the Palace, for the couple at least! The small room adjoining the spacious master bedroom had been converted into a sort of nursery for Usir. His mother had insisted that he be there so that she alone could look after him at night, without the help of any guards or other princely attendants, who would have had to occupy an adjoining room transformed by Nut into a small private sitting room. In fact, everything had been planned so that the royal couple could remain alone, with the son needing no supervision despite his very young age, as he spent all his nights sleeping peacefully, not even asking for his mother's milk before the Sun appeared in a sky that was less and less calm!

However, the couple enjoyed a peaceful honeymoon. The Annals do not say much about the perfect understanding that reigned from that day on between Geb and his young and pretty wife, but what is certain is that the son who was born on 4 January 9841 was the most "mortal" of all! He was just as acclaimed as the first-born at his presentation, although he cried non-stop during the ceremony and nearly choked on his own fury during the three plunges into the baptismal font.

Nevertheless, he was given the flattering name of Ousit, in the hope that his throat would not burst with sobs, and that later on, when he became the long-awaited symbol, this anger would no longer exist. But for the time being, the baby was very exclusive; he wouldn't let his parents sleep in peace; they had insisted on doing for him what they had recommended for the Eldest, but to no avail. From the very first months of his life, he was fiercely jealous of his brother!

Nevertheless, some eleven months later, the couple were surprised to have twins! They were named Iset and Nekbeth, on 23 February 9840, still in the pre-Christian calendar, rectified to contemporary dates. The two little girls were equally adorable, leaving the many visitors speechless with admiration! Iset was as blonde as Nekbeth was brunette! And while Iset laughed even more than Ousir, Nekbeth remained silent and serious.

A veritable nursery was needed for the four children, of whom Ousit became the tyrannical despot, jealous not only of his brother but also of his sisters, towards whom his devious spirit flourished. He would scream for the pleasure of screaming and having try to calm him down. When he had a nervous breakdown, or when he was already imitating her perfectly, he would only condescend to stop when his mother rocked him, humming a melodious tune!

This triple paternity, in such a short space of time, had soaked Geb's Wisdom in the best springs, and he was establishing himself as a Master of Justice and Goodness. This enabled him, despite his family's happiness, to know that Time was numbered!

It was at this time that misfortunes struck him deeply. His revered father, the old Monarch Abou, whom he had neglected somewhat in recent years, died quietly one night on his bed. The ex-Master had not undressed and, probably sensing that it would not be long before he joined his Ancestors in the Kingdom of the Blessed, he had put on his beautiful ceremonial tunic! Queen Petsout, his beloved wife, was a little ill and had preferred to rest that night elsewhere than in the royal flat on the upper floor of their Palace. Her grief was therefore immense and her illness, suddenly worsening, hastened her departure for the Beyond. A few days later, his soul had also left what had been his physical body, and was able to join Abou's soul.

Nout tried to console her husband as best she could, and showed him that the image of his grandchildren that Abu had taken with him could only make him happy for eternity! Indeed, that very evening, he had been seen in the company of the two little girls, making them jump in turn on his lap, and making them laugh out loud.

The accompaniment of the two embalmed bodies (to enable them to reach the Blessed Shores - seventy-two days were needed - to the specially built antechamber giving them access, after the weighing of their Souls, to the Kingdom of Eternal Life) took place with great pomp before tens and tens of thousands of people!

It was 21 March 9838, when the inhabitants of Aha-Men-Ptah had just forty-six years and four months of reprieve left to live on their land, to understand the extent to which, through their own fault, it was already sinking into unfathomable chaos!

The Master, returning from the long funeral ceremony, was meditating sadly on the future that awaited him and his people. He was in the 'Ak-Menou', the Hall of the Ancestors, whose entrance was at the end of a small inner courtyard behind the Temple, and which is the only building to be built on a different axis, its diagonal having to follow the north-south line so that the resting place is parallel to the eastern horizon, where the Sun sets when it disappears in its celestial boat to sail on the Great River, in the Kingdom of the Blessed!

From the threshold of the double door, made of finely carved sycamore wood, appeared the eight ritual chambers making up the whole of the antechamber intended for 'mortals' meditating in the memory of the 'absent', who were in the Ak-Menou and could not be disturbed.

Geb had followed the purification ritual step by step; he had bathed in the pool in the first room, and in the second he had perfumed himself with the ingredients provided for this purpose. In the third room, which he then entered, he was dressed by the two Pure Priests, guardians of the premises. Preceded by them, the Master entered the next room, where two small oil lamps were placed silently on the floor, after which he found himself alone, stripped of all impurity, ready for deep personal meditation. This fourth room had only a low door as an opening, and was completely bare. Geb lay down on the paved floor and prostrated himself, his forehead touching the granite. It was here that the purification of the soul was carried out after that of the body.

He then entered the fifth room, where he chose the various perfumes and incense that he would burn in the room that followed. There was a whole ceremony surrounding this choice, as well as the lighting of the incense on the white marble altar in the sixth room. The next room contained the food and sumptuous gifts he had had brought the day before, to be placed in the last and eighth room, where the life-size representations of his father and mother had been sculpted in the most veined pink alabaster: "the ancestors' living-room". Here, with a jubilant heart, the Elder of the Living asked for, and received, the protection of the Ancestors.

However, Geb's requests were so important that he had few illusions about their intercession! If his father, who was alive and well on the ferry, had been there to support him, it would have been much better!

In Ath-Mer, however, people seemed calmer, perhaps realising that it would be better to follow the government's directives regarding the precautions to be taken in the event of a "catastrophic event". The situation was very different in the Provinces that were still part of the union within Aha-Men-Ptah! Good words and even prophetic sermons were no longer listened to. And if they were heard, the exhortations provoked only sardonic laughter, showing that the end of the central State was approaching. Its break-up was once again being demonstrated, with the example of the Provinces that had left the union not serving as a lesson! However, even the smallest dissenter knew that in these cursed places, civil wars were still being fought between factions vying for supremacy in terms of freedom... which currently consisted of bloody pillaging, theft, rape and murder!

However, in the five Provinces that made up the country, the climate was becoming so bad that the Courts dedicated to dispensing justice were overwhelmed and rendered unusable in some places, due to a lack of means to protect the Judges, a lack of preventive means, as the "guards" had not been provided for in sufficient numbers, and also a lack of effective means of punishment, as the prisons did not exist and the underground dungeons had not withstood the internees who, having rebelled, had ransacked everything, There were also no effective means of punishment, because there were no prisons, and the underground dungeons could not withstand the internees who, having rebelled, had ransacked everything before leaving to join the ever-growing stream of bandits and rebels who had taken refuge in the forests or in the many underground tunnels beneath the towns!

The various 'clans' that were forming saw this troubled period as an opportunity to amass fortunes with impunity, as the army was not yet sufficiently trained to fight lawless rebels! Fortunately, as each of these factions was unwilling to recognise any authority higher than its own, the central government was not yet in any real danger.

That's why another ten years went by, with ups and downs, during which the Master's character soured! His authority, threatened on all sides, could not rise again: all he had to do was try to make it last until the last moment, in the hope that this would save what could still be saved from the Great Cataclysm! But Geb was far from suspecting that he was not yet at the end of his tether, and that the hardest part of the job lay with his own children! In the space of a decade, the progression of qualities - or faults - had been constant, and in the direction marked from birth by their reactions to baptism! The eldest, Ousir, who was now twelve, had become a blond angel, always smiling at everyone, including his younger brother Ousit, who was becoming very vindictive and increasingly angry with everyone, including his parents. He was more hypocritical when it came to his two sisters because, with their ten years, they were the joy not only of the King and Queen, but of entire population *of Ath-Mer*, who cheered them as soon as they appeared in town hand in hand! Nekbeth, a brunette with ebony hair, and Iset, a blonde with ashen hair, grew more beautiful every day. Nekbeth never lost her seriousness, but her eyes were often pierced by strange glimmers of irony or mockery, and she let her sister laugh when she was happy! Iset often laughed, for both of them. Except when she was with Ousir, whose company she enjoyed more and more, and who was already teaching her so much about nature, animals and even people. This made Ousit furious, and she never wanted to be alone with him, any more than her sister did.

The end of July 9828 arrived, leaving only thirty-six years minus a few days to live for the tens of millions of potential dead, who went about their usual business...

Geb was forty-six years old, another decade gone by; his beard was greying somewhat. Nut was two years younger, but still as radiant with life and beauty as in the early days of their marriage. Usir had passed his majority, but he was not yet helping his father to learn the administration of Aha-Men-Ptah, his reluctance to give orders being great. But his general education was such that his knowledge far exceeded that of his teachers in the scientific and mathematical subjects for which he had an innate gift!

Ousit, naturally lazy, found it harder to learn, and only his resentment pushed him to develop his intellect! The two sisters, on the other hand, had become like goddesses, each with a very particular type. Iset never left Ousir, whom she had first loved as the source of all knowledge, then simply adored as an incarnation of Knowledge and Kindness. Ousit, who had tried to enslave Nekbeth, had only succeeded in triggering a memorable battle from which he had almost come out with his eye out!

While the King had laughed at this altercation, without trying to get to the bottom of it, his wife had shuddered, recognising a certain evil side to their real son that had troubled her greatly. She also watched this attachment between Iset and Ousir develop with a certain apprehension. What had amused her when they were seventeen and fifteen, was now seriously worrying her when her blond daughter was twenty!

She decided to take the matter up with her Monarch-husband, who was wiser than she was and who would certainly be able to give her good advice in the matter! Geb's initial reaction was one of great disappointment, as he had had a great deal of work to do in recent years to maintain a semblance of unity in the Provinces still under the central jurisdiction. He was often on the move, and his last trip lasted eight months! So he hadn't noticed a thing...

With his eyes open, he quickly became convinced that not only were the two children in adoration of each other, but that they were made for each other! Indeed, since Usir was not born of him, he would not be committing any act reprehensible to God by taking as his wife a mortal born of the same mother, but conceived very differently and by Geb! It was high time, in any case, to teach the Elder, as well as his three children, the truth about past events that had been carefully hidden from them!

After immediately referring the matter to his wife, the Master sat down that evening in his study, in front of the assembled family, to recount in detail the events leading up to Usir's birth and what had followed. Nout's face flushed red and, with the benefit of hindsight, she came to see it all as normal! The children's bewilderment is easy to guess, and so are their reactions!

Ousir said nothing, remaining dreamy, with just a few deeper gleams in the depths of his eyes; Iset stared ecstatically at her lord and master, telling herself that she was worshipping not her father, but the son of God, which would make things much simpler! Nekbeth gave a gentle, expressive pout as she embraced the two lovebirds, as if to give them a blessing in advance that she knew would be favourable to them, but it made Ousit froth with rage, and he spoke of connivance and a plot hatched against him, because the Throne should belong to himself, the only son of Geb and Nut...

The Master intervened vehemently and an altercation ensued that would stop at nothing! Definitive words were spoken, causing Ousit to leave the Palace in a hurry, uttering words of vengeance, revenge and murder!

Nut wept for a long time, consoled by her husband and her three other children; she only calmed down when Geb set the date for the union between Usir and Iset, as soon as possible given what had happened, i.e. at the beginning of the second week to come. And Nekbeth had the last word, pointing out that on that day, 16 May 9817, everything was written in the combinations of the stars with the marriage of the Eldest and the departure of the Youngest, and that from then on nothing could change in any direction other than that of the Great Cataclysm!...

And indeed, only a quarter of a century remained before Aha-Men-Ptah was swallowed up!

CHAPTER ELEVEN

SIT: SONS OF THE ("MESIT BETESOU")

> *Alas! Alas! Alas!*
> *Sad is this "Eldest of God" nation!*
> *It is becoming more and more careless and unconscious:*
> *Increase your unconsciousness! Spread your carelessness!*
> *Multiply your blasphemies! Repent of your indecency!...*
> *Alas! Three times alas! Poor Aha-Men-Ptah!*
> *You will not even be able to mourn your dead,*
> *for you will not be able to count the multitude!*
>
> ANNALS OF AA-NOU'B HOR
> *(Book of Time Past)*

The wedding of Ousir and Iset took place with a minimum of pomp. There were few guests, as Ousit's absence had limited the festivities, the shame of this scandal tarnishing the royal family's aura a little more. But the happiness of the couple was a pleasure to behold, all the more so as they themselves, who cared little for others, were living an enchanted life!

The tense atmosphere that reigned in the Royal Palace, as much as outside its walls, did not lend itself to festivities! Ousit, who had left the capital in a rage following the inadmissible slur over his immediate inheritance of the throne, had further accentuated the rift! Nut smiled with difficulty at the two children united before her, but at what price!... As for Geb, his gloom was mingled with incipient anger, as he wondered why he was persevering in the path of Wisdom, actively preparing, despite widespread irony, the Exodus of this carefree and unconscious population who couldn't care less about their future!

His eyes lit up, however, when he realised that his daughter was watching him. He gave her a reassuring sign that could not have fooled her! In spite of this strange marriage, she would be happy, at least before the sad events occurred that turned all lives upside down, including hers!

Yet it would be from this union that the founding branch of future Egyptian dynasties would be born! The "Son" would be God's "Second Soul", and in a quarter of a century he would be able to guide the panicked survivors to the distant land on the banks of a Great River that was already destined for them. But several millennia of a trying Exodus would pass before they got there, and one generation after another would pass on the torch to the next, until the Promised Land was finally reached, and would take the name of this *'Second Heart of God'* who had saved them: Ath-Ka-Ptah!...

Nekbeth frowned, for it was she who had just made this rapid retrospective of thousands of years *into the future!* It wasn't the first time she'd noticed that she could 'see' beyond the present! She had never told anyone about this peculiarity she possessed within herself, nor about this faculty she was feverishly developing, which consisted in projecting herself into the future! It was for this reason that her sister Iset, as well as Ousir, had all her affection, for she knew their feelings of goodness and justice not only between themselves, but for everyone; whereas her own brother Ousit had appeared to her on several occasions not only as a vile and evil being, gifted with evil instincts, but, since she had 'seen' him as the destroyer of the family, he had become an object of repulsion. She had watched him leave the castle with relief!

At that very moment, while she was wondering where he might be, she saw him deep in the forest of Akni-Bet, in the westernmost province of the country, in open rebellion against the "Central Power", where a fratricidal and murderous civil war was bloodying the opposing factions. Ousit, dishevelled, beard untrimmed, dressed in a mud-stained tunic, addressed a group of rebels like himself, giving them a belligerent and venomous speech against the rulers of the kingdom, i.e. his own fathers and brothers!

Nekbeth shivered with despair. She quickly raised her head, which she had unconsciously bent over the bowl in front of her, as if to get a better look at the details of what was happening, to catch a glimpse of her beloved mother, who was observing her keenly!

For some time now, the Queen had come to terms with the fact that she had not conceived a single normal child after Ousir! And Iset's twin was not going to escape this rule in one way or another! As she was also very kind and helpful, her 'gift', which made her more than just a mortal, had to be on a beneficial level other than that which had affected her Divine son, but from which she had suffered the repercussions!

Seized by a sudden impulse, the Sovereign asked him this question:

-Nek... Tell me where Ousit is and what he's doing?

Faced with this precise question, which she had not expected, the young girl felt herself turn pale, for she could no longer shirk her responsibilities. Everyone was going to know; she didn't look away to answer:

-He's no longer called Ousit! He has renounced his ancient lineage for the simple name of Sit! He has taken refuge in the forest of Akni-Bet, where he is at this very moment gathering brigands of all kinds to form a revolt against the King. This is why the name he has chosen is being hailed from all over the forest: "Mèsit Bétésou", the son of the rebellion!

A great silence fell around her, and then throughout the room, as she spoke her words. The guests froze, and Geb himself seemed to have turned into a statue! Everyone was repeating the phrases over and over again, the better to assimilate them, finally grasping their full meaning, but not daring to give an opinion or a conclusion on the supernatural implications! Ousir had slowly straightened up, leaving behind for a brief moment the woman who had been the sole object of his thoughts since the marriage had been decided. He approached Nekbeth, who whispered in a tone of deep distress:

- Ousit will enter into open battle with you, and this battle will bloody the skies for all eternity!...

The Queen, very pale, who had approached in her turn, heard these words and felt herself faint, realising that her premonitory nightmares were not simply harmful illusions! Her daughter had a power that confirmed her most horrible imaginings! Nevertheless, she leaned towards this girl who felt so miserable at having nothing but sad news to give on this festive day, and whose process she had in fact triggered! She put her arms around her shoulders to calm her down and kissed her on the forehead.

Mother and daughter smiled at each other, and Nut made Nekbeth get up and lead her out of the Feasting Hall, where no one thought of having fun any more!

Geb, who had approached Usir, beckoned to follow. Naturally, Iset got up and apologised to her many friends for accompanying her husband.

The guests, now alone in this immense room overflowing with victuals, did not dare resume their conversations aloud. As for the harpists, singers and dancers, who were about to enter the circle reserved for the artists' frolics, they didn't know what to do!

An-Nu, who had remained placidly seated in his place, immediately began a serious conversation with his eldest son, who was seated on his right and who had been assisting him for some time at the great ceremonies, as his initiation as Pontiff was not long in coming. Although twice Nekbeth's age, this son had a penchant for this brunette child with braided hair, whom he had seen born and grow up, but also become more beautiful as the years went by! He was irresistibly drawn to her reserved but very pleasant air. His studies had kept him away from any female intimacy, and he had found himself a Priest before he had taken a wife, then a High Priest in silent contemplation before this almost child, so pretty and already matured, that Nekbeth had become! And the Pontiff, following the evolution of his eldest son's feelings without the latter suspecting it, had never spoken of marriage with him. But the moment had come!

The intelligence and shyness of both of them combined admirably. After what had just happened in that room, the old Priest felt the time had come to open his son's eyes, by showing him that his attraction was an even more powerful feeling and that he would willingly give his assent to a union between these two beings.

Meanwhile, Nut had taken Nekbeth back to her room, helped her undress and put her to bed, just as she did when she was much younger and wanted a good bedtime story. But on that memorable evening, her mother's comforting silence had an even more powerful effect on the adult daughter than an old family story! As soon as she was asleep, the Queen tiptoed out of the room and returned to the banqueting hall... where there was no-one! The guests had left, judging that as they had more important things to do than enjoy themselves, it would be indecent of them to do otherwise! So Nut joined her husband in his study, where Ousir and Iset were still! What a strange wedding night they had there, thought their mother, truly appalled at the turn events had taken! Geb was in the process of explaining to his children that although the situation was hardly improving, they did have a clear advantage thanks to Nekbeth's gift of clairvoyance. It was an invaluable asset that would serve them well in the future!

The Queen intervened by remarking to her husband that it was time for these children to think about something other than politics, which caused the Monarch to burst out laughing and the young couple to blush with confusion, but they took the opportunity to slip away immediately. And so the wedding party, which had begun with a banquet, came to an unorthodox end!

Hundreds of kilometres away, at the very place Nekbeth had mentioned, an important council was being held, chaired by Ousit, who had effectively become Sit, thus showing everyone that he did not recognise himself as Ousir's brother, and was therefore the legitimate heir to the crown! Despite his young age, he had unquestionably become the leader of the "Sons of the Rebellion", and his main objective was above all the destruction by annihilation of all the members of the royal dynasty who had deposed him!

The Akni-Bet forest was undoubtedly the largest and thickest in the Kingdom. It had been a favourite refuge for rebels from the very first disputes. Then several bands of looters, who had taken advantage of the unrest to ransack food warehouses to be used by participants in the future Exodus, hunted down by the new army, had fled to the depths of this forest where, bringing supplies, they had been welcomed as heroes!

No-one ventured there any more, not even the game that once abounded! Several clans had taken refuge in natural shelters, notably caves in the hills, where many bloody battles had been fought before Sit's arrival!

When he had fled after his father's revelations about Usir's birth, the young Prince had come straight to this place whose inviolability he had often heard praised. He knew he would find rebels ready to do anything if he knew how to talk to them! In a short space of time, he had united under his banner most of the bands of outlaws of all stripes who lived there, under the catchy name of "*Mèsit Bétésou*", these "Sons of the Rebellion", who were to tragically go down in the history of Aha-Men-Ptah! They included not only those who had been robbed and rebelled against, but also bandits and murderers!

That night, they all took the oath that was to become famous and be recorded in the Annals, but which, alas, would bloody the population and separate it into two irreconcilable kingdoms for generations, right down to the very depths of the second country, which would be born on the banks of the Nile several millennia later!

Proudly, Sit presided over the conspiracy, as if he were the true Master:

- We, the Mèsit Bétésou, are going to take an oath as the Sun illuminates the Kingdom of our ancestors, the only god we recognise because it is he who allows us to live! This is as certain as his coming in the morning, when he will let the souls of our ancestors rest in their turn!

He stopped speaking for a few moments, so that everyone could get a good idea of the blasphemies he was uttering, which were causing a strange fever to rise inside him. Approving murmurs bursting out here and there, he continued:

- Be propitious to us, O Sun, creator of all things! Inspire us with your victorious strength, and draw our hearts into the swiftness of the impetuous torrent of your combativeness to overthrow everything that might stand in the way of our victory! We will solemnly swear this evening not to cease the struggle that is about to begin until Aha-Men-Ptah is free from the tyrannical yoke of Geb the Despot, who is deliberately inoculating the population with the fear of a cataclysm, so that he can rule with impunity according to his own will, filling his coffers with the sweat born of the anguish sown by the priests in his pay!

A long cry of hatred rose from the crowd of outlaws gathered in the clearing, filling Sit with pride and ease, and he stretched out his arms in front of him in a gesture that he wanted to be solemn. As soon as silence had returned, he raised his voice fiercely to take the oath. The long litany that sealed the foundation of the "Mèsit Bétésou" was:

May our enemies be enveloped in flames
[of the fire they predict!
May their bones be charred like their flesh!
Let them come here to the scene of their torment!
May their new army be annihilated by ours
[to the death!
Let their blood flow in streams and form a
[new Grand Fleuve
May they be tamed, defeated and killed all those who
[will stand up!

Impale and slit the throats of all those who
[will be in the way
Let our fists stop the breath of all those here who will not observe the oath taken at this moment
WE SWEAR IT!...

After faithfully chanting each phrase after Sit, screams punctuated the triple:

"We swear it", repeated with arms raised by the hundreds of assistants present, who from the next day would echo everywhere the slogans of the new and terrible institution of the "Mèsit Bétésou", whose Head was Sit, the renegade son of Geb, who wanted to take over the direction of government affairs, not as Master, but as Father of the People, where everyone would have a share identical to his own!

The days passed once again, with intense military training for the rebel forces. The forest of Akni-Bet became increasingly teeming with men-at-arms training with their sharp-pointed stakes. Time also passed in the rest of Aha-Men-Ptah, where the King was trying to get the men interested in defending their property against these "Sons of the Rebellion" who were ransacking and pillaging shamelessly in various commando operations on the borders of the loyal provinces.

Iset gave birth to a son, who was named Hor, and who became Hor-Our: *Horus the Elder* in mythology, who established himself after the Great Cataclysm!

The round of the hours seemed to accelerate its movement, as if the spiral had only one hurry left: to bring together all the elements of the disaster so that it could happen with full knowledge of the facts! So much so that Nut, fully aware that she had passed the point of no return, would wake up almost every night with a cold sweat on her brow. Geb, who stayed up very late because he was prone to insomnia, would hear noises in his wife's rest room and come in to wipe her face with a ready-made, perfumed cloth, trying to console her as best he could, and reassuring her a little when he promised that the whole family would soon be reunited.

A short ray of joy ran through the whole household shortly after Hor's birth, when the marriage of An-Nu's eldest son to Nekbeth took place. It was above all a religious and mystical celebration, very different from ordinary nuptial ceremonies, because the bridegroom would soon be the Supreme Pontiff!

Each of us unconsciously awaited and dreaded the fateful date prophesied for the engulfment of the entire continent! Those who believed it were feverishly hastening preparations to move their essential belongings; those who didn't care were openly committing misdeeds, with increasing impunity, as the army had been sent to three provinces in an attempt to re-establish a much compromised order! The soldiers, outnumbered by the rebels, were routed everywhere, and an appalling slaughter ensued that left Geb speechless!

Ten more years went by, and the Monarch's hair turned completely white, while the Queen's turned beautifully grey. But the situation had become very critical, with only two states still loyal to Aha-Men-Ptah!

So Hor turned ten, and celebrated in the company of a little sister two years his junior and two brothers, six and five years his junior! Ousir and Iset, in the midst of their family's happiness, gazed happily at their little household, and all this cheered up Geb and Nut who, of course, were present at these joyous feasts. Such youth could clearly not bear the considerable burden that would soon fall upon them.

Sit had become the commander-in-chief of a considerable army, which continued to be called "Mèsit Bétésou", this name having brought good luck to its promoter. In the provinces subject to his despotism, the people, if not the army, had found that they were being squeezed even harder and were being forced into the destructive hordes. The bronze foundries were beginning to produce a complete armament for the troops. It would not be long before the great day of the invasion of the last loyal states arrived. In the meantime, he lived with his hatred, dreaming of a dazzling revenge. Sit thought with delight of the moment when he would hold that imposter Ousir at his mercy, just like Iset who had scorned him, and how he would revel when he ordered their heads to be chopped off and saw them roll at his feet. And so, time passed.

The Eldest Son of Nut was thirty-two years old when he agreed to comply with his father's oft-repeated wishes and become the new Master, taking over the power that was wavering on all sides. The ceremony took place without guests, and only in the presence of the College of Priests, presided over by the new Pontiff, the son of An-Nu, who was officiating in this role for the first time.

As he uttered the ritual words, Usir suddenly felt like the Master, as if he had really been invested with this role by God himself! An exceptional mission awaited him, and it was up to him to see it through.

He listened attentively as the choir of Priests repeated four times, at each of the directions of the golden circle, the phrase he had spoken earlier, which he had done without conviction, not really feeling its meaning until now, when he heard it several times:

I am Your Son, whom You put on the Throne of humanity to guide it. You are transmitting to me Your Power over all the Earth. By accepting this kingship now that You have begotten me in the human image, I become Your legitimate heir. May I be worthy of it, until my Son, who is also yours, replaces me.

The young Master's first actions were to urgently consolidate the links between the capital and the two States that were still loyal. New agreements with these Princes normalised relations that were beginning to become very loose. But on the first day of Uzir's reign, 14 April 9805 BC, the continent of Aha-Men-Ptah had only thirteen years and three months to remain above water!

From that point onwards, the Monarch set about creating a new army that would not only fight the rebels, who were now far too powerful, but would also specialise in protecting the ports and warehouses, which were collapsing under the weight of all kinds of foodstuffs, clothing and skins. This year would also be responsible for guarding the thousands of boats that were disappearing from certain ports and being used as firewood, which could easily be chopped down! There was therefore a major reorganisation to be undertaken to facilitate, when the time came, the rapid evacuation of the population still loyal to the Master.

In the rest of the country, where a few spies managed to obtain the information that Nekbeth did not provide directly to the King, the enormous mass of material stored for the Exodus had been pillaged, gutted, ransacked and rendered unusable by the armed hordes making up the "Mèsit Bétésou". Sit had become the "Lord", a title he had preferred, as it suited the supremacy he enjoyed over a territory three times the size of that still under the control of Aha-Men-Ptah. He now imposed an iron dictatorship, sowing terror and death among those who simply whispered that he was not the legitimate heir to this supposedly Divine throne!

He was securing his hold around the only two remaining states, certain of his imminent total victory. So much so, in fact, that he could not have received more poorly the two ambassadors Usir had sent him with an offer of peace to complete, in the newfound community, the preparations for the departure of all humans from the eight states that would soon disappear.

This Embassy, along with the long monologue in favour of an agreement for the departure to be carried out jointly, sent Sit into a frightful rage! He didn't believe in this nonsense at all, and saw this interview as an attempt to make him feel sorry for all those who were not yet under his authority, as an attempt to obtain a total pardon!

But all bowed to his power, and there was no question of leaving a despoiling brother alive with impunity once he had regained his throne. So he sent the ambassadors back to the Royal Palace at Ath-Mer, in a crate: their bodies and severed heads...

This silent, terrifying response foreshadowed the horrific slaughter that would soon precede the far more catastrophic and radical slaughter on the Day of the Great Cataclysm! Soon, there was no doubt about Sit's terrible determination to end it all with a fratricidal slaughter. In the months that followed, the capital began to be sealed off, becoming progressively more isolated as a prelude to a total blockade. The "Lord" wanted the "Master" to surrender completely, and he was going to try and starve Ath-Mer. There were just three more years to tick away on the clock of the Great Year! Hor was thus twenty-four years old when his rebellious uncle invaded his seventh state, and his first act of power was to order the immediate destruction of the four thousand small 'Mandjit', the unsinkable boats that would have ensured the survival of at least thirty thousand people in the province!

If this "Lord" was thus proving to his troops that he did not believe in such "nonsense", Hor, with all his fighting spirit, could not remain inactive in the face of such vandalism. As the rebels had only one final assault left to make to occupy the capital, the situation deserved to be taken in hand by a "young" man. So the man who humorously wondered whether he could be called "heir to the throne" went to see his father to explain a defence plan he had in mind.

The tactics Hor explained to his father seemed so "mature" that Usir made his son his commander-in-chief. Since the rebel leader now had around three hundred thousand men and plenty of weapons and food, the regular army would have to put just as many soldiers in position!

This active and hasty preparation took Sit by surprise. The invasion had to be postponed at the last minute or risk a war of attrition, the end of which no one could have predicted.

And the last three years of Aha-Men-Ptah passed in a continual state of vigilance, with the two camps entrenched opposite each other, and in feverish preparations for attacks and defences, the results of which were constantly called into question! Hor, increasingly impetuous and full of energy, foiled all his uncle's tricks. And Nekbeth was a great help! She had also strongly advised him to create a second line of internal defences to better protect the area directly surrounding the Royal Palace, the last legal bastion of what had once been the beautiful 'Coeur-de-Dieu'.

The last few weeks passed in anticipation of the first clash of forces. It was now inevitable, and it seemed increasingly likely, according to spy reports, that it would happen on the eve or the day before the "Big Day". There was nothing anyone could do to stop it!

Hor was putting the finishing touches to the advanced fortifications himself, in the castle gardens, so as not to be caught unprepared. Especially as he knew that his uncle had received large deliveries of weapons, which did not bode well.

Until that day in July 9792, when, with an appalling roar, the invading army enveloped the loyal warriors, three rebels against one guard, with extremely large reinforcements having arrived the day before hostilities broke out. Sit, having noticed the many inexplicable escapes, had taken all the necessary precautions for a surprise attack!

On the evening of 26th, the capital fell prey to the invaders, who ransacked the city, with the exception of a few rare pockets of valiantly defended resistance. Theft and pillage, rape and orgies were perpetrated during the night, in the glow of the fires, sinister omens that foreshadowed the final upheavals of the land, which, however, nothing had yet predicted. But the disaster at Ath-Mer was complete.

Together with the rebel commanders, Sit had occupied the Court of Justice and improvised a staff meeting to discuss the continuation of military operations. However, the Lord had not decided to order an invasion of the Royal Palace himself. His hesitation was understandable, and his lieutenants had to admit it reluctantly after a short discussion.

Their own troops, drunk on booze, stupor and blood, were in no condition to face the elite, highly-trained defensive corps that was waiting for them. They were ready to defend every inch of ground dearly, Hor, at their head, having assured them that there would be no quarter given and no prisoners taken.

So cunning was far preferable to force! So the Council of Rebels decided, at the suggestion of their leader, to set a trap for Usir directly, as the only way to thwart Hor's vigilance. An emissary was therefore sent to him, tasked with making him believe that his younger brother no longer felt any animosity towards his family, that on the contrary, he was now animated by peaceful feelings and that he was eager to put an end to this fratricidal war by an agreement that would spare the honour of both parties. Through this envoy, Sit offered an armistice as the first token of his good faith, on condition that Usir himself came with the parliamentarian to discuss and sign the clauses of the cessation of hostilities that would inevitably result from this meeting. Despite the warnings of Geb, who had been hastily called to the rescue by Nut in tears, and whom Iset had immediately gone to warn, the young Master made it known that he had to agree to go to this meeting, as the younger brother's offer had a chance of being serious, even if this hypothesis was not very credible. It was vital for everyone to make every effort to reach an agreement, even a provisional one, as the elements could be unleashed the very next day.

Another stele, known as the Metternich Stele, is dedicated to the exploits of Horus against Set.

His wife, hanging on his arm, distraught with grief, didn't know what to say to prevent the tragedy she foresaw! And Nekbeth was not at the Palace to explain what would happen during the meeting. Ousir agreed that going to this meeting presented some danger, as it looked very much like an ambush, but he had to go anyway. The end of their world was too close for him to pass up a single chance to make peace before tragedy struck. The population had to be free to rush towards the boats that were still intact in some places.

The Master hugged Iset tenderly, as if he were due to return very soon, but in the depths of his soul, the Divine part of him said that it was a journey of no return. He reluctantly accepted the guard of honour his father had imposed on him as an escort, which consisted of sixteen men and an officer. He left happy to leave Hor in charge of the castle, knowing that his son would valiantly defend all the Palace's installations. -

At Ath-Mer, however, the leaders of the "Sons of the Rebellion" were impatiently awaiting the return of their emissary. Lookouts were placed on the surrounding terraces, from where, with the light of the fires illuminating the sky on all sides, they scanned the horizon to be the first to indicate who would be arriving with the special envoy! Sit already saw himself as the Master of the Kingdom!

After crossing his capital in flames and ruins, Ousir and his retinue reached the road leading to the Court of Justice, where he had already been announced. As soon as they passed through the entrance gates, the guards of the royal escort were killed by spears and arrows through the heart or head before they could make the slightest defensive move. The rebels had been massed in the inner courtyard and it was more of a butchery than a battle...

Usir was only wounded in the shoulder, as orders had been given to spare him. But he was dragged unceremoniously to the room where the chiefs and Sit were gathered. On the way, the broken shoulder was dislocated by the violence of the men who were pulling him by that arm, screaming.

Drunk with his complete triumph, Sit came and bent over his hated brother, dismembered and bleeding at his feet, but who wasn't complaining and was looking at him with infinite sadness. It was this that unleashed his irrational fury! He seized the sword of one of his captains and repeatedly pierced the wounded body, without a single complaint. Tired in his madness, he ordered each of his chiefs to strike a vengeful blow themselves. They did so, some with insults, others with vengeance, but three remained silent and thrust their spears into the dying man with revulsion.

Without a murmur, Usir expired, probably with the sole regret of not having been mistaken about his brother, who denied the need to unite in the face of impending adversity, just as he denied his family. And all of them, like him, would soon surrender their souls to this God whom they didn't want to recognise as their Father either!

This ultimate thought was far from Sit, who was frothing at the mouth at having seen his hated brother die so quickly. With a howl, he cast a haggard glance around him, looking for something to wrap the corpse in, so that it would rot while keeping this soul, which would then decompose and not bother him in his sleepless nights.

With a triumphant shout, he spotted a large dried bullskin hanging between two rooms. He seized it with an angry fist and pulled at it. He laid it on the floor, then pushed the still-warm body onto the leather with his foot. He motioned to two of his assistants to close the edges. Then, using a leather strap from one of the hangings, he carefully tightened the whole thing himself, tying it up as tightly as he could, so as not to leave any air passage or the slightest gap through which Usir's soul could have escaped!

A sigh of relief escaped his throat as he contemplated his handiwork! Conquering the Palace would now be child's play. To ensure that nothing remained of this hated carcass, Sit ordered one of his commanders to take four men to carry the "parcel" to the inlet, where it would have to be dumped after being weighted down. The water would carry it far away, where the crabs and carnivorous fish would feast on the remains once the salt had loosened the thong and opened the bullskin... a very long time from now!

The "Lord" then climbed to the upper floor, where a number of prisoners were awaiting the victors' goodwill. He chose one of them to watch the dawn, the long-awaited moment when he would break the blockade he had instituted and make the final assault on the

Palace! The clamour of the fine victory that had just been confirmed by the departure of Usir's corpse accompanied his ascent, making him dream of his ascent the next day, which would be the long-awaited consecration as Master of Aha-Men-Ptah!

At the same time, Nekbeth, who had come at Iset's request, had a terrible and tragic vision of the events unfolding at Ath-Mer. She immediately sent word to Hor, who and his loyal officers were making sure that all the guards were at their posts for the decisive clash.

After being told what had happened at the Court of Justice, he urged his sister to go to the bottom of her vision and tell him what had happened. Crazy with horror, she fainted, unable to bear the atrocities she 'saw' being committed from a distance, without being able to do anything to prevent them. Carefully looked after by everyone, she soon came to, and offered to accompany Hor if he tried to leave, to help him avenge Ousir.

At that moment Iset reappeared, haggard. She had finally fallen asleep, overcome by fatigue and anxiety, overcome by a heavy sleep. She had been woken by a shrill cry, only later realising that it was she who had been screaming out her husband's name. That scream at the end of her premonitory dream instantly anchored the idea in her mind: Usir had been killed!

She rushed out of the room and arrived in front of Hor and Nekbeth to realise that she had not made a mistake. In view of her nervous state, the young chief decided that the two women should stay together inside the palace, while he went immediately to deal with his father's vengeance.

In a short space of time, he assembled two thousand troops, to whom he explained what had happened and what he expected of them. With rage in their hearts, they all set off for Ath-Mer in a vengeful cohort. The Sons of the Rebellion blockading the Palace were very sullen. They had heard the cries of victory and had been waiting in vain for a relief for several hours in order to join in the slaughter themselves, but their impatience was sorely tested. They were arguing out loud, shouting at their officers for not sending anyone to find out what was going on. So they didn't see it coming, nor did they hear it approaching, like a sledgehammer levelling everything in its path, the two thousand guards who smashed into the rebels' foreheads without difficulty, mercilessly killing everyone in their path! Hor followed in the footsteps of his companions, hacking his way through with his axe, which he picked up on the spot because he had broken his spear driving it too hard into an enemy chest.

With his troop virtually complete, he quickly arrived at the Court of Justice, where he had to face up to the fact with horror: the place was empty of *living people!* On the first floor were the mutilated bodies of murdered women, the only bestial remains of the passage of the Sons of the Rebellion. Drunk with fury, he sent out a few scouts to gather information. In no time at all, he knew how to catch up with his father's murderers, seek justice and bring his body back to the Palace.

Along the way, the small army liberated several districts from the brigands who had decided to spend the rest of the night with the inhabitants. Hor's force was thus doubled, as the able-bodied men decided to join the regular troops. Sit, who had been warned by his lookouts of the arrival of a real army, had first fled at full speed, before deciding to retreat to the nearby woods.

Shortly before dawn, the entire capital was liberated, but completely devastated! Hor regrouped all available forces, knowing that his uncle would have to do the same in a clearing where he would have the advantage, as he was used to living deep in the forest.

When the Sun was to appear... no one saw it. It rose on the last day that humanity was to live. Time was over on 27 July 9792. An unreal dawn broke, the last of this era in which the Sun moved in front of the constellation Leo, usually resplendent in a dazzling golden light, the prelude to a beautiful, hot summer's day!

That morning, the star of the day seemed to be absent from the sky... as did the sky itself, for a thick fog of diffuse, reddish light, oppressive in its thickness, smothered everything! It absorbed not only noise, but also daylight and the air, making it suddenly wheezy and difficult to breathe. A bitter, pungent odour, similar to the natrum that embalmed the bodies of the dead, wafted through the air and made all the living tremble as they recognised the foul taste.

When people across the continent awoke, they realised that something unusual was happening. And man's deepest nature resurfaced, giving rise to an irrational fear in the face of this dramatic unknown.

In the capital, where no one had slept a wink during that bloody night, everyone knew that the day had come to settle accounts with God, and that nothing would be credited to this careless and unconscious humanity. The fratricidal sacrilege of the night was to be punished by God.

The panic that ensued is almost indescribable! The Annals recount it at length, but in reality it was similar to any terror engendered by such terrifying circumstances. A large proportion of the able-bodied population ran to the Royal Palace to seek refuge with the "Master" to whom anything was possible. The poor people did not even remember that the day before they had been openly mocking the man whose protection they were suddenly seeking, and who a few hours earlier had been trying to persuade them to hasten preparations for the Exodus.

At the castle, meanwhile, a sad wake was being held in anticipation of the appearance of daylight. Geb and Nut were in the company of *An-Nu-Père*, the other members of the family looking after the refugees who had come during the night, but Iset had taken Nekbeth with her to join Hor and find Ousir, even if he was dead.

Having arrived too late at the Court of Justice, the young women held a short meeting to decide what course of action to take. Iset was going to catch up with her son at the edge of the wood, but her sister pointed out that her husband was not in that direction but in the opposite direction, on the edge of a beach. It was then that she was the first to realise how strange the atmosphere was, blurring even her vision. She understood immediately and explained the situation to Iset. It was therefore decided to go to the as a matter of urgency, where she could at least die next to her husband. This selfish sentiment did not shock the kindly wife of the young An-Nu, who knew that her own children were safe with him.

The morning was progressing, but no one would have *been* able to tell the time because the sun was still invisible, in a day when the dark redness of the impalpable dust of this strange fog was just beginning to lighten, taking on a blood-red hue.

Hor also understood that not only had the time come for the human settling of scores, but also for the heavy dispute between God and the creatures He had modelled in His image! He had goose bumps and found it hard not to show his own fear in front of his panicking troops! If his soldiers had known where to go, they would have fled in a hurry; but their young leader had given them the assurance that he would take care of getting them and their families out in time.

Because he hadn't completely lost his mind, he correctly thought that the state of fearful effervescence that reigned within his army must be identical, if not worse, among the rebels! The time had come to strike a decisive blow. He called his commands together and gave the order for a general assault to take the whole wood and exterminate everything that moved in it, without distinction. All he asked was that Sit's whereabouts be revealed to him in good time, so that he could hear from him what had become of his father before he was put to death.

This stimulus galvanised the entire army, which was sorely needed in the unusual, total and suffocating silence. There was a surge of ghost-men who could not see those in front of them more than two metres away, nor the trees they were narrowly avoiding.

In this almost reddish glow, the clash between the two armies was as violent as it was sudden. They suddenly found themselves face to face, and for a long hour the outcome was uncertain! The shaggy faces of the men could hardly see the frightened faces of the others. The fury of men was suddenly doing everything in its power to destroy the fruit of centuries of civilisation, while this cursed land had only a few hours of survival left. And Divine fury unleashed its Almighty Power!...

The first tremors of the earth's crust occurred, slight but sufficiently disruptive to stop the bloody and grotesque fighting at this moment when the warriors on both sides were living out their final hour.

CHAPTER TWELVE

THE GREAT CATACLYSM

> *The fountains of the Great Cataclysm gushed forth from the heavens, bursting through the Divine Sluices of Leo.*
> TEXT OF THE PYRAMIDS

> *On that day the fountains of the great deep gushed out and the floodgates of heaven were opened.*
> OLD TESTAMENT
> *(Genesis VII, 11)*

The time had come! Walking along the path that ran alongside the surrounding wall, the An-Nu tried to pierce the unpleasant reddish darkness, to contemplate the golden serenity of the God-Temple one last time. But nothing could be seen through the slimy stench of the appalling mist.

He reached the double door of the great portal before he even saw it. A huge crowd, motionless, kneeling and prostrate on the sticky flagstones, was distraught. The old Pontiff could have triumphed easily, but in truth he took no pride in the general distress. Everyone was going to die. It was no longer time to revel in a victory from which he would derive no benefit, the time had come...

In his omnipotence, the God of Eternity was going to punish his creatures for the countless sins they had committed, and he, who had failed to prevent them, would suffer the same fate. Sinister creaks rose up from the depths, making the feet tremble and then, growing louder, the whole body! The weeping, the cries for mercy, the screams, the anguish of an entire crowd trying to implore what they had scorned and denied, seemed supremely vain.

Muffled creaks created disturbances in the reddish glow that tended to lighten overhead, and their vibrations put a strain on eardrums, some of which burst. Geb appeared at this point, weary and exhausted, but keen to make his presence felt in the absence of his son, the Master, to whom the people were turning for help. Clamour of satisfaction arose at the sight of him, for he appeared once again as a Son of God, and therefore as the Saviour.

The old Monarch managed to straighten his waist, which was buckling under the years of a long reign, made particularly hard by the foolishness of the people who were cheering him on that morning! He no longer felt equal taking back an authority that was no longer his, but only that of an angry God. The situation would have been ridiculous, if this tragic outcome had not been predicted so often and so long thought out before its fulfilment.

So when the old man reached his faithful friend An-Nu, he shrugged his shoulders in helplessness; saving his people, who had been so reckless, selfish and godless, was becoming increasingly uncertain. Nevertheless, he took the only possible decision: he decreed an immediate general exodus. Everyone was to prepare to leave their homes, their lands, their possessions and their country of Aha-Men-Ptah, with no hope of ever seeing it again...

The departure to the port had to be orderly and the embarkation rigorous, otherwise too much haste would derail the most arduous part of the programme, which had been carefully planned to avoid panic. The royal soldiers would be on hand to help anyone who arrived.

The time is fulfilled! Osiris takes upon himself the burden of humanity's faults by crowning himself with the dead Sun, so that the new Sun rising in the east may be God's new instrument.

Without waiting any longer in the Temple, the crowd quickly dispersed, terrified in spite of themselves, in order to prepare a summary bundle of strictly necessary items as quickly as possible.

In the roadstead of the royal port, thousands of "Mandjit" boats, reputed to be unsinkable, had been stored and rigorously guarded, with full survival equipment on board: barley cakes, quarters of dried and salted meat changed every year, watertight jugs of water. The Old King immediately sent emissaries to the four dockyards, so that the gates could be opened wide immediately and the soldiers could take up their positions so that the departures could take place in the best possible order.

These initial arrangements, in the absence of Usir and Hor, should already have enabled several hundred thousand people to leave in good order. At the same time, evacuations were being organised at the Palace for all the families living there, as well as on the Priests' estates. Everyone was moving what they still had to carry onto the boats that had been allocated to them for several years. For them, the precautions taken over several decades were paying off.

The reigning An-Nu, the eldest son, calmly gave his orders from the special place in the royal roadstead where his 'armada' was waiting. All his directives were followed to the letter, and treasures of all kinds piled up in the holds of the largest galleys, which were beginning to be slightly shaken by deep eddies. But the fog, as heavy as ever, made it impossible to get an accurate idea of the scale of the potential disaster, and even the sounds were very muffled. So even his family embarked calmly, except for Nekbeth who was still absent, but he was not too bothered by this, convinced in his heart that she was in no danger and that they would meet again...

As for the people, they jostled and ran down the stairs, trying to drag behind them an incredible jumble of utensils! Panic gripped all these poor people, who were suddenly faced with a reality so often ridiculed that it was impossible for them to comprehend its true excess.

A hundred kilometres away, volcanoes that had been dormant for thousands of years suddenly to contract. The underground fires became powerful enough to emerge and their pressure became so great that they threw a shower of powdered earth high into the sky, combining with the fog and falling as far as Ath-Mer. A solid rain of small rocks and waste of all kinds fell on the crowds on their way to the ports, crushing some and knocking others out, and all hell broke loose.

There was a stampede towards the harbour, everyone abandoning everything precious to run faster. In the harbour, an animal fear swept away all human feeling; the soldiers, who were resisting only with difficulty their own anguish, were suddenly knocked down, crushed and trampled underfoot by a haggard horde storming the frail papyrus boats, woven extremely tightly, then coated with resin and finally with bitumen to make them impervious and indestructible.

The terror that gripped them, and the horror of the incredible event that was taking place, made them lose all sense of security. Instead of boarding with just ten people or, at worst, fifteen, they stormed the first "mandjit", fighting to the death to cram in twenty or thirty. So much so that the first flotilla sank before leaving with all its occupants. Thousands of poor, distraught people perished before they had even left the port of what would not be AhaMen-Ptah for much longer!

The volcanoes, once again active, spat out the Divine wrath, covering the neighbouring villages in lava. The terrified inhabitants, who had huddled in their homes, were buried in seconds beneath a glowing river.

Thousands of tonnes were spewed out in a matter of seconds from a dozen freshly opened mouths, carving out a thousand new routes with each tremor. The most solidly established mountains could no longer withstand the tremors imprinted on the ground: flanks ripped open on all sides, others shattered and vanished into thin air.

Two poor women, far away, isolated, were trying find a corpse. Nekbeth was guiding her sister through the muddy, stinking meanders of the barely visible shoreline. The soldiers who had accompanied them at the beginning had almost all fled! Only three remained, also ready to flee if they had thought they could get to a place of embarkation in time. The "seer" was having great difficulty concentrating on "seeing" exactly where she had described the skin containing the murdered body of Ousir.

She knew that a low branch of a large sycamore tree, flush with the bank of a small cove of very characteristic shape, was gripping and immobilising Usir's body. But it was obvious that the terrible swells now appearing in the sea risked breaking this fragile mooring and dragging the body away for good, especially as she couldn't ensure a good "sighting", given the prevailing apocalyptic atmosphere.

Worst of all, Nekbeth knew that what was preventing her from "seeing" was her own concern for the fate of her husband and children! Since she 'knew' that he was in port with the whole family, she had lost all 'contact'. The panic around her and the thousands of dead bodies meant that she could no longer see anything worth seeing.

And the little group was wandering around a restricted area, admittedly, but one in which there were many small roads hidden by the thick fog. So we had to explore them one by one! Iset was beginning despair and her sister, alas, no longer dared to assure her of a result! They were the only beings left in this vastness where the animals and birds had already fled to God only knew where. Was it worth continuing the search if they too were to die?

Sit was asking himself the same question now, albeit thinking about the battle being waged by the Sons of the Rebellion! Most of the brigands had fled in all directions at the first contraction of the earth beneath their feet. They had been painfully aware of this more serious warning, where all their notions of balance and justice had been trampled underfoot! The ground was rising, falling, cracking, practically in a suffocating silence, the entrance to a hell whose existence they had denied. They, who had never ceased to mock the superstitions that foretold the end of Aha-Men-Ptah, suddenly felt guilty and thought only of going to a more peaceful place, where they could recover their spirits and rely on the grace of God.

It was at this propitious moment that Hor chose to launch the last of his followers into the assault on a mound that was just waiting to be conquered. He himself suddenly appeared to the rebels, less than three metres from the assembled leaders, slashing one and knocking out the other, like an avenging God! And these lawless warriors abandoned everything, running deep into the forest, up mountain paths, for over an hour. They arrived at the

Dantesque river unaware of its fiery descent from hell. They were all buried and reduced to ashes before they had time to turn back.

Their leader, who had isolated himself from his staff shortly before the attack with two officers to plan where to place traps, had heard nothing of the short battle between the two sides, and even less of the noises, which were absorbed by the reddish 'fog'.

When they returned, their stupefaction reached its peak when they saw nothing but cripples and the dead, surrounded by countless swords and abandoned maces. Sit finally understood the vanity of his rebellion before God and that he had helped to speed up a process that was now irreversible. Everything was lost, even his honour. He remained alone, dazed, hesitating, trying to recover his shred of Divine spark that he had once thrown in the rubbish because it came from his mother Nut! The surrounding atmosphere had taken over all consciousness...

The soldiers, who had retreated downwards and towards the sea, had come up against the main body of Hor's troops, whose leaders had agreed amongst themselves to halt their forward progress there, in order to evacuate as quickly as possible, and to inform their leader.

A final battle pitted the two armies against each other, and the perfectly controlled government troops cut the rebels to shreds. Afterwards, the chiefs advised the son of the deceased Master that it was best to let the rebel leader die alone and guide the fugitives to a new destiny.

Hor gave everyone the freedom to leave in good order, but decided to stay behind himself in order to pursue his uncle and kill him so that his father could be avenged. Immediately, a new rush sent the soldiers in the opposite direction, towards the ports where they knew they would find their families... perhaps. In this forest, not far from each other, only two men remained, each sitting under a tree and meditating sadly on the tragic events and the raging elements...

The "Mèsit Bétésou" no longer existed, and their name would be lost forever! Sit thought bitterly, reluctantly admitting the power of the Divine, of the abandonment of everything he had been driven to! But to flee where? He thought Hor was lurking nearby, ready to avenge his father's death!

If he wanted to escape, he had to take the lead and kill this nephew with his own hands, who would give him no rest if he remained alive. Hor, still meditating not far away, was coming to the same conclusion, namely that there would be no respite if he did not pursue the murderer with his vengeance. All sense of caution gradually left him and he steeled his hand firmly with a heavy bronze sword. The final, now inevitable, human clash seemed to suspend the onward march of the raging elements.

The same could not be said of the royal port or the still sheltered roadsides of the capital's harbour! The tumult reached a climax, for it was no longer a few thousand people who were panicking in terror, but several hundred thousand who were crowding together, choking, struggling and killing each other, with not a single soldier left to protect the public property, in other words the boats.

But the total lack of visibility, which stunned the crowd, nonetheless pushed them towards the edge of the pier. There was an irresistible surge that threw the front rows into the water, the "mandjit" sinking with their overflow of passengers. The others, managing to overcome the human tide, embarked away from the bottleneck, taking their time so as not to sink their frail skiffs before untying the mooring ropes.

At that precise moment, the rebel horde arrived in the harbour and, like a steamroller, threw everything in its path to the right and left. Anything in the way was pushed into the water. They knew only too late that they were running towards their own deaths much more quickly than if they had taken their time, calmly, to reach these famous "mandjit"!

In fact, they made the same mistake as those who had preceded them, by overloading the boats too much; in their haste to embark, they only realised this when they saw their boats sink. Their weight dragged them to the bottom, creating a second layer of corpses that piled up on top of the first. But others, who thought themselves better inspired, had directed their steps towards the royal port where the great galleys were hastily, but rather calmly, piling up their cargoes. The flood of rebels unleashed a slaughter that left only the strongest surviving, the "Mèsit Bétésou".

Fortunately, the An-Nu and her family, along with several Priest ships, had left the quay. Although they were close by, hidden by the reddish screen, they saw nothing, and heard nothing, of the murderous episode that bloodied the last day of Aha-Men-Ptah!

The two chiefs were approaching each other, unaware of it. Sit, however, more accustomed to tracking in the forest, sensed that his nephew could not be far from him. The fog, which seemed to be thickening, protected him by making him invisible, and the "Son of the Rebellion" stopped to try and locate him in this total silence. The pause helped his intentions because, at the same moment, a thick cloud of this mist was torn away by the wind, revealing a small knoll overlooking the path he was walking on, barely twenty metres ahead and overhanging. There, Hor stood in a meditative pose, scanning the opposite side, luckily for him.

Suddenly, L'onde was overcome once again by his desire to destroy the members of this hated family, forgetting that he was still part of it. He had to kill the nephew, just as he would kill his two sisters. So, as soon as the mist had cleared Hor's silhouette, Sit approached his young relative with hushed steps.

The cracking of the earth's crust resumed its terrifying symphony, reverberating with a heavy, sinister echo. The lava flows, which had been advancing slowly, reached the edge of the forest and began their destructive work, snapping the age-old trees like chaff, burning them in their wake and wiping out every shred of plant and animal life beneath a layer of fiery matter.

In the sky, which seemed to be collapsing in its turn, there were muffled explosions, but their sudden dazzle startled both the rebellious uncle and the younger son awaiting his revenge: the thunder joined in and the lightning demonstrated once again to the two protagonists who were about to be confronted that Eternity belonged to God. But this celestial warning had no immediate effect, as a foul-smelling vapour preceded the disaster created by the molten river. Their nostrils suddenly prickled, this bitter, acrid smell made the two men gasp.

Sit, who was only three steps below his nephew, was overcome at that moment by an irrational fear. So, without further ado, he threw the mace he was clutching tightly in one hand. It struck Ousir's descendant hard on the right shoulder, shattering it clean off!

His cry of pain was lost in the roar of the forest being consumed; he collapsed as one, dropping his sword, and his left knee struck against a ridge of hard rock, preventing him from falling below, but breaking his kneecap in the process. Breathing heavily, and trying to regain his balance to see where the foul being who had struck him from behind was, he lifted himself up but fell back heavily.

Drunk with rage at the sight of Hor still alive, Sit picked up the sword that had fallen at his feet and, striding forward, he threw the blade with all his might. It hit the face, planting itself in a place the rebel could not see, his nephew's two hands holding the bronze in front of his face and quickly becoming stained with blood.

Sit, now certain of being the victor, fled at full speed without further ado, for he could see an enormous, blackish, glowing wave, its ghostly embers crashing closer and closer, tumbling down from the surrounding heights. So Hor had no chance of getting out of there alive... or even dead! Nor could his soul try to trouble him.

The lava flowed with a monstrous hiss, raising huge clouds of burning steam closer and closer to the son of Usir, now alone and abandoned to the sole will of the Divine. With one shoulder broken, one knee shattered, his right eye gouged out and the other bloodshot, it seemed Hor had only moments to live! But he was still alive, despite being immobilised on his promontory... and unable to see anything.

His uncle seemed to have gone, presumably believing him to be dead, so he said a final prayer of thanks, asking God to save Iset and the other members of his family. He was happy to disappear forever in exchange for the lives of others. Blood flowed from his wounds and he had little time left to dwell on his pain. He could hear the infernal fruit growing near him, but he didn't want to give in to the panic of the invisible!

Already, the river of lava was cutting through the nearby trees, and the boiling steam overtook him, enveloping him in a matter of seconds. A single moan escaped from his throat, where the air could no longer pass, and he fainted. He thought he was dead for a moment, but God ensured that this impression did not last. The Creator had chosen this type of cauterisation to close all his bloody, festering wounds, and at the same time prevent him from attempting any rash action which would have caused him to fall down his hill and die a charred death. The lava was unable to overcome this hard granite rock and swirled around it, surrounding it as it descended, but preserving it. Hor remained safe...

Still saddened by the sea, Nekbeth finally reached the place she had been looking for. The little bay was there, misty though it was, but the huge sycamore tree stood out clearly from the edge of one of the banks. All she had to do was approach it and bend over the lowest branch, which should be dipping in the water, to find the bull skin containing Usir's body.

In no time at all, the search was over: it was indeed the place they had been looking for in vain. Iset breathed a sigh of relief; the delay in leaving this cursed land had not been in vain! The two sisters carefully brought the skin ashore, and the soldiers placed it on one of the small empty 'mandjit' boats that had probably broken their moorings and been washed ashore by the strong current.

After a short discussion, the Queen ordered her sister to leave the shore with the body and the soldiers and try to rejoin her own family. It was time she thought about herself. Iset would set off alone in search of her son. With her husband sadly dead and already buried in that skin, it was up to the mother and her alone to save the eldest son, if that was possible. So she returned alone to the Royal Palace, so that Geb and Nut could be kept informed of events and so that they too could leave Aha-Men-Ptah. She did so just as the last quarter of the faithful were begging the old Monarch to accompany them as they fled. But the penultimate Master claimed he still had a lot of work to do before then, and his wife herself was reluctant to press him, anxiously awaiting news about her son and Hor, who had disappeared in search of her. Iset arrived in the meantime.

Faced with his daughter's decision to leave for the forest, and reassured about the fate of her twin, he regained his former authority to dictate his conduct to everyone. No one dared contradict the old Master, not even his wife, who knew from the pang in her heart that she would never see her beloved King again!

Geb ordered Nut to leave with the notables and her followers without further delay, to reach the canal at the far end of the park, where the two large special galleys were moored, ready to return to the open sea. Another land would need a Mother, the Lady of a new Heaven, who, in the absence of Usir and Hor, would have to teach the survivors how to rebuild a second country, a second 'Soul' which, after AhaMen-Ptah, would become Ath-Ka-Ptah.

The violence of the elements at that moment overcame Nut's hesitations; she nodded briefly to hide her despair and quickly left the room so as not to burst into tears in front of her husband. The enormous explosion she heard came from a gigantic crater that had suddenly opened up beneath the feet of the capital's many fugitives, just as they passed through the "Gate of Oblivion" to skirt the Resting Place of the Blessed and descend towards the sea! The huge gaping hole swallowed up the bronze gate, hundreds of living people and the thousands of dead in the cemetery in one fell swoop.

Geb, who had decided to accompany his daughter into the depths of the woods for her last outing, had mounted a stallion to go faster. When he saw the unleashing of the elements and the chaos everywhere, he thought it was too late to try and save Hor. But Iset wouldn't give up; courageously, she spurred on her horse to force it to advance towards a hill high enough to protect her and allow her to find her bearings, as the fog finally lifted a little. The old King did the same, not wanting to go back any further. At the top, a sycamore tree stood out majestically, as if inviting her to pray; she hastily dismounted her horse and threw herself to the ground, bursting into tears:

- You, Sycamore Tree, who gave birth to Hor's son: spare him on this day cursed by You! You are the Master of Light, and the Master of the Darkness that surrounds us today: make the Sun appear again and allow me to find my son Hor!

With her forehead resting on the sticky grass, full of pain and pleading, Iset did not look up at her old father, whom she could feel standing behind her, distraught; she was waiting for an answer from God, just as her mother had received one from another sycamore tree. She barely had time to make the connection when a gigantic bolt of lightning burst from the cloud that was gradually coming into view, drowning the majestic tree in its blinding light. The ground beneath her shook strongly, as if in response. She straightened up and threw herself into the arms of her old Monarch father, always there when needed to offer comfort. He calmed her gently:

- *You have your answer, my Iset! God has heard you.*

- *But what should I do, Father? Time is running out...*

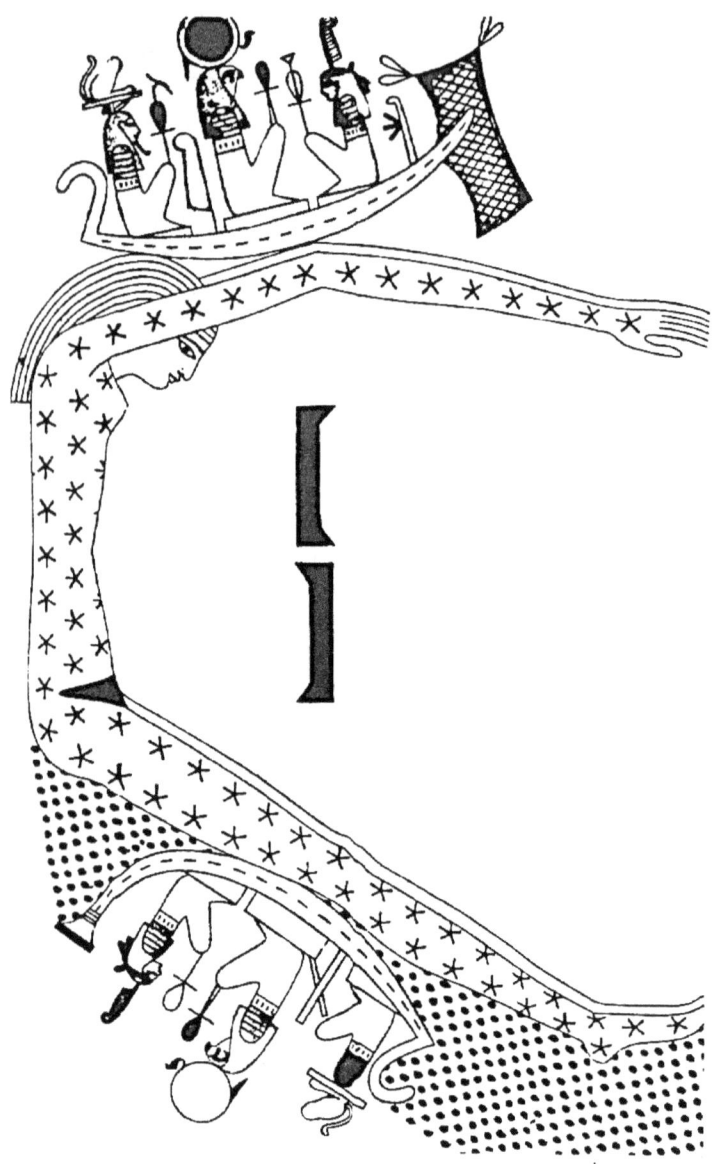

Nut protects the new boat arriving in the East after the Great Cataclysm.

What she couldn't yet know was that she had already received an effective response. A few kilometres away, a little above where

Hor lay, the earth had split open into a gaping crevasse, into which rushed the thousands of tonnes of molten lava that continued to eject from the dozens of active volcanic vents. They would no longer threaten to engulf the islet on which the son of Ousir, son of God, lay. Already, the level of the igneous mass was dropping; the glowing river tan, it would take little time for the rest to flow below. There was already silence around the inert, bruised body, just as there had been around Geb and Iset! The sycamore tree appeared in all its splendour in the restored calm. So it seemed that the prayer had brought a lull in the wrath of the elements, making it easier to find Hor! But where to look?...

She raised both hands in supplication, towards the top of this tree which, she was certain, would allow her the Supreme dialogue. Her prayer came from the depths of her being, instantly, before she could even think of clever compositions of phrases, for she would have been immolated on the spot if she had had to, to bring her son back:

O Ptah-Hotep[12], King of Heaven: open your floodgates, so that the fire you have unleashed on Earth may be controlled! Save the son of Thy Son! Command that this day of the Great Cataclysm not become the day of the Great Mourning... O Ptah-Hotep, King of the Earth: quench the thirst of the ground, so that the thirst You have unleashed on the Earth may be satisfied! Save the son of Usir! Order the Great River to open up all its reserves...

Six millennia later, this prayer is still engraved in several tombs in the Valley of the Kings in Luxor, as well as in Sakkarah and Denderah!

And the annals of the "Four Times" book also state:

- The Earth darkened again over the whole country, but Iset's prayer had been heard; a rain began to fall, which in turn was

---

[12] "God-of-Peace". This is the phonetics of the two opposites PTH + HTP which form the ONE.

reddish and unspeakable! It quickly accelerated the rate at which its drops hit the ground, proving that the very Springs of the Great Abyss were in the process of emptying! Rain by day, rain by night, accompanied for some time by the sound of immense flames crackling overhead. And in a second human wave, the strongest men and women trampled on the children and the weakest in order to flee more quickly. Dazed, their eyes full of the despair of the whole Earth that was about to sink, they forgot that they had once been Men. But it was too late. They climbed the public buildings that were still standing, but the palaces themselves had collapsed. They climbed the ancient sycamores that once stood proudly, but the trees themselves crumbled. They hid in the caves adjoining the springs, but the broken rocks closed in, imprisoning, crushing and suffocating them. Thus was completed the first act of destruction of the "God's Elder People", on that first whirlwind day of the Great Cataclysm.

There is an abundance of texts on the horrors of the floodshanded down by Tradition as a warning to future generations, but interpreted by Champollion's followers in a very distorted way.

Ath-Mer, the proud capital whose name means the Heart of the Eldest Son, has been drowned and returned to the nothingness of oblivion, just as impiety had turned it into a nothingness of incomprehension. Mankind, with its millions of voices, has uttered many complaints and regrets too late to be heard by the Father.

Already there is no trace of life in this world that had been so alive. With His finger, God has wiped out the multitude He had created. For the storms unleashed by the countless orgies were irreversible. For the fratricidal battles could only drag the cursed children into the bottomless abyss of Ameuta, phonetic for the rest of what was Aha-Men-Ptah, i.e. the Kingdom of the Dead!

Future generations of survivors will no longer even ask the question: "Where is the Elysium of the Orient? Because the millennia of the future will lose even the memory of this gigantic underwater tomb, if not under the pseudonym Amen ta, located *after* the cataclysm in the West!

For a time, only the Sages of the successive An-Nu would tell the descendants of the survivors about the period of Fear and Dread they experienced when the Sun, traditionally entering Leo, changed its course on the day of the Great Cataclysm. They even perpetuated this period as a sign of warning, so that no one would defy Divine Power again.

But they too died out, and the comprehensible History of Aha-Men-Ptah with them. From that moment on, the process of the Eternal Return of things was triggered. Oblivion fell upon the whole Earth, and everyone did what they had to do to ensure that another Day of Great Cataclysm would happen again. A final choice will have to be made once again, which will either widen the "Bed of Despair" even further, or finally set in motion the thousand years of peace of a "Golden Age".

But let's go back to 27 July 9792 BC, when torrential rain covered the land of the 'Elder Heart' with a reddish liquid mantle. Within a couple of hours, the layer of lava had solidified and cooled enough for Geb and Iset to get back in the saddle, heading deep into the charred trees. The mounts put their hooves down on a path less strewn with pitfalls, which led them under the hill where Hor was immobilised, *invisible* because he was lying down.

The Queen, in despair, not knowing which way to turn in the face of the total desolation everywhere, decided to climb this eminence in the hope of finding her bearings. Like her father, she was soaking wet and had to coordinate her movements by jerking one leg in front of the other. Geb supported his daughter during the arduous climb. A few metres from the top, they saw the body lying there, shaking...

Iset let out a howl of joy, causing the young man to sit up and soliloquise, asking God not to abandon him. He thought he was hallucinating. His mother couldn't be that close to him... But a hand came to rest on his shoulder, and the voice he loved so much, recognisable despite the sobs that interrupted it, said to him:

- *Fear no more,* O *my son who has avenged your father, God has guided me to you in order to save you.*

With a cupped hand, the mother delicately collected the rainwater dripping from the rock and sponged the blood from the punctured right eye; then, helped by Geb, she carefully cleaned it, before washing the left eye, thanks to which Iset's reddish face suddenly appeared, transfigured. Hor could see his mother, and he let out a howl of joy as the rain that was pouring down on him mingled with tears of joy!

He tried to lift himself but would have fallen back heavily if his grandfather had not rushed to support him and show his daughter the state of his knee. With Iset's help, he loaded the young man onto his shoulders and they slowly made their way back down to the horses, which were waiting patiently in the torrential downpour.

Helped by her father, Hor grabbed hold of the mane and managed to pull herself onto the back of the stallion, who did not flinch. Geb then forced his daughter to get on the other horse, before telling her in an authoritative and unanswerable voice:

- Iset, now you must obey immediately, because time is running out for the survivors. Ousir had set aside a 'mandjit' in the small shelter by the lake. Sacred in case of urgent need. Perhaps he knew that the day would come when it would be useful to find it. That day has come. Meet up with the two of you at this shelter and head out to sea as quickly as possible. There's only one pair of oars and it's a light boat. I'd be too much dead weight, and I've still got work to do at the Palace. I'm going to take the shortcuts down. Don't worry about me, that's an order! Just look after your son. Go now!

- But I... Father, I...

- Go!

There was nothing more to say, and Iset set off, followed by the other horse, which put itself beside hers. All along the way, she reassured her son with comforting words, with the aim of making him forget Geb's absence, as well as his own pain, for the state of his knee, not to mention his eyes, must have been the source of intolerable pain. They embarked without further difficulty. Iset rowed vigorously in order to reach the "Mouth of the Gap" before nightfall, the inlet where they would be safe and where they could perhaps board a larger boat with other survivors who could give Hor some care.

They had been away from the coast for around ten minutes, having valiantly crossed the small and large canals, when the first real earthquake was triggered, shaking all the land and making most of it disappear, while dazzling lightning streaked the sky before being lost on the surface of the water in dantesque spurts.

While Hor, leaning against the bench where his mother was struggling to stay on course, remained insensitive to the convulsions of the environment on the brink of annihilation, the last survivors left here and there this earth that had sought its annihilation and was atoning for it on this day. The Times were over, just as Man had wanted them to be! Don't the texts in the Annals make this perfectly clear

"Man: these were your thoughts; these were the thoughts of Heaven."

CHAPTER THIRTEEN

MANDJIT

Still sailing towards the West!
The mallet was taken, the stake driven,
the bowstring lowered,
the West had been reached:
Hor-Our was saved!

ARRIVING AT TA MANA
(Text by Oumbos)

During that night that never ended - the night of 26 to 27 July - all hell broke loose in the waters of the strait to the south of Aha-Men-Ptah, where the narrow continent almost touched the land of what is now West Africa. This was the famous "Mouth of the Gap", which linked the two parts of the eastern sea, and on which the enormous waves of the "Mandjit", reputed to be unsinkable, sailed and should therefore reach the western shore safely by following the path of the sun.

The horizon to the west was ablaze with fires, turning it blood red. But was it really the west? A tidal wave, further amplified by the gale-force wind, was literally crushing the waves, creating crevasses several metres deep and dragging the 'mandjit' to the bottom, bending under the weight of the water they were carrying, but pulling themselves up valiantly, albeit with increasing difficulty.

After a relative lull, during which the terrified survivors saw the burning coastline sink and then disappear into the sea in countless eddies, there was a second tremor that was felt more keenly because it was of underwater origin.

It unleashed a terrifying cyclone which, with the roar of increasingly violent whirlwinds, pulverised all the frail boats caught in the eddies.

Alone on this liquid immensity, the surviving sailors, exhausted and half-mad with terror, had not yet reached the limit of the impossible. In a sky that was still reddish, but relatively serene, they suddenly saw the Sun move abruptly, rushing forward accompanied by daylight. passing over the panicking heads of the sailors, while their arms clutched the edges of the boats as if seeking some comfort, then disappearing over the horizon in a few minutes, bringing back the night, in the midst of which the stars also followed the same rapid rhythm. The Moon appeared in its turn and suddenly crossed the sky to sink into the waves! And the madness seemed to subside, as did the celestial disorder...

Complete darkness had returned in the space of an hour! No one could have said, had they wanted to, how long this extraordinary day would last, and even less whether it would be followed by another day. The horizon remained crimson, and full of an otherworldly sound, ghostly and elusive! The shipwrecked men in distress were crying out at the top of their lungs in their insurmountable anguish; they believed that their last hour had come, just like that of a world that had once been theirs, and in which they no longer recognised anything! Everything was gone, except the night!

The sea had spread out dramatically; the strait that joined the two seas, which had not been crossed, had disappeared. In the distance, a coastline was boiling, but no longer identifiable. The steam and flames coming down to the waves transformed every profile. The fires at the end of the horizon echoed their sinister creaks over this poor, wandering, groaning humanity, whose lives depended solely on the "mandjit" they occupied while waiting, no longer for a welcoming land, but for their final hour.

A jet of glowing embers shot miles into the horizon, lighting up the stormy sea. A rain of fire fell in dazzling sprays, while the discordant, infernal sounds of the blast terrorised these helpless beings. It really was the end of Aha-Men-Ptah, which was hard to imagine for all those who, like them, had lived there for countless generations in peace, in the best and most peaceful of worlds. And yet, this earth was disintegrating, breaking up, liquefying completely as it mixed with this infinite water, becoming one with it.

Those with good eyes saw, against the purple background, the black mass of the last mountain ranges in the distance, sinking and disappearing beneath the liquid element: nothing! There would be nothing left!

The new tidal wave that followed this submarine upheaval didn't reach the "mandjit" until half an hour later, when calm seemed to have returned. The sea was crushed by the first huge wave, a dozen metres high, which carried everything in its path for several kilometres at dizzying speed... and suddenly found itself in the middle of a terrible storm. The violent wind threw hundreds of people into the sea, but many had had the good idea of tying themselves to the masts with the thongs that had held the sails, which had long since been blown away, and were held against them, thin but solid.

Such was the case for Iset and Hor, tied together to the mooring peg of their disabled boat; such was also the case for Nekbeth, and also for Nout and his retinue. The same was true of Sit, who had managed to embark alone, and who was counting on eventually landing somewhere and finding some of the 'Sons of the Rebellion' who had escaped the scourge like him.

Hor, reduced to a state of total inertia by his broken knee and his spirits much lowered by the intolerable pain caused by his gouged eyes, nevertheless realised how lucky he was to be alive in the company of his beloved mother. The "mandjit" allowed them to sail while waiting for a shore to land; but was there one left? The young man began to think, forgetting his wounds. If he'd had to die, he wouldn't have been rescued on this unsinkable boat, which was certainly rocking them back and forth, but which was actually carrying them to get them "somewhere"! He tried remember how such a cataclysm was possible...

He had learned from the Master of the "Combinations of the Father" that the Earth was a large ball, similar to the Moon when it appears full. Observation, accompanied by meticulous calculations of the geometrical figures composed by the planets and the stars, showed a long series of celestial movements that were highly differentiated, but linked together by a single vast universal Law. Logical reasoning should certainly show him that this earth could not disappear everywhere.

The scientific reasoning we used in 1975 proves that our globe rotates in several different directions, either on itself or around the Sun, at astonishing speeds... especially if you consider that we appear to be immobile! The result is that the rotation differs between the largest diameter, at the equator, and the smallest: the poles. One constant is that increasing progress in the direction of rotation cannot fail to produce an effect that is the opposite of that which attracts us towards the ground.

Hor could not have failed to learn from his teachers the classic example that has been handed down to us from the dawn of time: "If you bend a bow, it will shoot all the further the stronger your hand is pulling on the string!

This property made it possible to deduce from the earliest antiquity that there was an offset in the general movement of the balls circulating in the celestial vault, including that of the Earth.

Denderah's texts on "MathematicalCombinations" leave no doubt on this subject. They state, among other things: "The time taken by the Sun to return to a rigorously observed location, from one sunrise to another, at the moment when it appears just in front of the brightest star in the constellation of Leo: 'the Heart' (today: Regulus) lasts 365 units, plus $\frac{1}{242}$ of a unit. This time is shorter than that taken by the stars to complete the same cycle: 365 units, plus $\frac{1}{256}$ units. The annual difference in this time is therefore the fifty seconds of arc of the great celestial circle that joins the twelve zodiacal constellations by crossing them.

This means that, necessarily, for a reason unknown to humans, there is a precession of Time in Space at the beginning of each spring. Let's make these facts even more precise in our modern language, with the developments they entail, because they are always in continual contradiction with the attempts at scientific explanations made by astronomers and physicists. So what are we talking about?

According to Newton, who has been trying to re-address this question ever since the ancient treatises on the "Divine-Mathematical Combinations" were lost or hidden, the cause is none other than the bulging of the globe over its equatorial region. It follows that this part of the world gravitates more strongly towards the Moon and the Sun than the rest of the sphere. And this excess of gravitation in this part must have the effect of continually diverting the plane of the terrestrial equator, and forcing it to retrograde on the plane of the ecliptic, precisely by fifty seconds of arc per year. In other words, Newton concludes, if the Earth were exactly spherical, the equinoxes would always coincide with the same points on the ecliptic, and the equinox would never occur!

At first sight, astronomers immediately adopted this rather simplistic theory, which was a bit like an oracle in that it removed some very embarrassing question marks! D'Alembert tried to translate it algebraically against all logic, but the result was the opposite of what was observed! Full of perseverance, he resumed his work, thinking that he had omitted some vital data, and then, with no change in the result, in his frustration, he threw it into the fire! Then he put the handle after the axe, imagining a cause for this precessional movement that brought his calculations into line with observation!

The diurnal rotation of the globe, which neither Newton nor any of his colleagues had considered, provided the cause. This led Lalande[13] to say: "The solution of this question is one of the most difficult parts of the calculation of terrestrial and celestial

---

[13] *Abrégé d'Astronomie*, p. 1064

attractions; Newton was mistaken, and d'Alembert was the first to solve the problem. Euler, Simpson, and several others have practised on this subject, and I have given it with the greatest clarity in my astronomy."

But had d'Alembert really solved it? If the problem had been purely mathematical, there is no doubt that his solution would have been satisfactory. But this is not just a question of numbers. It is a question of organised and predestined mathematical combinations, which the ancient masters had solved *exactly*, *albeit* quite differently. In fact, following their very long and patient observations, the Ancients had recognised without any possible error that the annual revolution of the stars was nothing but a vain optical illusion, just like that of the Sun under another aspect. In reality, the Earth, and the Earth alone, rotates in various motions, which gives rise, in appearance, to circular configurations of several different amplitudes in the Sun and the stars, which, although they too are animated in their particular systems, are immobile and fixed in relation to us.

Now, although the Earth is delayed in its annual movement, and the plane of its equator is continually diverted and forced to retrograde on the ecliptic, it nevertheless completes the same revolution in Time every year.

Consequently, we cannot accept that the 'illusion' produced by motionless stars can be different from the identical illusion produced by the Sun in space!

The question was therefore to understand how it could be that the illusory revolution of the stars, and the equally illusory revolution of the Sun, are not isochronous - and therefore identical - since the only real rotation is unique and always the same: that of the Earth!

In other words: how can it be that one and the same constant cause produces different effects of movement on immobile bodies? Why, therefore, do the stars complete their full revolution while the Sun is still fifty seconds of arc on the same circumference, but backwards?... This, in a nutshell, is the question that remains unanswered.

Simple common sense proves that these two stellar and solar revolutions, which are purely illusory, should be completed at the same time. So how does the equinoctial line retrograde on the ecliptic plane? It's easy to answer, imitating our dear Monsieur de La Palice: because it is retrograde by the simple apparent fact that it is retrograde! But this is a blatant position of principle! It would be better to state this other nonsense: It is retrograde because the illusory revolution that drives it is discordant with those of the stars and the Sun, because if they were all concordant the line of equinoxes would not retrograde at all!

The vital question therefore lies in this lack of concordance between the annual revolution of the Sun and that of the stars, *and not in the figures*, which are merely secondary results reflecting the unexplained event. We must not allow ourselves to be distracted from the main aspect of this serious question by secondary considerations that are no more than appearances.

It was precisely by guessing only at the primordial mathematical and Divine "combinations" of the days of Creation of the celestial movements that the Sages of Aha-Men-Ptah were able to foresee the consequences of certain disastrous geometrical configurations and thus predict the place and date of the Great Cataclysm.

The problem therefore needs to be posed correctly, not only in algebraic form, like d'Alembert, but also in a way that gives a positive result in all its combinations. Let:

- Since the rotation of the Earth is the sole cause of the illusory revolution of our solar system, how is it that there appear two annual revolutions that are different from each other, so the line of equinoxes retrogrades annually on the ecliptic by fifty seconds of arc of a circle?

The two different revolutions stem from the fact that the Earth's annual path is an ellipse, albeit of very small amplitude, the apparent path of the stars takes place within a perfectly circular circumference, like the twelve zodiacal constellations on a celestial equator of just 360 degrees!

Equinoctial precession is therefore not the effect of a disturbance caused by the attractive gravitation of the planets in our solar system, but a normal mechanical effect of the 'eclipticity' of the Earth's orb, due to its 'anomalistic' inequalities. Gravitation only intervenes in the sector of Time, and not in that of Space, which is primordial for all human life on Earth and gives rise to all the differences!

So, when the Sun has really completed its annual revolution in what we call the Heavens, i.e. an apparently complete turn, *its double*, which is in reality the "combination" left by the Earth's revolution, will find itself backwards by the famous duration of precessional retrogradation, by fifty seconds of arc, mathematically irrecoverable in Space!

So that at a certain moment 'M', the double, instead of preceding the real, will find itself preceded by it. The line of the equinoxes will be carried forward to the very point where it was the previous year, thus clearly creating the break that is so easy to understand.

The equinoctial points. once they have reached the major axis of the elliptical orbit in their retrograde course, are forced forward by the action of the planets in our system, and yet are pushed further back by the effect of the "anomalistic" inequality, would no longer be able to do anything other than oscillate on either side of perigee and apogee on the plane of the ecliptic drawn at the moment of rupture, until the moment when the broken equilibrium is transformed into catastrophe, which was clearly calculated and 'combined' in the case of the Great Cataclysm.

The more or less accentuated pivoting on the invisible axis, which can go as far as a total tilt depending on the configuration, thus brings east to west, and vice versa. As a result, the Earth having tilted, and given its double, the Sun, the same appearance, the latter, instead of continuing to rise in the west, did the opposite and appeared in the east every morning, although it had strictly the same course as before. But the survivors bound in the 'Mandjit' awaiting a new day did not know this! Only Hor had acquired the Science of combining 'Combinations' and their powers.

This determined that the Great Year of 25,920 was in reality nothing more than a chimera, since it would be difficult for the globe to continue its evolution in Space over more than 180 degrees, or 12,960 years! This inevitably leads us to talk about another vital 'coincidence': the one that triggered the precessional phenomena at just the right moment, i.e. when the first humanoids appeared, to enable them to develop and evolve in a slow but progressive cyclical fashion over this period of approximately 12,000 years on 180 degrees!...

Plutarch, in his "Life of Plato", gave Copernicus his first idea of the system wrongly attributed to this scholar. He learned from this book that "disciples of Pythagoras, including Philolaus of Crotone, had placed the Sun at the centre of the world and set the Earth in motion around this fixed point!

Anyone can read this passage in any edition of the "History of Mathematics" (book III, 4), which was itself shamelessly compiled for the use of the Greeks, the heliocentric system of "Mathematical Combinations" in use at Heliopolis, a Hellenic name from that period, incidentally, but which meant exactly the same thing in hieroglyphic: the "City of the Sun". There, the solar globe was deified as Master of the solar system, which was understandable, because if the daytime star had disappeared once again, there would have been no more Life on Earth!

It is certain, and the Greeks recognised it, that this combinatorial science did indeed come from Egypt, and that the Priests of that country attributed it to texts of an antediluvian Tradition. No other people, until our so-called "Modern" times, possessed enough of this so-called astronomical science to understand and demonstrate that in the natural mechanism regulating cosmic movements, there were Divine anomalies that enabled men to harmonise their actions with God and Heaven.

There is a curious remark to be made here; it is that Pythagoras taught his familiar disciples that the stars were similar to our Sun, and that they all possessed, in all probability, a planetary system similar to our own. Now, knowledge of this Truth presupposes a particularly highly developed science, because we have only known this with certainty since the great telescope on Mount Palomar was put into operation, where we were able to see systems so far from our own that they remained totally invisible until then.

If we now accept the accuracy with which the apparent revolution of the Sun, the retrograde revolution of the equinoctial points, was defined, it would be unwise to consider as certain the veracity and reality of the famous zodiacal planisphere in the Temple of the Lady of Heaven at Denderah, which, although it has come down to us after the Temple was rebuilt, has nonetheless retained its original configuration.

The one where all the stars are placed in such a way that they can only represent a single day: that of the Great Cataclysm of July 9792... This will be the subject of a separate study, but we must return to the company of the 'mandjit', hundreds of whom wandered in search of a day, a glimmer, a light of some kind, that would enable them to see if there was still a coast somewhere where they could land.

The passage of time increased the dangers involved, as the small, light boats, although unsinkable - as they had amply proved! - were showing signs of obvious fatigue! The bitumen, which held the resin firmly to the papyrus, was cracking.

Hor thought to himself, as he felt the drops sprayed violently towards his face, where the deposited salt hurt horribly, that the "mandjit" could hardly hold out for many more hours!

But what was the point of lamenting in such circumstances when man was solely responsible for his own troubles and the catastrophe. Apart from the intelligence he had lost over the centuries and which he would have to patiently relearn, he was just an animal like any other. The image that God had modelled for him came from the fact that the Creator had breathed a Soul into this carnal envelope, as he had learned. All that was a long way off. He would have to learn everything all over again to live!

Suddenly, a cry from his mother brought him back to reality. He took advantage of this to open his valid eye wide, but it was still so misty that he could only see the very vague, dark shape of an asexual profile. He asked:

- Is the "mandjit" in trouble, mother?

- No! That's the day that seems to be breaking on your right.

- To the right? But that's impossible! We're on the wrong track, Mother, otherwise the Sun would be in the west!

- It's on the right, Hor; and it seems to be east, because the coast is usually visible from the east.

This new enigma left him speechless; what could this Divine trickery be hiding, which was now flouting all the natural laws of "mathematical combinations"? It was time for a solution, for spirits were getting lost in all these apocalyptic meanders! From all the boats, a chorus of lamentations arose at the sight of the inexplicable solar movement!

The survivors were understandably anxious; but as the day dawned normally, in contrast to the day before, the steep coastline became increasingly visible and was recognised by some of the sailors, which was a great relief.

As the scarlet ball appeared above the earth's horizon, still purple from the remnants of the night, howls of joy erupted from every inhabited point on the sea, reverberating from "mandjit" to "mandjit". Life was returning to normal everywhere as the dazzling sun rose; it was barely possible to remember the horrifying day of the previous day. This burst of enthusiasm only lasted a short time, however. If the day resumed its normal course, praise be to God, certainly: but why be so displaced in Space?...

Iset knelt down, resting her forehead on the watery bottom of the boat, before raising her head a little and saying aloud:

- How many have disappeared, O God of Eternity?... You have chastised us severely, but we humbly thank You for allowing us to live today. To show us Your Power, and to remind us of It constantly, so that we live in Fear of breaking Your Commandments, You have changed the course of the Sun! From now on, it will follow another path, which will remind us of Your Wrath until the end of Time! And the Sun, which rises over the Eastern Earth, will now set over the sea, in the place that was Your Heart: Aha-Men-Ptah, and which from this day becomes: Amenta, the "Kingdom of the Dead", millions of dead!...

The Queen of the Sunken Kingdom rose to her feet and came to lean on her son's shoulders, before crying out to the approaching boats, for they all recognised Iset, their Celestial Lady: "To all of you, I say it in truth: if you are ready to start living again in accordance with God, who made you in his image, the world will soon be lit up by a 'Second Soul': *Ath-Ka-Ptah*, which will be our second homeland, purified, warmed and resurrected by this second Sun! For its rays will be the life-giving forces that ensure our resurrection.

A few hours later, the hundreds of "mandjit" began to dock on land that everyone agreed would be called Ta Mana", or "the place of the setting sun", as the sun would no longer rise there!

The "mandjit" became the "boats that had accompanied his double course", so the "Meskit" were those of the new day, reclaimed thanks to the "mandjit".

In less than twelve clock hours, everything had been consumed! The Earth had tilted sharply on its axis, freezing the continent of Aha-MenPtah, a tropical region, at the same time as it engulfed it, and the torrid heat had caused the glaciers that had 'fallen' in southern Morocco to burst open!

As for the texts that recount all these facts, they make the Sun the primordial element, whose presence alone makes all life possible. They even elevate it to the rank of God's instrument: "The Majesty of Ra returns to what was the 'Elder Heart', but beams down from the opposite horizon, for they now rest only on the dead! Hor-the-Elder will recreate Life where the Sun now rises, on a second Heart."

The "mandjit", which transported the survivors at the end of their marine exodus, were duly celebrated. The survivors gave them a special feast, intended to perpetuate their memories forever. This is why, many centuries later, gigantic stone boats of exact proportions were built, some of which have been found, always facing west, as at Abousir and Sakkara, on the edge of the desert plateau bordering the road near Giza. This is why a real 'mandjit', in its original wood, was dismantled piece by piece and buried under the Great Pyramid, the Beloved-Who-Loves-The-Light.

The one at Abousir, some thirty metres high, is monumental. The very name of the place where it was erected is significant: "the Father of Osiris", hence God! The "mandjit" itself was rebuilt on the orders of Ni-Ousir-Râ, pharaoh of the Vth dynasty, whose name is: "Descendant of Osiris and the Sun", who wished to perpetuate the "Amenta".

THE GREAT CATACLYSM

Usir, "Master of the TWO LANDS"
Aha-Men-Ptah and Ath-Ka-Ptah.

The orientation of the boat is obviously east-west, with the bow pointing absolutely west, i.e. towards today's setting sun. The deck and various accessories have disappeared, victims of vandals and sand. But the boat itself still retains its superstructure, as well as its remarkable hull, reputed to be unsinkable, with ingeniously softened lines, as were those of the papyrus 'mandjit', woven and tarred.

The stone boat at Abousir, on the very edge of the plateau, is probably as important an archaeological wonder as any, but it has always been greatly disdained by Egyptologists, who have never understood the highly symbolic value of this monument. It stands proudly, victoriously one might say, just as the Sun is about to disappear and sink below the horizon, before the eyes of the tourist who has come to admire the unforgettable spectacle. With very little imagination to supplement the texts, the suggestion is perfect of this "mandjit", sinking irresistibly into the shadow of the night of the Great Cataclysm!

What it also suggests to the new initiates of this new land, this second-soul-of-God, is that the "mandjit" was also the saving boat for Iset, Hor-Our, Nekbeth and so many others like An-Nu, not forgetting Ousir and Sit, without whom Ath-Ka-Ptah could not have been born!

CHAPTER FOURTEEN

CHRONOLOGY OF AHA-MEN-PTAH

> *Where is the man who can appreciate time, estimate the day,* and *understand that he dies every moment?*
>
> SENECA
> *(Letter to Lucilius)*

> *It is really fighting a battle to try to overcome the errors that prevent us from gaining knowledge of the truth; and it is losing a battle to receive a false opinion on a matter of some importance.*
>
> DESCARTES
> *(Discourse on Method)*

The ancient texts provide the key elements for reconstructing the Chronology of Aha-Men-Ptah. Bibliographical references are appended at the end of this volume. Although there are not many references on this subject, many Greek authors from the beginning of the Christian era provide additional information which, when added together after deleting any that are too fanciful, forms a coherent whole.

It has recently been established, particularly since the recent discoveries at Negadah, where tombs predating Menes are legion, that the very origin of the first arrivals on the territory that was to become Ath-Ka-Ptah or Egypt, dated back to a time much earlier than the first king of the first dynasty: more than a millennium at least before the first Pharaoh. Which adds a further advantage to this chronology.

The jewels buried with the still rather poorly mummified bodies, the pottery and other luxurious objects that accompanied the dead into the afterlife, undeniably date from this very remote time, amply demonstrating the culture and knowledge of the people who reached this place with their Knowledge, and who in a short space of time absorbed the natives, who were still living there in the Stone Age, similar, according to archaeologists, to those living in the Chelléenne period in the Somme, in France.

It is therefore through post-diluvian rock and tomb engravings that the chronological sequence of these ancient "Masters", monarchs who were "Sons of God" in an "Elder" land, has been established. But there are also the famous Abydos tablets, the texts from the foundations of Philae and Esnea, the texts from Dendera, and the hieratic Canon, a fragment of which has been found and is kept in the Turin Museum. Finally, there is Manetho's famous chronology, which was the starting point for all manner of elucidations for two thousand years, before it was realised that the mathematics used needed no interpretation to be clearly legible! In fact, the dating goes back to the beginning of the history of these people, in their first country, twenty-six thousand years ago, with their arrival in Egypt well before the first dynasty, which began with Menes, 4,241 years before the Christian era. But until a few years ago, according to the Bible, this historical fact was an aberration!

Manetho, despite his Greek name, was an Egyptian, a priest as well as a historian, born in Sebennytus in the Delta. He lived in the third century BC, during the reign of Ptolemy Philadelphus. This wise and learned emperor asked Manetho, when he had become Priest of Heliopolis and therefore guardian of the Sacred Works of the Ancient Homeland, to write him a complete history of the Pharaohs (i.e. the "Descendants of the Elder") in as accurate a chronology as possible.

It must be understood that the very function of this Priest, who was "the Keeper of the Sacred Texts of the Elder", was of the utmost importance, for he regulated the Solar Rites of Heliopolis, according to the content of these texts. He was one of the most senior figures in the complex priestly hierarchy of the Egyptian clergy.

Having clarified this, here is the complete chronology of this people, the one that *goes back to the Origin of AhaMen-Ptah*, with the Divine dynasties, those of the Heroes, then those who lived in Egypt, this Ath-Ka-Ptah, or Second-Soul-of-God. The historical concordance with chronology is complete, proven by the celestial harmonic movements and their easy dating. This already allows us to affirm that the multiple "coincidences" here can no longer be "coincidences", but that they are natural actions dependent on a Law of "mathematical combinations" willed by God, so that they can be foreseen by Man, and so that he can avoid cataclysms by behaving according to the Divine Commandments!

In the "Chronological Canon" preserved in Turin, the ninth, tenth and eleventh lines contain a general summary of times prior to Menes. They give a duration of existence of 13,420 years until the advent of Horus (Hor), who is noted as the first "Hero"; and 23,200 years for the Divine successions prior to Hor, i.e. a total succession of reigns spread over 36,620 years until Alexander.

It is easy to imagine the howls of the censors and exegetes who, until the beginning of the [twentieth] century AD, maintained that Adam, the first man begotten by God, had been begotten a little over six millennia earlier! But the Councils changed this precept, and recent Popes have brought Church historians back to a little more discernment, thanks in particular to the report of the Vatican Biblical Commission in 1948.

The affabulation so much advocated twenty centuries ago by Le Syncelle thus falls of itself to become a chronological reality once again. Manetho had merely copied texts from the archives, but those who could read the hieroglyphics on the foundations of the Temples of Edfu, Esnea and Karnak could find them engraved in their entirety according to the most precise data traditionally preserved by the "Masters of the Measurements".

This sequence of reigns, dated in Time and materially accessible to future generations for their studies, has been rightly reproduced in Space, on the Denderah planisphere, so that no one is unaware that these are not coincidences, but a logical sequence of "Combinations", willed by God and prophesied by the Pontiffs.

Ptah, therefore, the Unic God, the Creator, at a certain moment, transformed an earthly creature into His image, so that the created environment could serve Him in all things. He touched it with His grace, and this particular species completed its rise so that it could always stand upright. Little by little, he began to use the particle of Divinity included in his brain, and the mind came to him. Man thought, and his reflections created intelligence, which took its place in the Soul. The centuries, then the millennia, refined it: he used fire, melted metals, made weapons, and one day, his supremacy was asserted over the rest of the earthly race!

But God soon noticed that His image had also changed in spirit! It was now divided into an infinite number of clans, tribes, peoples and countries. Each of them wanting to ensure superiority over the others, this led them all to ignorance of the Divine Commandments and to impiety. So time had passed on humanoids who helped each other to become men who hated and killed each other!...

Chronologically, the Beginning of Humanity was the time when God decided to *judge* humanoids to make them His image. This time of reflection enabled Him to weigh the new Souls according to His own criteria of Good and Evil. This lasted for the time of the Sun's passage, for 12°, in a celestial constellation (i.e. for 864 years) to whom was given the name of: Khi-Ath, or 'the Judge of Hearts'. It was Ptah-Nu-Fi who gave him this name when he wrote down for posterity the leather scrolls of the 'Divine Mathematical Combinations'. He justified this name by saying that "the hearts of the first human beings were weighed before their souls could be measured to determine their exact content of Good and Evil". This led shortly afterwards to the introduction of the concept of Libra, and to the naming of the same constellation.

After these 864 years, the Sun moved on to the next constellation. It then left the Khi-Ath group of stars for a very pure group of stars, at which time a young virgin, touched by Divine grace, gave birth to Ptah-Nou-Fi, the God-sent-from-Heaven to teach the peoples and who was the first scholar. Quite naturally, he gave this constellation three ears of corn as its symbol. Why did he do this? Because his mother, symbolising Heaven (Nut), God, the Creator, and he, the Son, future generations, was the triad from which all humanity sprang!

More popularly, this celestial constellation later took the name of the Virgin, so that humanity would remember that it descended from Nut in this constellation. In this way, souls became accustomed to reflecting in the very spirit of God, so as never to break the thread linking them to Heaven.

In 2,592 years, the time spent travelling the thirty-six degrees where the Sun appeared, the people, taught by the seventy-one direct descendants who succeeded Ptah-Nou-Fi, created an evolved civilisation, having learnt the art of living in unanimous accord with the celestial rhythm.

When the star of the day, continuing its slow navigation along the Great Celestial River (the Milky Way: Hâpy), was in the next constellation, the seventy-third descendant of the Elder (the Pâa-râ) undertook to rule the country alone as soon as he was crowned. He had very strong muscles, of which he was very proud, but a small brain, which he was less aware of! So he liked to flaunt his exceptional strength at the slightest opportunity, rather than talk in fine words! It was obvious that after all the blood mixing, his Divinity was much diminished.

And so, on the very day of his coronation, an almost miraculous event took place, which is well remembered in the Annals, and which has come down to us by way of the name of a group of stars! This young Master, therefore, had been annoyed for some time by the constant boasting about the prowess of the lions who frolicked around his home and whom no one wanted to brave. At the time of his coronation, he saw a bold lion approaching the place of worship, thus disturbing this pompous and traditional ceremony, so he dropped his crown to jump more easily to the ground from the high esplanade where the ceremony was taking place, to pursue the animal.

It was a splendid adult male, who, in less time than it takes to write it, was caught and strangled with his bare hands!... The huge crowd, who had rushed to the terraces to enjoy the details of the struggle, applauded wildly at this unprecedented feat, which left no doubt as to the favours God was bestowing on the new Monarch.

The name of the lion, Er-Kaï, was therefore given to the constellation where the Sun entered on the day of the Master's consecration. And so he decided to call himself: Meri-Ptah-Er-Kai, i.e. the "Lion-Love-of-God". It should be noted, in connection with this account, that the name Er-Kaï became synonymous with: "Strong as a lion", and that the Greeks named Er-Kaï after Heracles, who became Hercules in our language.

Seventy-one generations also succeeded him during the solar journey to this constellation, *Er-Kaï*, but in lesser times. The many misalliances led to the degeneration of these descendants, who lost all control and whose last representatives sank into total blindness. God's wrath manifested itself against them without further ado.

The celestial order was disrupted by a retrograde movement of the sun's path through space! So this is the first report of such a phenomenon to reached us!

During the government of this one hundred and forty-fourth Master, when the star of the day was at the thirty-second degree in the constellation Leo, the elements were unleashed, overturning entire continents, placing seas in place of land and vice versa. The magma, with its weight of billions of billions of tonnes, caused the Earth to rotate on its axis, and it found itself inverted, at the fourth degree of the same constellation of Leo!...

The solar movements were then carefully observed by the first King of this IIIrd dynasty, who noticed that the Sun was now following a direct ascension course, after having moved backwards for several millennia. But of course, it came back on itself in Leo for 1,440 years. He therefore took the name: Mou-Kaï-Ptah, or "Just-in-God's-Force".

This patronymic name aptly defines the new fear that the Divine Power inspired in His creatures! But this dynasty established a primary script in symbolic characters that enabled the intelligence of the people to evolve spectacularly. This is why *the Lion: Er-Kai*, symbolised not only Strength, but also God and the Sun.

Then the star of the day left the constellation of Leo and entered Nut again, *the Virgin of the Three Thorns*. The people soon realised that this name had been given for a good reason, which once again demonstrated the Divine Power. The Queen of that time, who had received the name of her illustrious predecessor, as tradition dictated, gave birth to a Divine first-born son.

It was he who, under the name: Ath-Aha-Ptah, i.e. the "*Second-Age of God*", took advantage of the perfect writing of his predecessors to help people understand the Divine commandments and the importance of observing them. He organised the rites of prayer and offerings, punishment and punishments.

The 2,592 years during which the Sun was again in Virgo, but in the opposite direction, were devoted to peace and justice, and humanity developed all the physical sciences and perfected the methods used in agriculture. Then came the era of the Khi-Ath who judged hearts: *Libra!* This time, solar navigation took place all along the river, and lasted for the 1,872 years planned. Here too, a sort of Golden Age was established during this time, thanks to the obedience of an entire people to Divine laws. The few minor disputes that needed to be settled were settled without difficulty once a year by the Master, who sat in an inner courtyard of the Temple-God. He was seated on a cubic green granite stone, four cubits square, with a golden balance beside him. He stood there from sunrise to sunset, during the twenty-six days of its annual revolution in this constellation. The Master's decisions were final and, as his verdicts were just, no one raised their voice... So the last Masters fell asleep in a Faith that was no longer anything but Law, and took themselves for gods!

It was for this reason that the entry into the next constellation was awaited with perplexity by some and anxiety by others. This group of stars did not yet have a name, as the Sun had not yet entered it since the beginning of the written Annals. This created a climate of fear and a certain unease in the circles close to the King, an unease that grew as the fateful date of the passage into the next era drew nearer.

Several serious accidents occurred during the intervening years, one might say, of the changes in the astral influxes of the constellations. In the seventeenth year of the reign of the Master reigning at the beginning of this new Time, the Monarch died crushed under the rubble of his Palace, which collapsed one day beneath him, without anyone understanding why. His son, in another building, was safe; but the following day, when he was being fetched with great pomp for the coronation ceremony, he was found dead, undoubtedly killed by himself! Today, we would add, as a result of a nervous breakdown.

The priests, seeing the finger of God in it, called the constellation Hétet, "The Destroyer", which was transformed into Tèti, the name of the Scorpion, a few weeks later. The people had given it this name following the suicide described above, as the scorpion can also kill itself by stinging itself with its stinger when impelled to do so by an evil instinct.

It was a nephew of the first king who came to the throne in his turn. To ward off fate and win allies on all sides, he took the name Hètet-Tèti, 'the Scorpion-Destroyer'. In fact, he reigned for a long time and was a bloodthirsty despot. He enslaved the world under his yoke, having decided that only his justice would be valid and that he would exercise it at any time of the year.

Eighteen hundred and seventy-two solar revolutions took place in this destructive constellation, during which sixty-one Masters succeeded one another, accentuating the Divine wrath through their injustices and the continual battles they waged, because once again, human decadence was precipitating.

The last King, the sixty-fourth of this cursed dynasty, was so depraved that he never married. Living without female companionship and having no concubines, he died without leaving any children. His succession ushered in an era of rebellion and civil war, with legions of pretenders to the throne.

A younger half-brother, however, who should have been one hundred and twenty-third among the possible candidates, managed to establish himself as the fourth contender within three weeks. With a loyal company of archers, he decided to put an end to it all by having not only the three possible future 'Masters' killed, but also their main friends and relatives. After that bloody day, there was no longer any obstacle to his becoming Monarch. He was accepted by the frightened Priests without protest. His name was naturally Maka-Sati, 'The Invincible Arrow'. This prompted the College to officially name the constellation into which the Sun had just entered Sati, or 'The Arrow'. The Greeks later named it Centaurus, or Sagittarius...

As Manetho had access to the Heliopolis archives, he was perfectly familiar with the text of the Annals of Antiquity. But Eusebius, Josephus and the others, who even at the time had the works of this priest in their hands, and in the script of their own language, retained only the bow-hunting on the day of the coronation! Which just goes to show how little interest these Latin historians took in chronological dating.

This Maka-Sati, the first king of this VIIth dynasty - which would be the last entitled "God-Kings", and which was in the Sati constellation - had organised a hunt in the nearby forest, to the north-west of the Royal Palace. At the time, it was a hunt for huge animals: the âa-n'abu, now totally extinct, but now known as mammoths.

This race of giants - peaceful, but dangerous because of their mass - was the last to exist in these remote times, and now only digested certain young plant shoots. As they proliferated and formed large herds, they became a real scourge, not for the population, which they completely disdained, but for barley cultivation! When a herd of a hundred animals arrived in a field, there was nothing left to do but say goodbye to the harvest. In less than an hour, the earth was levelled and flattened.

One day - it was the day of MakaSati's coronation - driven by hunger, a horde approached the Palace fields. To open his reign in style, he organised the famous mammoth hunt! Apart from himself, there would be just eight other hunters, armed only with their bows and a quiver containing just twelve arrows. The guests would be able to watch the spectacle from the terraces, as beaters were to bring back the odious beasts that had committed the crime of lèse-majesté by devouring the royal barley. The Monarch and the eight hunters would wait there for the stampede... at the very edge of the forest.

Mounted on a black stallion, and followed a few paces behind by his eight servants, Maka-Sati was listening distractedly to the confused noises made by the touts, when suddenly two enormous dark grey masses emerged: two *âa-n'abu!*

Instead of turning around and fleeing, the young King stood proudly on his horse, holding it firmly under him with his calves, and, picking up his bow with the speed of lightning, he cocked it with an arrow that he barely aimed and did the same with three others in less than ten seconds. The second behemoth fell at the very feet of his horse, an arrow having pierced each of its eyes; as for the first, it had collapsed a few paces away, struck down in the same way by the two previous arrows. The eight hunters hadn't even had time to move! All the spectators had contemplated this feat of arms, undoubtedly favoured by God. That's why Maka-Sati was glorified from that day on and for all eternity as the "Horseman" with the invincible arrow!

This Monarch, however, despite his physical power and his quick instinct to defend himself, was devoid of the Divine part of his ancestors. He was born of a human couple, and his highly elastic conscience caused this last dynasty of God-Kings to degenerate completely, after sixteen generations of Monarchs who reigned for seven hundred and twenty years. The last: Maka-Aha-Sati, reigned a nameless terror whose savagery was never equalled and who, unfortunately, because of this, dominated his people for sixty-four years! This brought the Sun to within ten degrees of the constellation Sagittarius!

A geological upheaval then occurred, accompanied by strong earthquakes and a flood. The whole thing was not caused by the Earth's axis pivoting, but by an instantaneous advance of 72° in its rotation, which meant that on the same day the Sun was no longer at 10° in Sagittarius, but at 21° in Aquarius. This was the name given to a time when water was clearly being poured in by the bucketful!

The new ice cap at the North Pole had sunk beneath the waves, tearing up the territory of Canada and creating what is now Hudson Bay, the coasts of Alaska and Greenland, separating the latter territory by a vast arm of the sea from the continent of Aha-Men-Ptah. The same thing happened all around the globe along this parallel, leaving the North Pole frozen into an immense isolated territory.

So here's the chronological summary from Aha-Men-Ptah to this mini upheaval:

Méditation et Création (864 ans)	DIEU	Ptah (DIEU-UN)	Khi-Ath (Balance)	864 ans
Iʳᵉ dynastie Divine (2 592 ans)	+ 71 Rois	Ptah-Nou-Fi (Envoyé du Ciel)	Nout (Vierge)	3 456 ans
IIᵉ dynastie Divine (2 448 ans)	+ 71 Rois	Meri-Ptah-Kaï (Lion-Aimé)	Er-Kaï (Lion)	5 904 ans
IIIᵉ dynastie rois-dieux (1 440 ans)	+ 33 Rois	Mou-Kaï-Ptah (Juste et Fort)	Er-Kaï (Lion [1])	7 344 ans
IVᵉ dynastie rois-dieux (2 592 ans)	+ 71 Rois	Ath-Aha-Ptah (Second-Aîné)	Nout (Vierge)	9 936 ans
Vᵉ dynastie rois-dieux (1 872 ans)	+ 63 Rois	Mou-Ath-Ptah (Cœur-Juste)	Khi-Ath (Balance)	11 808 ans
VIᵉ dynastie les demi-dieux (1 872 ans)	+ 55 Rois	Hetet-Teti (Le Destructeur)	Têti (Scorpion)	13 680 ans
VIIᵉ dynastie les demi-dieux (720 ans)	+ 16 Rois	Maka-Sati (La Flèche invincible)	Sati (La Flèche)	14 400 ans

Le mini-cataclysme qui bouleversa l'hémisphère Nord de la Terre à ce moment-là, porta notre globe à effectuer un bond en avant sur lui-même, et sur le même axe, qui le poussa du 10° degré du Sagittaire au 21° degré du Verseau, que les « Combinaisons-Mathématiques » calculent avec précision, afin de débuter dès cet instant précis une chronologie exacte. Nous sommes au 21° jour, du 2° mois de l'an 21 312 avant Christ.

---

1. Le Lion, à partir de ce jour, est repris en position directe par le Soleil, qui continuera à naviguer sur sa voie direct jusqu'au Grand Cataclysme.

The Manethonian chronology is therefore accurate, since it gives a total of 36,000 years since Divine meditation. Now, we find this same total to within a few details: 14,400 + 21,312 + 244 years to Alexander = 35,956 years. This leads us, for greater understanding, to present the same study in graphic form:

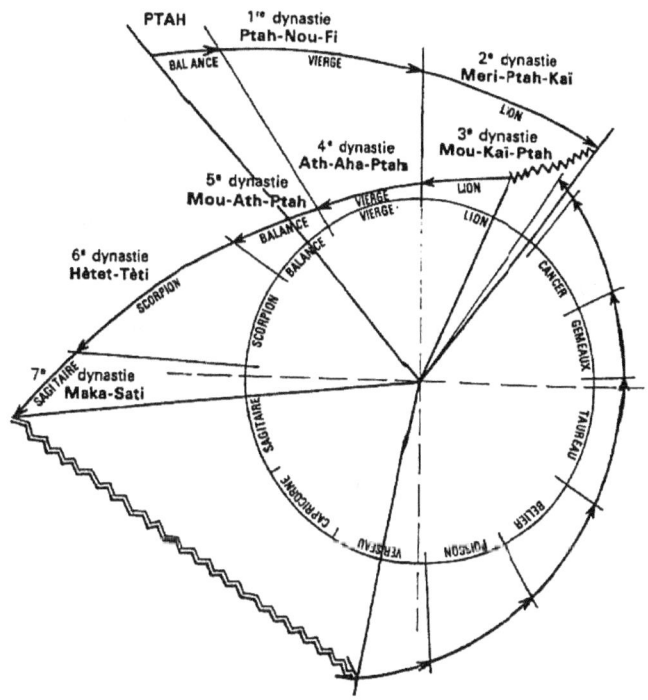

After the upheaval of the earth's axis, which brought "the sky" forty days forward on the celestial equatorial ecliptic and caused the intense disturbances described a few pages earlier, the continent, amputated of its sunken northern province, nevertheless remained the Great Aha-Men-Ptah, oriented differently and with almost all its land above the equator.

The Priests then elected a Pontiff, the first, who would direct matters relating to Divine Law, and consecrated a second-degree relative of the deceased Master, who would rule over the people and be invested with power in matters not relating to the spiritual domain.

The latter was still a young man who, born with good aspects of the 'Combinations' of the Fixed Ones, had been noticed by the High Priest. As a result, he was admitted to the novitiate of the "House of Life" in the Temple of Ptah, where he stayed for six years, learning everything that, on the face of it, was likely to make him a Sage. It was certain, however, that the atmosphere of decadence in which his environment was immersed had not even touched him.

Through him, a first dynasty of "Heroes", or "Manes", was established on this new day of 21 February 21,312 BC, as a Master aware of the realities demanded by God in Aha-Men-Ptah. This second chronological period lasted 11,520 years, ending with the Great Cataclysm, which saw its last "Master", the Son of Nut: Usir.

Before the first King of "Heroes", the VIIth dynasty of demigods came to an end after 14,400 years of history, with an advance on the earth's axis, which saw the Sun appear in the constellation of Aquarius:

Soleil dans constellation	Durée en années	Durée avant le Christ	Durée totale avant 1975	Durée depuis Méditation	Durée depuis les « Héros »
Sagittaire	1 576	21 312	23 287	14 400	—
		Mini déluge amenant le Soleil à 8° du Verseau			
Verseau	576	20 736	22 711	14 976	576
Poissons	2 016	18 720	20 695	16 992	2 592
Bélier	2 304	16 416	18 391	19 296	4 896
Taureau	2 304	14 112	16 087	21 600	7 200
Gémeaux	1 872	12 240	14 215	23 472	9 072
Cancer	1 872	10 368	12 343	25 344	10 944
Lion	576	9 792	11 767	25 920	11 520
... *En ce jour-là « Le Grand Cataclysme » amena le Soleil à se lever à l'est...*					

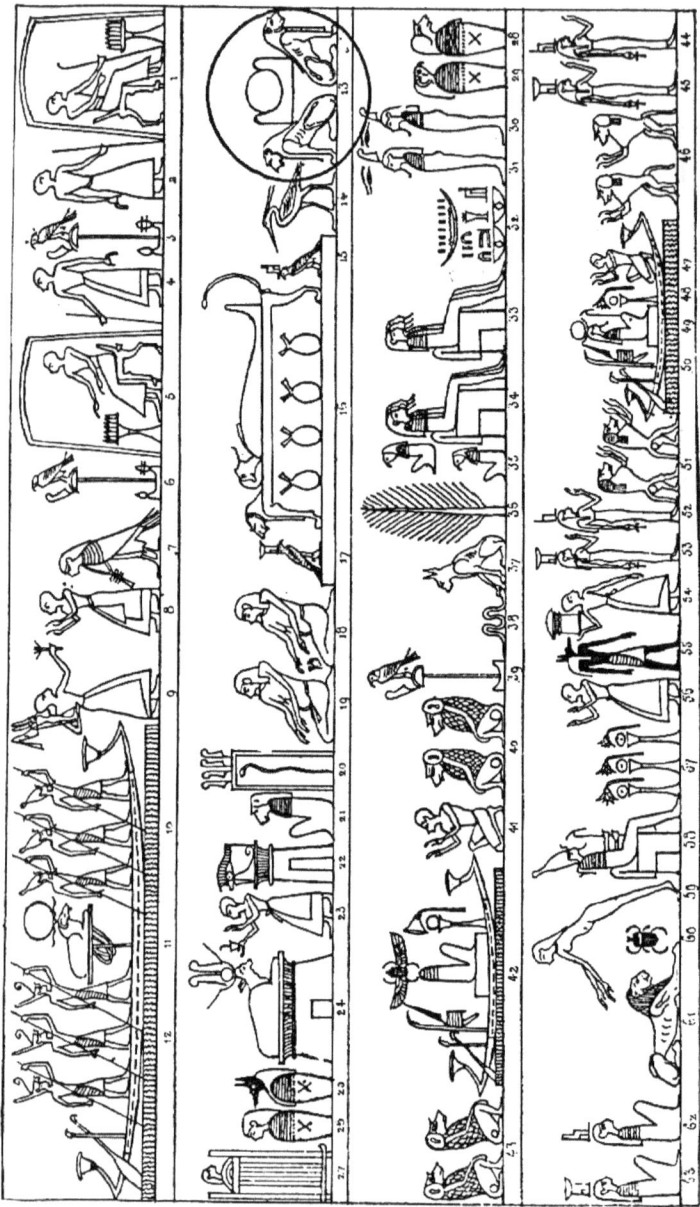

Chapter XVII is the only chapter in the Book of the Dead to have no hieroglyphic text. It consists of this single engraving which unequivocally narrates the "Great Cataclysm", in LION!

And the third dynastic period, which began with the valiant survivors of the sunken continent landing on a second earth, began its Chronological Annals with Hor: Horus the Pure.

A very interesting translation, albeit very approximate, of the text known as the "Memphite Theology" has been made by the professor of oriental archaeology Henri Frankfort:

It happened that they fought;
which means that Horus fought with Set.
And Geb said to Horus and Seth: "Forget it!"

The survivors, the authors of the original manuscript, were reminding their successors six thousand years later of a reality that had become incomprehensible! History was transformed into a mythology adapted to a new environment, where these "old books" had become a series of fantasies, each more fanciful than the last!...

It is likely that Hor, who had not yet entered the legend to become the deified Hor-Our, was thinking of this distant future, still tied up in a "mandjit", with his mother Iset watching over him tenderly, as the boat rolled helplessly from wave to wave on a furious sea, shaken by the jolts of an entire continent sinking beneath the waters.

Immobile, his body stiff with damp and clotted blood, he was nonetheless very much alive and extremely lucid. He could feel a gentle hand gripping one of his legs tightly, as if to keep it glued to the wood and prevent him from rolling into the abyss that would have dragged him to this sunken Kingdom, now home to millions and millions of dead. Dripping with water, he held the bottom of the broken mast, watching through the lashes of his able eye for a shore that might be accessible, where the Creator, who had spared them, would allow their 'mandjit' to run aground.

The hollow of the enormous waves usually prevented him from doing so, and the noise they made as they crashed against the frail yet resilient hull hurt his heart as well as his ears! Each time he wondered he and his mother would end up in the bellies of the crustaceans! And his faith was waning, all the more so because he was also asking himself an agonising question: how many survivors could survive?...

Nekbeth, for her part, was not troubled by the mountains of water that loomed like cliffs in front of her boat. She knew that she would see the end of it at the moment chosen by God. The whole world seemed to dissolve in the diffused light given off by a new Sun, which didn't even intrigue the young woman. After the storm, calm would return, as would life. New builders would construct a second homeland, and everything would begin again. But that would only make men understand their own iniquity and the futility of constantly believing that they themselves were gods!

Contemplating the bull skin at the bottom of her boat, which contained the remains of her venerated father Usir, the young woman did not, however, allow herself to seek vengeance against the murderer of her own brother Sit. She knew that their father would never have wanted that. And that it was he, in that protective leather, who inspired her to think of mercy. But what was this skin protecting?... The more Nekbeth observed this mass, the less she "saw" a dead person! It seemed inexplicable to her...

Suddenly, a deep joy came over her, and as she looked up at the Sun, which was comforting people's hearts, she realised that a miracle had been performed. Tears flooded her eyes; she was convinced that somehow Usir had been resurrected! Her Father, to demonstrate His omnipotence in all circumstances, would give life back to His Son!

Nekbeth didn't know how, but she was confident!

BIBLIOGRAPHY

THE MAIN DOCUMENTS STUDIED FOR AN ANAGLYPHIC UNDERSTANDING OF THE TEXTS

DESCRIPTION OF EGYPT. - Recueil des observations et des recherches qui ont été faites durant l'expédition de l'armée française, 1st ed. 9 vols. of text and 12 vols. of atlases and drawn documents (1809 to 1813).

BIBLIOTHÈQUE DE L'ÉCOLE DES HAUTES ÉTUDES. -Maspéro: *Genre épistolaire*, 1872; Grébaut: *Hymne à Amon-Râ*, 1875; Virey: *Papyrus Prisse*, 1887; Jéquier: *L'Hadès*, 1894.

ANNALES DU MUSÉE GUIMET. - Lefébure: *Hypogées royaux*, 1886; Amélineau: *Gnosticisme*, 1887; Mahler: *Calendrier*, 1907.

BIBLIOTHÈQUE ÉGYPTOLOGIQUE. - Works by French Egyptologists: Leroux: two volumes, 1893; Maspéro: *Mythologie*, 1894; Dévéria: *Mémoires*, 1904; Chabas: *Œuvres*, 1905; de Rougé: *Œuvres*, 1909.

ARCHEOLOGICAL SURVEY. - Griffith: *Hieroglyphs*, 1895; Davies: *Ptahhetep*, 1897; Crowfoot: *Meroe*, 1911.

ALTERTUMSKUNDE AEGYPTENS. - Sethe: *Horusdiener*, 1903; Schaeffer: *Mysterien des Osiris*, 1904.

EGYPT EXPLORATION FUND. - Naville: *Pithom*, 1885; Petrie: *Denderah*, 1900.

EGYPTOLOGICAL STUDIES. - Lefébure: *Mythe osirien*, 1874; Révillout: *Chrestomathie*, 1880.

And in alphabetical order, the authors

Authors	Works	Dates
AMÉLINEAU E.	Studies on the Boulacq payrus	1892
- -	The cult of the predynastic kings (article in the "Journal des Savants" of 1906)	
AMPÈRE J.-J.	Transmission of professions in ancient Egypt	September 1848
BAILLET Auguste	Duties of the High Priest of Ammon	1865
BERGMANN	Hieroglyphs Inschrifften	1879
BIRCH Samuel	Select Papyri of Britisch Museum	1841
BRUGSCH Émile	The Book of Kings	1887
- -	Old geographical dictionary	1877
BUDGE Wallis	Papyrus of Ani	1895
BURTON James	Excerpta hieroglyphica	1825
CAPART Jean	The feast of striking the Annou	1901
CHABAS François	The Harris papyrus	1860
CHASSINAT Émile	Denderah (6 vols.) I.F.A.O.	1911
DAVIS Charles	The Book of the Dead	1894
DÉVÉRIA TH.	Papyrus of Nebqeb	1872
DEVILLIERS	Denderah	1812
EBERS Georges	Ebers papyrus	1875
EINSELOHR August	Before the reign of Ramses III	1872
ERMAN Adolf	AEgypten Leben im Alterthum geschildert	1885
- -	Egyptian grammar	1894
FRAZER J.-G.	Totemism	1887
GAILLARD Claude	Le Bélier de Mendès	1901
GARDINER Alan	Berlin Papyrus	1908
- -	The Admonitions of an Egyptian Sage	1909
- -	Hieratic texts (pap. Anastasi and Koller)	1911
GAYET Albert	Pharaonic civilisation	1907

GOLÉNITSCHEFF	*Papyrus No. 1 from St Petersburg*	1876
--	*Hieratic papyrus no. 15*	1906
GRÉBAUT Eugène	*The two eyes of the solar disc*	1879
GRENFELL BERNARD	*The Amherst Papyri*	1891
GRIFFITH	*Two Papyri hieroglip. from Tanis*	1889
GROFF William	*The name Jacob and Joseph in Egyptian*	1885
--	*Orbiney papyrus*	1888
GUIEYSSE Paul	*Hymn to the Nile*	1890
HORRACK PH.-J. (de)	*The Lamentations of Isis and Nephthys*	1866
--	*The Book of Breathing*	1877
JOLLOIS J.-B.	*Denderah*	1814
LANZONE Rod.	*The home of spirits*	1879
LAUTH Fr. J.	*Pharaoh Meneptah*	1867
LENORMAND Fr.	*The first civilisations*	1874
LE PAGE-RENOUF P.	*Religion of Ancient Egypt*	1880
LIEBLEIN J.	*Research into Egyptian chronology*	1873
--	*Hieratic papyri from the Turin Museum*	1868
--	*Dictionary of hieroglyphic names*	1871
LIEBLEIN Dr J.	*Research into the civilisation of ancient Egypt*	1910
LORET Victor	*Ritual for the festivals of Osiris at Denderah*	1895
--	*Manual of the Egyptian language*	1896
MARIETTE Aug.	*Description of the Great Temple of Dendera*	1875
MARTIN Théodore	*Manetho's opinion on his chronology*	1860
MASPÉRO Gaston	*Ancient Egyptian religious literature*	1872
MORET Alexandre	*The ritual of divine worship*	1902
--	*Kings and gods*	1911
--	*Egyptian mysteries*	1911

MORGAN J. (de)	*Research into the origins of Egypt*	1897
NAVILLE Édouard	*The Litany of the Sun*	1875
- -	*The religion of the ancient Egyptians*	1906
PETRIE W. Flinders	*Religion of ancient egypt*	1906
PIERRET Paul	*Horus on the crocodiles*	1869
- -	*Hieroglyphic vocabulary*	1875
REINACH A.-J.	*Prehistoric Egypt*	1908
RÉVILLOUT Eugène	*Contemporary chronicle of Manetho*	1876
ROUGÉ Emm. (de)	*Origins of the Egyptian breed*	1895
SHARPE Samuel	*History of Egypt*	1870
VIREY Philippe	*Ancient Egyptian religion*	1909
YOUNG Thomas	*Hieroglyphics*	1823

Almost the entire bibliography was consulted at the Bibliothèque des Fontaines, near Chantilly, in the Oise region, where the Jesuit Fathers, who are the librarians, watch over 600,000 philosophical and religious volumes with great care, while at the same time providing access to anyone interested. Our thanks go to them.

OTHER TITLES

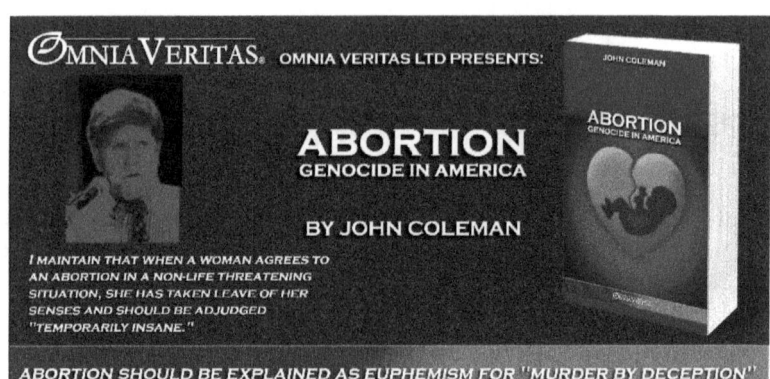

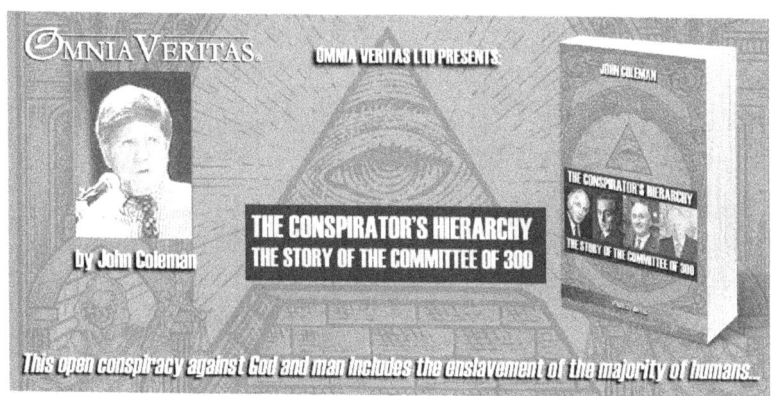
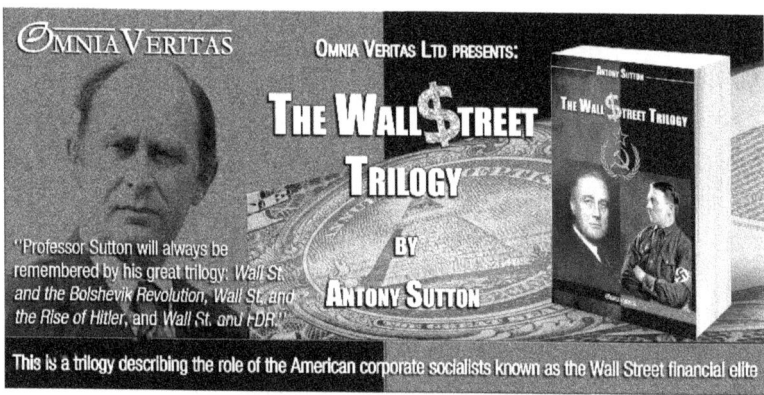

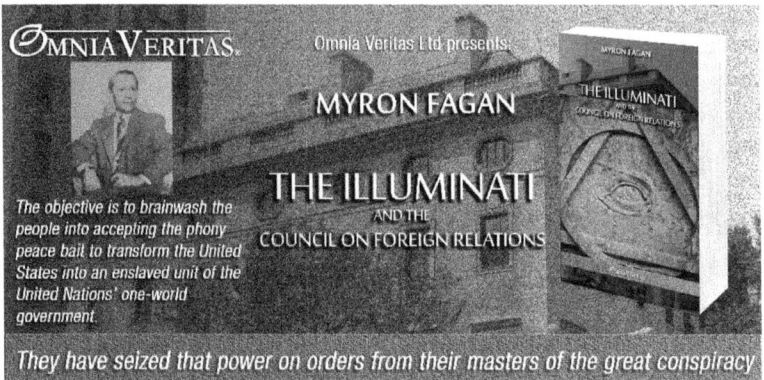

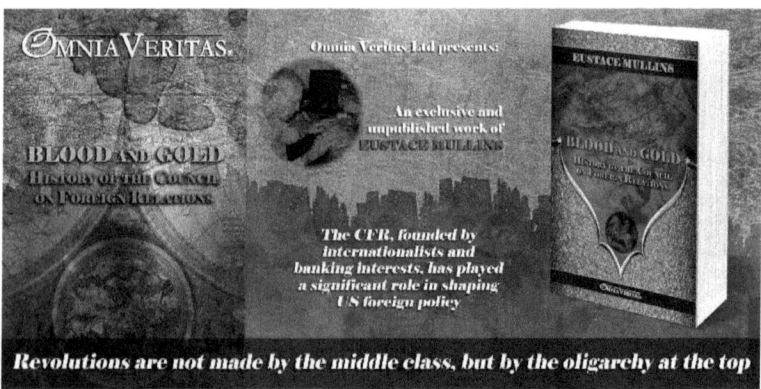

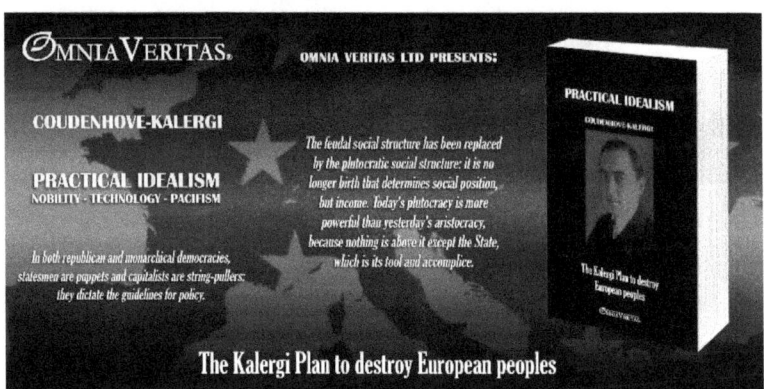

www.ingramcontent.com/pod-product-compliance
Lightning Source LLC
Chambersburg PA
CBHW050130170426
43197CB00011B/1782